COCHINEAL RED

Also by Hugh Thomson

The White Rock
Nanda Devi

HUGH THOMSON

COCHINEAL RED

Travels through Ancient Peru

Weidenfeld & Nicolson

LONDON

First published in Great Britain in 2006
by Weidenfeld & Nicolson

1 3 5 7 9 10 8 6 4 2

A CIP catalogue record for this book
is available from the British Library.

ISBN 13-978 02976 45641
ISBN 10-0 297 64564 1

Typeset by Input Data Services Ltd, Frome

Printed and bound by Butler & Tanner Ltd,
Frome and London

The Orion Publishing Group's policy is to use papers that
are natural, renewable and recyclable products and made
from wood grown in sustainable forests. The logging and
manufacturing processes are expected to conform to the
environmental regulations of the country of origin.

Weidenfeld & Nicolson

The Orion Publishing Group Ltd
Orion House
5 Upper Saint Martin's Lane
London, WC2H 9EA

www.orionbooks.co.uk

CONTENTS

ILLUSTRATIONS

Unless otherwise indicated all photographs are by Hugh Thomson (© Hugh Thomson 2006).

Moche portrait head. (© Museo Larco – Lima, Peru).

Scene with captive. (© Museo Larco – Lima, Peru).

A pair of llamas. (© Museo Larco – Lima, Peru).

Donna McClelland: Drawing of 'The Arraignment of Prisoners', showing the sacrifice ceremony, taken from a Moche fineline ceramic bottle in the American Museum of Natural History, New York. (© Donna McClelland).

Chavín: entrance to the temple.

The 'jaguar heads' which were originally supported on the walls of the temple.

Juan Manuel Castro *Colibrí de Nasca (Nasca hummingbird)*. (© Juan Manuel Castro 1997).

Maria Reiche studying the Nasca lines. (Private Collection).

Hiram Bingham in front of his tent at Machu Picchu, 1912. (Yale Peruvian expedition).

Hugh Thomson and Gary Ziegler on the 2002 Cota Coca research expedition.

Press coverage. Daily Telegraph article on discoveries at Cota Coca.

Between pages 234 and 235

Chavín: the Lanzón in its cruciform gallery.

Petroglyphs at Toro Muerto.

Huari head.

Gordon McEwan with the recently discovered Huari turquoise figure.

The miniature figure in his hand.

A *quipu*. (© Museo Larco – Lima, Peru).

Qoyllurit'i: *chu'uncho* dancers with their feathered head-dresses.

Ukukus with their whips and furred costumes.

An ukuku with one of the crosses high on a glacier.

Massed ukukus beside a glacier at dawn.

The mountain bowl of Sinakara at 14,000 feet.

The Island of the Sun: the pilgrimage route down the island.

Pilko Kayma at first light.

Machu Picchu seen from Llactapata.

Machu Picchu seen from Llactapata through the doorway of the Overlook Temple.
Looking from the Sacristy at Machu Picchu towards Llactapata.
Sunlight down Llactapata's long sunken corridor at dawn.
Hugh Thomson in the field-tent at Llactapata.

Endpapers: Weaving from Huilloc, near Ollantaytambo (author's collection)

Every effort has been made to trace copyright. We will be happy to repair any omissions in subsequent editions.

COLOMBIA

N
W · E
S

Quito

ECUADOR

Guayaquil

Tumipampa
(Cuenca)

Tumbes

Putumayo

Napo

Tigre

Putumayo

Amazon

Marañon

Huancapampa

Chachapoyas

Kuelap

Sipán

Chiclayo

Cajamarca

BRAZIL

El Brujo
Chan Chan   Trujillo
Moche Pyramids of
the Sun and Moon

Pucallpa

Casma   Chavín de Huantar
Las Aldas   Sechín

PERU

Ucayali

Supe   Caral

Pacific Ocean

Lima   Jauja

Pachacamac

Huari

Ayacucho

Urubamba

Apurimac

Quillabamba
Machu Picchu
Urubamba
Cuzco
Pikillacta

Pisco   Tambo Colorado
Paracas

BOLIVIA

Palpa
Nasca

Island of
the Sun

Sillustani

Toro
Muerto   Puno

Aplao

Arequipa

Lake Titicaca

La Paz

Tiahuanaco

The Inca Empire
(Tahuantinsuyo)

COLOMBIA

ECUA-
DOR

PERU   BRAZIL

Cuzco

BOLIVIA

Pacific Ocean

CHILE

ARGENTINA

300 Miles

PERU

• Pre-Columbian settlement
○ Post-Columbian settlement
······· Inca roads

CHILE

0   100   200   300 Miles

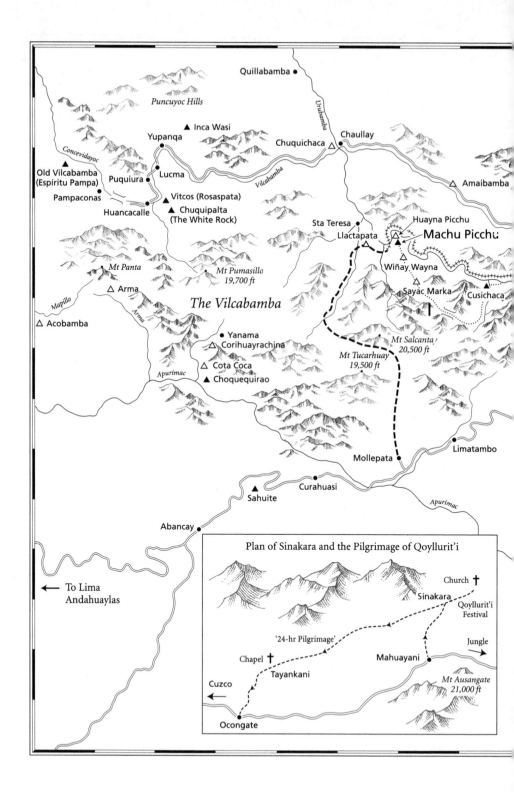

Quillabamba •

Puncuyoc Hills

Concevidayoc

▲ Inca Wasi
Yupanqa

Chuquichaca
Chaullay △

Urubamba

Old Vilcabamba
(Espíritu Pampa)
Puquiura • Lucma

Vilcabamba

Amaibamba △

Pampaconas

Huancacalle

▲ Vitcos (Rosaspata)
▲ Chuquipalta
(The White Rock)

Sta Teresa •
Llactapata △

Huayna Picchu
▲ **Machu Picchu**

Mapillo

• Mt Panta

△ Arma

Arma

Mt Pumasillo
19,700 ft

The Vilcabamba

Wiñay Wayna
△

△ Sayac Marka
Cusichaca ▲

△ Acobamba

• Yanama
△ Corihuayrachina

Apurímac

△ Cota Coca
▲ Choquequirao

Mt Salcanta
20,500 ft

Mt Tucarhuay
19,500 ft

• Limatambo

Mollepata •

▲
Sahuite

• Curahuasi

Apurímac

Abancay •

← To Lima
Andahuaylas

Plan of Sinakara and the Pilgrimage of Qoyllurit'i

Church ✝
Sinakara
Qoyllurit'i
Festival

'24-hr Pilgrimage'

Jungle

Chapel ✝
Tayankani

Mahuayani •

Cuzco
←

Mt Ausangate
21,000 ft

Ocongate •

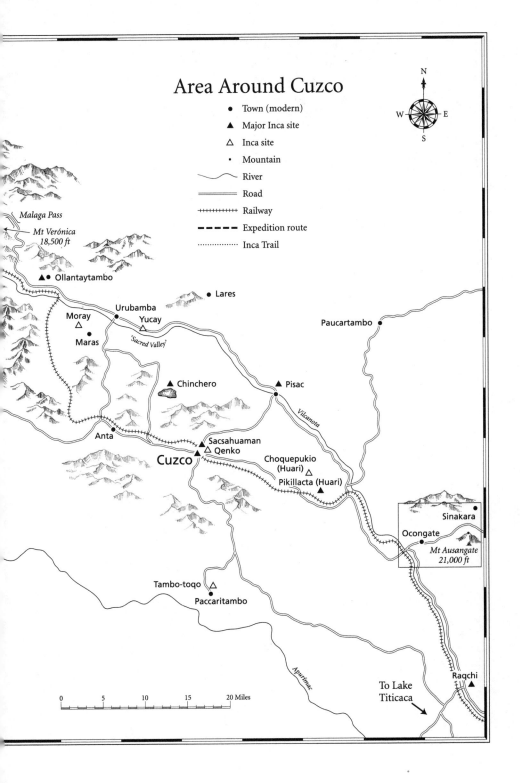

Area Around Cuzco

- Town (modern)
- ▲ Major Inca site
- △ Inca site
- · Mountain
- River
- Road
- Railway
- Expedition route
- Inca Trail

N · W · E · S

Malaga Pass

Mt Verónica
18,500 ft

▲• Ollantaytambo

• Lares

Moray
△

Urubamba
Yucay

'Sacred Valley'

Maras
•

Paucartambo

▲ Chinchero

▲ Pisac

Vilcanota

Anta

Sacsahuaman
△ Qenko

Cuzco

Choquepukio
(Huari) △

Pikillacta (Huari)
▲

Sinakara
•

Ocongate
•

Mt Ausangate
21,000 ft

Tambo-toqo △

Paccaritambo

Apurimac

To Lake
Titicaca

Raqchi
▲

0   5   10   15   20 Miles

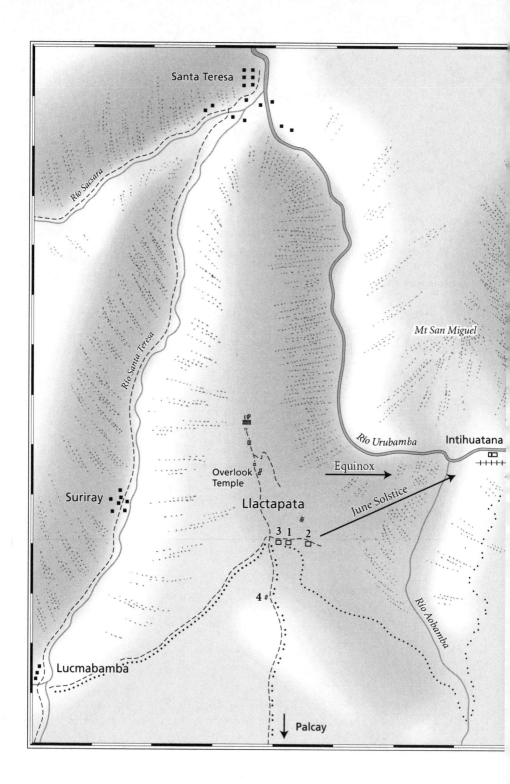

Santa Teresa

Río Sacsara

Río Santa Teresa

Mt San Miguel

Río Urubamba

Intihuatana

Suriray

Overlook
Temple

Llactapata

Equinox

June Solstice

3 1   2

4

Río Aobamba

Lucmabamba

Palcay

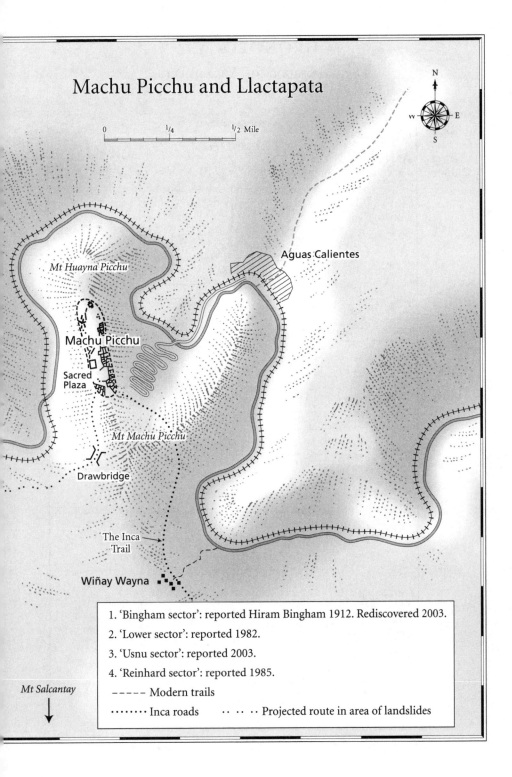

Machu Picchu and Llactapata

0   ¼   ½ Mile

N
W · E
S

Mt Huayna Picchu

Aguas Calientes

Machu Picchu

Sacred
Plaza

Mt Machu Picchu

Drawbridge

The Inca
Trail

Wiñay Wayna

Mt Salcantay

1. 'Bingham sector': reported Hiram Bingham 1912. Rediscovered 2003.

2. 'Lower sector': reported 1982.

3. 'Usnu sector': reported 2003.

4. 'Reinhard sector': reported 1985.

- - - - - Modern trails

········ Inca roads   · · · ·· Projected route in area of landslides

CHRONOLOGY

The Civilisations of Ancient Peru

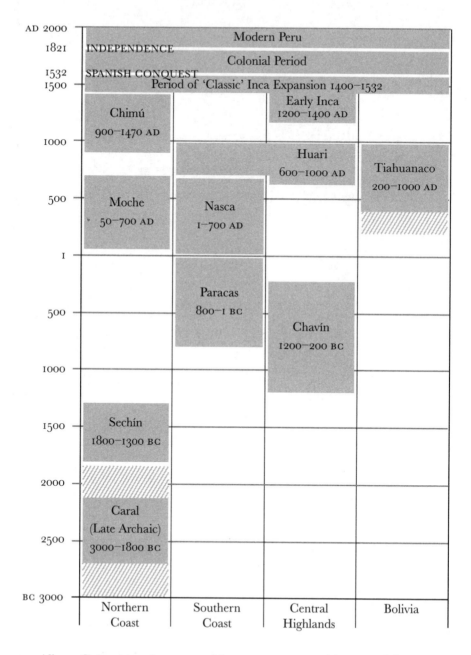

	Northern Coast	Southern Coast	Central Highlands	Bolivia
AD 2000	Modern Peru			
1821 INDEPENDENCE	Colonial Period			
1532 SPANISH CONQUEST				
1500	Period of 'Classic' Inca Expansion 1400–1532			
	Chimú 900–1470 AD		Early Inca 1200–1400 AD	
1000			Huari 600–1000 AD	Tiahuanaco 200–1000 AD
500	Moche 50–700 AD	Nasca 1–700 AD		
1		Paracas 800–1 BC		
500			Chavín 1200–200 BC	
1000				
1500	Sechín 1800–1300 BC			
2000				
	Caral (Late Archaic) 3000–1800 BC			
2500				
BC 3000				

All pre-Columbian dates are subject to constant revision and debate.

INTRODUCTION

This book is an exercise in compressed time. Into the year described I have poured many of my feelings about Peru over the past twenty-five years, and I have likewise used it to explore five millennia of ancient Peruvian history as I travelled through the country.

The impetus for this came from my continuing investigations at the Inca site of Llactapata, near Machu Picchu, as it became increasingly difficult for me to understand the Inca mindset without a fuller understanding of the thousands of years of Andean culture that preceded the Incas.

The story therefore begins with Llactapata and the Incas before returning to the dawn of Peruvian civilisation at Caral in around 3000 BC and moving forward through the millennia up to the present day.

In a book spanning 5,000 years of Andean history, there is an inevitable concentration on the 'summits in the range', to the exclusion of some of the smaller civilisations. I was drawn to explore the principal and defining cultures that left enduring monuments, from the great pyramids of the coast, with their tombs and murals, to the temple-cult of Chavín, buried in the mountains, and the lines of Nasca.

There is a virtue to this broad-brush approach, in that it can help to see ancient Peru as a continuum rather than as many individual and discrete cultures. Andean culture developed in lurches and in different places across Peru, but a book such as this can give a panorama, showing how consistent the development of their way of viewing the world seems to have been, and how different it was from ours.

One problem for more serious-minded archaeologists is that ancient Peru seems to have flirted with every element of archaeology that the public most like to sensationalise and which as a consequence professionals like to downplay: human sacrifice, stargazing, wild sex, psychedelic drugs and the mummification of the dead, let alone leaving treasure concealed in pyramids. It is with some relief that archaeologists in the past averted their eyes from such tabloid behaviour and concentrated on dating the phases of a culture's pots. Some also tried to avoid any charges of sensationalism by using peer-language of a studied dullness.

But ancient Peru was a place full of wild energies and of what in the sixties would have been called 'alternative lifestyles'; any account of its development needs to grapple head-on with the more lurid aspects, as a new generation of archaeologists have started to do. The very illiteracy of the Andean peoples – so patronised by the Spanish conquistadors – seems to have channelled their creative energy into other forms of imaginative expression.

To help guide the reader through these different and exuberant civilisations, a chronology is included, as well as a glossary. Rather than constantly interrupt the text with footnotes, the 'notes and references section' indicates external sources when they have clearly been quoted from. Where a translation from the Spanish original is not listed in the bibliography, the translation used is my own.

A constant theme of the book is how recent many of the discoveries in this area have been. Ancient Peru is still playing catch-up with the other great ancient civilisations of the world and many of its monuments have only just started to yield their secrets. As one archaeologist put it to me: 'Imagine if all the discoveries of ancient Egypt had been made so recently – the finding of Tutankhamen's tomb, of the Great Pyramid of Cheops, of Abu Simbel – and you have some idea of the great excitement at what has been happening in Peru.'

This was one of the most inspiring elements of my journey – the sense that so much of the evidence is only now being revealed. Moreover it is only in the last few years that the first Peruvian civilisations have been dated back to around 3000 BC, far earlier than elsewhere on the continent and far earlier than had ever been conceived possible before. Peru, it now seems, was the cradle of civilisation in the Americas, just as Egypt and Mesopotamia were in the Old World.

It is terribly easy to be complacent about the state of our current knowledge, as the medieval world was before Copernicus, and to assume that we know all there is to know – whereas in certain disciplines, like archaeology, we may just be on the initial shoulder of the exponential curve upwards that lies ahead. Nowhere does this seem to be more true than in Peru, still on the fringe of the world when it comes to the study of ancient civilisations and where there are many new discoveries to be made, whether in the field or in the library.

*

My first and principal thanks go to my family for their support while we lived in Peru and during the writing of this book: Sally, Daisy, Owen and Leo.

My companions on the research expedition to Llactapata included: Ramiro Abendanio, Nicholas Asheshov, Michael Boland, Barry Bond, Raul Cobos, Greg Danforth, David Espejo, Pío Espinosa, Amy Finger, Jeff Ford, Antonia Hall, William Heath, Eddy Kruppa, Sandy LaJudice, Beth LaTulippe, John Leivers, Kim Malville, Robert Mrocek, Nathan Poole, Roz Savage, Jack Vetter and Gary Ziegler. Particular thanks go to Kim Malville and Gary Ziegler for the shared collaboration in the analysis of our research, and to John Leivers for accompanying me on journeys around Peru and through the night at Qoyllurit'i.

The expedition was supported and approved by the Royal Geographical Society, the Explorers Club and the Mount Everest Foundation. John Hemming gave advice and support in mounting the expedition. R. Tom Zuidema helped analyse the findings. Earlier investigations at Llactapata by David Drew, Johan Reinhard and indeed Hiram Bingham himself all greatly aided our work there.

Simon Sherwood, Paul White, Filip Boyen, Joanna Boyen,

Laurent Carrasset and Yasmine Martin of Orient Express and PeruRail contributed greatly to the success of the expedition with their support and gift of facilities. Barry Walker, Rosario Velarde, David Guevara and the staff of Manu Expeditions showed their unrivalled expertise in organising the ground operations.

Charles Chadwyck-Healey kindly facilitated my study of the Hiram Bingham archives at Yale University. I would like to thank Rolena Adorno for showing me Bingham's house in Yale, and Richard Burger and Lucy Salazar-Burger for assistance with maps of Llactapata and for their hospitality. Mike Jay shared with me his pre-publication thoughts on the hallucinogenic substances used at Chavín.

Many archaeologists and anthropologists were generous with their time and knowledge: Henning Bischof, David Browne, Richard Burger, Johny Isla, Josué Lancho, César Leandro, Gordon McEwan, Perci Paz, Xavier Ricard Lanata, Vince Lee, María Rostworowski de Diez Canseco, Johan Reinhard, Lucy Salazar-Burger, Ruth Shady and Charles Stanish.

I would also like to thank the librarians of the Museo Inka and the Archivo de Bartolomé de las Casas in Cuzco, of the Sterling Memorial Library at Yale and of the Royal Geographical Society in London.

Those who accompanied me on journeys around Peru included Arabella Cecil, Paul Cripps, Adrian Gallop, Simon Leishman and Carlos Rey.

It would be impossible to list all those in Peru who showed me hospitality and kindness, but Nicholas and María del Carmen Asheshov, Ken Duncan, Barry and Rosario Walker, Wendy Weeks, Michael White and Clara Bravo deserve special thanks, while Carlos and Claudia Rey made us feel that their house was indeed our home.

John Gilkes prepared the maps: the map of Machu Picchu and Llactapata incorporates elements from a previous map of Gary Ziegler's. I am likewise obliged to Juan Manuel Castro Prieto for the welcome opportunity to include some of his black and white photographs from *Perú: Viaje al Sol* (Lunwerg, Barcelona, 2001).

Sections of the manuscript were read by David Browne, Fiona Cadwallader, Pedro Morales, Henry Shukman, Sarita Taylor, Patience Thomson and Wendy Weeks, to all of whom I am grateful, while of course remaining responsible for any errors.

My agent Georgina Capel and editors Francine Brody and Ion Trewin at Weidenfeld & Nicolson guided the book through to publication.

It is a curious Fact, as connected with the History of the Human species, that the Nation which gave its Laws and Civilisation to the rest of South America, should have proceeded from one of its most barren and unproductive Regions.

> Joseph Barclay Pentland, unpublished report
> on Peru for the British Government, 1827

If the ancestors of the people called Indians had known writing in earlier times, then the lives they lived would not have faded from view. As the mighty past of the Spanish Vira Cochas is visible until now, so too would theirs be.

> *The Huarochirí Manuscript,*
> compiled from native sources *c.*1598

No se puede dar puntada sin hilo. You cannot weave without thread.

> Peruvian proverb

There is no Quechua word for 'meaning'.

> Quechua dictionary

CHASING HIRAM BINGHAM
TO LLACTAPATA

A SINGLE DREAMLIKE IMAGE comes into focus: I am flying in a small plane through the Andes, clouds and summits peeling away to either side; the great massif of Mount Salcantay is lit up ahead in the distance above the clouds like a vignette on a Victorian postcard.

It is a landscape I know well and yet a view I have never seen, for this is the first time I have flown over the Inca heartland around Machu Picchu.

The plane is bucketing from between 15,000 feet to 17,000 feet as it swerves around the mountain ridges. We have opened the doors to use the thermal-imaging camera, and I am taking the odd hit from an oxygen bottle. The cold is intense. Perhaps it's the altitude that's making me hypoxic and the landscape hyper-real; nor am I used to sitting directly beside the pilot, who is called Juan. I am conscious that he is struggling with the map.

'*No sé donde estamos*, I don't know where we are,' says Juan over my headphones.

There is a scene in Howard Hawks's *Only Angels Have Wings*, set in the Andes, when Cary Grant as the pilot looks up to see a mountain wall emerge out of the clouds right in front of his nose. I have seen the film many times.

'Maybe we should go higher,' I murmur.

'You can fly the plane yourself if you want to,' offers Juan. This is not meant sarcastically. He genuinely thinks I'll be able to find our target better, having been there once on foot.

For a moment I think I will – isn't anything possible in South America, as Conan Doyle once remarked? – but sanity quickly returns. I have never flown a plane before. This is clearly not the moment to learn.

And then there is a break in the clouds and Mount Verónica does indeed loom up out of the clouds, looking startlingly large and close on the starboard side. Verónica is unmistakable. It is the mountain that dominates the highlands around Cuzco. Juan can put away his map.

We have hit the familiar, twisting runway of the Urubamba river; it is not long before Machu Picchu appears below. We get out our cameras like tourists, even though between us we must have spent thousands of hours at the ruins. But this is different. We are seeing the site from directly overhead, actually spiralling over it through 360 degrees, as if it was a pivot. Juan cannot resist showing off both the ruins and his piloting skills.

As Machu Picchu twists beneath us in its seemingly impossible position on a narrow saddle, the river curling right around it, I remember the Inca obsession with combining stone and water for their *huacas*, their shrines. The plane corkscrews and the day itself seems to have become impossible, like a video arcade game. A phrase flies through my head: 'I have been here before – I will be here again.'

*

Gary Ziegler shook my arm urgently and I took off the headphones. With the doors open, the noise and wind in the Cessna were intense. He pointed ahead. I could see why he was worried. The distant image I had seen earlier of Mount Salcantay emerging from the clouds had now been completely blanketed by those same clouds. They were swirling in from the Amazon, covering our destination, the area where the Llactapata ruins should be.

Our thermal-imaging camera was supposed to be able to detect the difference in temperature between stone buildings, which retain heat, and vegetation, which does not. By using it, we should be able to see through the cloud-forest to any ruins below the canopy. This was the theory at least, although it was only recently that such a camera had started to be used for archaeological surveys. We thought it could be the innovative technology we needed to locate lost Inca sites, the archaeological equivalent of those X-ray specs sold in schoolboys' comics to look through women's skirts, but hopefully more effective.

Thermal imaging had recently been used with interesting results at Maya sites in the central American rainforest, but not here in the Peruvian Vilcabamba, so we looked forward to mining a rich new seam. But we had not reckoned on the thick cloud cover that sometimes billowed into this part of Peru from the Amazon. While the thermal-imaging camera could penetrate through the banks of cloud, the resulting information was useless without a visual reference. It didn't make for easy flying either.

We were only able to afford this expensive infra-red equipment because Gary and I had been successful in an expedition we had led the previous year. Our expedition had made the first report of a previously unknown Inca site called Cota Coca, lying in a deep impassable river canyon. The discovery had brought interest and newspaper headlines around the world; more importantly, it had also allowed us to mount this new and better-equipped expedition to a place that had long fascinated me – Llactapata.

Llactapata was the place that had first drawn me to the Andes and the Inca heartland in 1982, as I'd described in my first book, *The White Rock*. Yet although we had found some ruins there, I had never been totally satisfied that we had uncovered everything. Now I had the chance to find out.

Gary was shouting in my ear as he pointed to exciting new features of the Urubamba range that could only be seen from the air. The noise from the open plane doors meant that I couldn't hear him clearly. But I knew Gary well enough to know pretty much what he was saying anyway.

This part of the Andes is indented by the deep river canyons that fall away towards the Amazon, and it is often difficult to cross from one valley system to another in what is a compact and intransigent topography. The cloud-banks would occasionally part to give us glimpses of whole new areas that had never been properly explored:

we could see rivers gleaming impossibly white, coiled lazily along the valleys with serpentine loops, and the thick vegetation that Hiram Bingham once characterised as 'the magnificent witchery' of the Peruvian jungle. In particular we were looking for those features of the landscape that we knew from long experience the Incas might have been drawn to, the high shoulders or cols with peaks behind them that mirrored the positions of Machu Picchu and other known Inca sites.

Now Gary was mouthing things like 'that looks a good ridge to climb some day', to which my characteristic response was to nod and hope we didn't ever put it to the test, as even from the air I could see some murderous vegetation on the way up.

Gary turned from his binoculars to synchronise his wristwatch against the digital and infra-red cameras. He loved all the technology. It was he who had first suggested we use the infra-red equipment from his experience of using it in Vietnam during aerial recon-naissance at night from a light plane. After serving in Vietnam, Gary had retreated to Colorado and the most remote horse ranch he could find, where he had got an old-timer to teach him the ways. Now he was a cowboy from his Custer hat down to the tips of his riding boots. But anyone who pandered to this preconception and assumed that Gary was some hick from the sticks (and the stuffier archaeologists often did this) would be brought up short by his erudition and knowledge. One of the things I valued most in my friendship with Gary was his infinite capacity to surprise.

The eminent Peruvian archaeologist Jorge Muelle had supervised Gary's doctoral work in Lima in the 1960s. Since then he had covered more of the Vilcabamba on foot than just about any serious investigator, and had put his training in both archaeology and geology to good effect in his interpretative work on sites.

Moreover, although Gary was certainly cut out as an action hero, he was more of a James Stewart than a John Wayne; tall and laconic, he had a slow drawl that could disarm the occasional frustrations of his colleagues when his disconcerting leaps of faith catapulted them into places they hadn't necessarily intended to go.

On the face of it we were polar opposites, different in age, nationality and background; far from serving in the army, I'd never shot a rifle in anger and was ambivalent about horses, in that I liked them to walk, not run. Yet as Amy Finger, Gary's loyal partner in both the ranch and his life, often commented, we were good for one another; while Gary prompted me to try the unexpected, I was sometimes able to focus our ambitions in achievable directions. And having led several expeditions together, we trusted each other totally.

Right now, I felt we might have bitten more off than we could manage. Gary's face was white from the cold. John Leivers and Kim Malville were behind us in the aircraft body, battling to get clear test shots with the infra-red camera out of the open plane door. I had an earful of static from the intercom. Juan and his co-pilot were pointing ahead. The clouds were resolutely not parting over Llactapata. They clung to the 20,000-foot peak of Salcantay at the hub of this particular mountain area. I remembered Elizabeth Bishop's lines:

> the pressure of so many clouds on the mountaintops
> makes them spill over the sides in soft slow-motion,
> turning to waterfalls under our very eyes.

Mount Salcantay's northern ridge ran down between two valleys: the deep Santa Teresa valley and the shallower and shorter Aobamba valley. The sharp serrated edge of the ridge just poked through the cloud bank, like a fish breaking the surface. It was a beautiful sight but also a bitterly frustrating one. There was nothing we could do. The plane circled up and down the two valleys and the ridge between them for as long as we dared, willing the clouds to part over the slope where we knew Llactapata lay. Indeed, we circled so many times that the locals below thought we were *federales* looking for coca or marijuana plantations.

John and Kim were trying to film out of the open door as the plane banked, and then playing back the data immediately to see whether we were getting any thermal-imaging readings. The thermal-imaging camera was small – about the size of a camcorder. It would obviously need more time back at base to analyse its findings fully; at least digital playback allowed instant access of the grainy black-and-white images, although as John commented in an understated, Australian way, 'It's a little difficult to work out where you are.'

I had a mental image of the camera printing out a neat graphic plan of an Inca settlement – a plaza, or perhaps some *kallanka* grouped around a courtyard – with the blurred lines and cross-hairs of similar images from the Gulf War. The news had been full of such disturbing images when we left home, with a plane's infra-red system locking onto a target. Coming to Peru had been a welcome escape from such visions of Iraq, although even here the war had pursued us. Our infra-red equipment had been classified as military hardware and needed a special licence to bring it from the States; the idea that it was being used to look for Inca ruins had met with scepticism from the State Department.

The flights were costing a daunting $1,000 an hour and even with the backing of a film company, which wanted additional documentary footage from the plane, we had to be disciplined in our use of time. This was already the second day we had been up in the air; the previous day had been worse for cloud cover. The problem was that we needed to film after some hours of sunlight, so that the buildings would be warm enough to register on the infra-red camera – yet before the afternoon cloud cover rolled in. This window of opportunity was a frustratingly narrow one.

The resulting costs of all the delay were causing tension in the plane. It was not an easy working environment. With the plane doors off in order to film, the cold, noise and turbulence were bone-crunching. Our infra-red team, John and Kim, jostled around the open Cessna door with the cameraman who was filming us at work. Trying to relay and translate instructions between the various camera crews and the pilots – a job that fell to me – was frustrating. At times both Gary and I found the multimedia technological environment all too much, certainly for the concentrated work we wanted to achieve.

At some point in the flight, the glass in my watch had shattered against a hatch, so I was reliant on the instrument panel for our flight time as well as our altitude. When I saw that we were already running into the red on the flight time, I consulted with Gary. He shouted against the wind, inches from my face: 'It looks like we may be screwed.' It was pointless – and expensive – to carry on, so after one final turn around the still-clouded site, we admitted defeat and started to fly back.

As the plane began its precarious descent to the mountain bowl of Cuzco, it seemed we were returning empty-handed. It would take time to analyse the infra-red video footage, yet given the flying conditions and the cloud cover, I couldn't believe we would be able to glean much new information from it. The expensive 'toys for boys' technology had failed.

So to find anything we would have to go to Llactapata on foot, clearing our way with machetes in the way we were used to from previous expeditions and as indeed I'd gone there first, twenty years before. However, I wasn't dispirited; in fact I felt almost a perverse relief that modern technology hadn't made such work on the ground obsolete, as I enjoyed it.

More than this, I knew we had a secret weapon with us, a precious piece of information I had coaxed from the archives at Yale University, which meant that even if the thermal imaging proved completely useless, there was a good chance we would still find what we were looking for.

*

It was the American explorer Hiram Bingham who had taken me to Yale. Indeed, it was Bingham who had first enticed me to Llactapata and Peru.

Hiram Bingham might be best known for his discovery of Machu Picchu in 1911, but he had also located a whole range of other Inca sites throughout the Peruvian Vilcabamba. Following in his footsteps, I had been there in 1982 with a small team that I had brought out from England to help relocate one such site which he had described and yet which no one seemed to have seen since. We had joined up with an energetic and capable archaeologist called David Drew, who was working with the local Cusichaca Project and had led us to the site. Since writing *The White Rock* about that first visit, I had also written an introduction to a new edition of *Lost City of the Incas*, Bingham's account of his findings at Machu Picchu. For this I had reread all Bingham's other available books and articles.

In doing so, I had become interested in a conundrum. The site-plan that Bingham had left of Llactapata, while of a similar size to the 'Llactapata' we had found in 1982 on precisely the same hillside, and in the right area, did not correspond exactly to ours. At the time I had put this down to a certain carelessness in Bingham's drafting. I was used to archaeologists endlessly patronising him as they are inclined to do when anyone is not an official member of their guild; his interpretation of Machu Picchu had also been criticised, so it was easy to think of him as an unreliable witness. I knew that Bingham had spent very little time there in 1912 – he was, after all, in the middle of excavating at Machu Picchu near by. And the site we had found shared many features with his and was the right size.

However, now that I had read more of his work and recognised how careful and conscientious most of his draughtsmanship was, it seemed even more remarkable that he would have got such details wrong.

Perhaps, I thought, the secret lay in his unpublished journals, which were kept in an archive at Yale.

*

I had never been to Yale before. Standing in front of the extremely large house that Hiram Bingham had once owned on Prospect Street, one could immediately see why he had caused such envy in his academic colleagues. Here was a tall, good-looking assistant professor who seemed to be permanently away on sabbaticals in South America and who became a media celebrity on finding Machu Picchu. Moreover he married a Tiffany heiress – hence the large house. Add to this considerable academic and political ambition, lightly concealed with a certain arrogance of demeanour, and one could understand why he was eventually cold-shouldered out of Yale, to become a senator instead. Even the Senate found him too much and he was eventually impeached.

Still, Yale had since recognised his achievements – and his loyalty in exporting most of the finds from Machu Picchu back to his *alma mater*, much to the legitimate annoyance of Peruvians. Most of those finds had been lying in cardboard boxes ever since, but now the Peabody Museum had a committed Andeanist as its director, Richard Burger, who together with his wife Lucy was mounting a major exhibition of all Bingham's takings from Machu Picchu.

I was lucky to arrive when I did. Richard's interest in the area meant that he could advise me on the complicated procedures for accessing the various Bingham holdings. He also led me to a dusty basement cupboard at the back of the Peabody where Bingham's old photographs were kept. He had been an assiduous and talented photographer; 12,000 prints had survived from his various Peruvian expeditions.

The room was not prepossessing. Hot-water pipes ran overhead, hardly ideal for conservation. It was more like a walk-in cupboard than an archive. The photos were kept in old metal filing cabinets that looked as if they had been removed bodily from Bingham's study on his death and hardly glanced at again, for there had been little interest in him since. Aside from a memoir by Alfred Bingham, which combined the rigour of a lawyer with the jaundice of a disaffected son, no one had written the biography of a man who could lay claim to being the greatest American explorer of the twentieth century.

It was a curious feeling to be sitting in this forgotten basement with an explorer's lifetime's work around me. Flicking through the dusty large-format panoramic pictures stacked on the filing cabinet because they wouldn't fit in, I was struck by how poetic some of the images were: cattle bathing in a highland lake; the high passes towards Anta; Quechua women weaving by their huts. Bingham was never just an archaeologist, and all the better for it.

His actual pictures of Machu Picchu and other sites were masterfully composed, some using the difficult Kodak Panoram Camera, with its ultra-wide aspect ratio. There were file after file of contact prints, numbered and dated. But the few shots he took of Llactapata seemed uncharacteristically rushed and partial: he seemed more interested in photographing his tent than the ruins, which was a bad sign.

Richard kindly also found the original sketch maps of Llactapata that Bingham had drawn on for later publication – there were a few additional details, but nothing remarkable. However, it transpired that the Sterling Memorial Library near by still had all Bingham's original field notebooks. Once I had been frisked for sharp objects and had surrendered all writing implements other than a pencil, I was allowed in to see them.

Naturally I turned first to his entry for discovering Machu Picchu on 24 July 1911. His handwriting was terrible, but it was an intoxicating feeling to hold Bingham's journal in my hands, with his excited scrawl: 'more ruins – even finer than Choquequirao.'

Then I turned to his description of finding Llactapata. To my surprise it was extensive, far more so than in his books. And as I read, I began to realise why Bingham had published so little on its discovery, for he was not a man who liked to dwell on his failures.

Bingham's journal records that on 1 August 1912 he left Huadquiña, the hacienda of the local landowner, at 7.30 in the morning and arrived at 'Surirai' at 9.00. The modern hamlet of Suriray lies in the Santa Teresa valley, so Bingham had clearly decided to approach the Aobamba/Santa Teresa ridge from that side.

At Suriray he scribbled hastily in his notebook: 'men here speak of ruins: Llactapata ruins; Cochapata – *laguna* [lake]; Mishihuanca – *lugar* [a place]; Palcai – old *pueblo* [settlement]; Pampacahuana – best ruins of all.'

By 9.30 he had reached a hut 600 feet above Suriray, noting that 'quite a little coffee' was being grown in the smallholdings he passed. By 12.00, after a hard climb, he reached a clearing at the top of the ridge and met Marcello Añanca 'who lives at Llactapata' (there is still a smallholding on the top of the ridge today). By 12.35, presumably having descended over the ridge, he saw the ruins which 'lie at 9100 ft, i.e. 1100 ft higher than MP [Machu Picchu]'.

He remarked on 'the wonderful view' and that the snow peak of

Salcantay was visible. He spent the afternoon looking at the ruins, but determined to press on to the other sites he had been told about previously at Suriray.

So the next day, 2 August, he rose at 5.40, noting that the clouds were rising rapidly from below and that Machu Picchu was already hidden in the distance. At 7.45 the sun burnt off the clouds and he left Llactapata at 8.05, never to return. He pressed on rapidly up the valley to the site of Palcay, which lies at the head of the Aobamba valley. He had spent just five daylight hours at Llactapata.

One might well wonder why Bingham did not spend more time examining a previously unreported site, but the journal made clear that he was handicapped in having a most unwilling team with him: three muleteers who had been pressed into service by a local landowner as a service to Bingham and who clearly did not want to be there. He spends far more time lamenting their deficiencies than describing the ruins themselves. Later in the same journey they deserted him.

He also had an atrocious journey. The cloud-forest vegetation is still extremely thick around Llactapata. An earlier team led by Bingham's assistant Kenneth Heald had attempted to head up the Aobamba valley, but had met with 'almost insuperable difficulty', as 'the jungle was so dense as to be almost impassable. There was no trail and the trees were so large and the foliage so dense that observations were impossible even after the trail had been cut.' Heald's team were further discouraged when an *arriero* was almost bitten by a poisonous snake.

Bingham arrived at Llactapata by an even more difficult route, up the steep-sided Santa Teresa valley. His handwriting seems to get even worse over this journey as he suffered from the worst the Andes could throw at him. At one point his only strong mule had fallen backwards, injuring herself, and her cargo had to be carried by the hostile porters (Bingham did not record their reaction to this additional load).

His decision to move on rapidly is also of a piece with his previous actions when he had first seen Machu Picchu the year before, in 1911; again he had spent just a few hours at the site before heading on rapidly to his next objective. Only later did he send a team back to clear the ruins. A certain impatience was characteristic of the man.

Bingham published very little on Llactapata. A few comments in *Lost City of the Incas*, written in 1948 towards the end of his life, described it as 'Llactapata, the ruins of an Inca castle'. He added: 'We found evidence that some Inca chieftain had built his castle here and had included in the plan ten or a dozen buildings'; 'it may well have been built by one of Manco's captains. It was on a strategic spot.'

In an earlier *National Geographic* piece of 1913, he had written of his regrets at not doing more investigation there, commenting:

> 'It would be interesting to excavate for three or four weeks and get sufficient evidence in the way of shreds and artifacts to show just what connection the people who built and occupied this mountain stronghold had to the other occupants of the valley.'

Yet his half-hearted and incomplete description of Llactapata gave little incentive to later expeditions to do just that and follow him. From the journals it was clear that he was suffering from 'explorer's fatigue': a combination of loneliness, difficult muleteers, difficult territory and perhaps a certain feeling of 'not another bloody ruin'.

Buried in this catalogue of woes was one detail that almost made me whoop aloud in the staid confines of the Yale Sterling Memorial Library. For beside the sketch-map of the ruins he had found, Bingham had jotted down some compass bearings for 'his' Llactapata:

> Machu Picchu Heights [Mount Machu Picchu] 67°.
> Huaina Picchu Heights [Mount Huaynu Picchu] 45°.
> Machu Picchu sacred plaza bears 52°.

These compass bearings had never been published. They were different from the bearings for the ruins I had seen in 1982. Bingham had given an exact triangulation point which, allowing for a small offset due to changes in magnetic north over time, should allow us to relocate the sector.

I felt like Long John Silver being given the map to Treasure Island. It was this which more than anything else made me want to return to Llactapata and make sense of a mystery that had puzzled me for twenty years. Regardless of whether the thermal imaging worked (and it could be argued this was a redundant 'belt and braces' approach), we should now be able to relocate 'Bingham's Llactapata', and establish clearly quite how extensive the site was.

For this was my other great excitement. It was not just a case of Bingham having found the 'right' Llactapata, and our having found a 'wrong' one in 1982. We were clearly talking about a much more extensive site than had ever been realised, of multiple sectors.

Gary Ziegler had come across another account of the area near Llactapata by Johan Reinhard, the celebrated discoverer of the so-called 'ice mummies' left on mountain peaks by the Incas as sacrifices. He had passed by in 1985 while investigating an Inca trail along the northern ridge of Mount Salcantay, the same trail that Bingham had taken when he left the ruins. While Reinhard did not try to investigate the main site at Llactapata, thinking that it had already been reported, he did say that he had come across a different and substantial building on the ridge-line above, at 9,960 feet: 'the ruins of a large structure or series of structures that have a nice view towards Machu Picchu'. Reinhard mapped the building.

So Llactapata was a puzzling site, in that each of the very few explorers who had been there seemed to bring back a different description and map of what should by all rights have been the same place. My growing suspicion was that we might be dealing with a far larger site than anybody had ever realised, and that previous explorers had each found a part of a much greater whole, like the Sufi parable in which three blind men hold the legs, tail and trunk of an elephant but fail to realise that it is the same animal.

The only way to prove this was to return with a large and thorough expedition that could examine the whole hillside.

*

So I felt remarkably relaxed when after hours of looking through the thermal-imaging footage back in Cuzco, we concluded that there was nothing there we didn't already know. I was helped in this unusual mental calm by one signal advantage. I was staying in the five-star Hotel Monasterio.

Previous visits to Cuzco had been on my own account and consequently in the cheapest place that had clean sheets, with hot water at the landlady's whim. But Simon Sherwood, the boss of Orient Express and a man with a keen awareness of the Andes from his early days trekking there with a backpack, had taken a personal interest in our expedition. One welcome by-product of this was a 'gold access-all-areas card' giving help right across the Orient Express empire. And in Peru, it really was an empire. The company had bought hotels in Cuzco, Machu Picchu, Lima and the complete train-set to go with it: both the famous old railway to Machu Picchu and the longer line over to Lake Titicaca. The Hotel Monasterio in Cuzco was the jewel in their crown, a restored seventeenth-century monastery with magnificent rooms set around cloisters.

Having just arrived, there had only been a short while to get used to the opulence. But I could see it was a taste I could rapidly – and dangerously – acquire. I had already spent a strange time staying at their equally five-star hotel in Lima after the flight from Europe. Arriving with my usual dirty backpack and trekking clothes for the cloud-forest, the exquisitely polite desk-staff had taken it on the chin and ushered me to what was described as 'The Presidential Suite' on the top floor of the hotel.

'But doesn't the president live in Lima anyway?' I had asked the bellboy as we ascended in the capacious and eerily silent lift.

'It's for all the other presidents,' he said.

A series of rooms with impossibly ornate Louis XV furniture opened onto a balcony with its private pool; there was a view down to the Pacific breakers below. The plane had arrived at night, and now all I could see was the waves breaking phosphorescent on Lima's ragged coastline.

Inside the suite were a bed and jacuzzi so large they could have accommodated a rock band complete with groupies. There seemed to be two bathrooms. Already feeling that I had betrayed my lack of worldly, let alone presidential, experience (and worrying what size tip was appropriate for such a prestigious suite) I asked why.

'One bathroom is for the president himself. The other is for his *funcionarios*, his staff.'

Of course. Resisting the temptation to ring room-service for cocaine and call-girls, I sank into a dreamless and air-conditioned sleep under a blanket heavy with embroidery.

And now in Cuzco I had an equally presidential suite and even a courtyard to myself. Just in case hubris followed, it seemed that mosquitoes had no respect for 'gold card' status. I'd been bitten more in luxury than I had ever been in the usual so-called 'fleapit' hotels. Perhaps Mick Jagger had experienced the same problem when he'd passed this way on one of the Peruvian adventures the Stones had occasionally indulged in.

Gary, Kim, John and I discussed our thermal-imaging findings from the flight. We had still not given up on the new camera. One problem was getting a stable enough platform from which to use it. Unfortunately there were no helicopters available in the area, which would have been far better than fixed-wing aircraft. The only previously operational helicopter company had been forced to close its exclusive commercial run to Machu Picchu; the locals had burnt the helicopter pad, on the grounds that if tourists (worse, very rich tourists) flew direct into Machu Picchu they would miss the enticing display of local handicrafts available when they came by train.

There was a good sight-line to Llactapata from Huayna Picchu, the peak above Machu Picchu, so we decided to go there and take more thermal-imaging readings from a fixed ground position. This had another signal advantage. It meant I could stay at the last of the three luxury Orient Express hotels, right by the ruins themselves, which had been built on the site Bingham had first used for his camp when he excavated at Machu Picchu; it now retailed at $500 a night.

*

'You guys are really something,' said Mike. Mike was the Canadian cameraman accompanying the expedition. His comments were only partly induced by appreciation of our collective skills. The fact that along the bar were lined up representative shots of every type of flavoured *pisco* helped; it looked like an alchemist's counter, with phials of clear, ochre and turquoise liquor, some containing floating herbs. The comparative tasting was going down a storm.

It had been arranged by Patricio, the engaging Italian manager of the Orient Express Machu Picchu hotel; on the strength of one evening's *pisco* tasting and a stay in his exclusive hotel we now rated him as a lifelong friend. We had already had a good day climbing Huayna Picchu, and even though, again, the thermal-imaging camera had not delivered what it said on the packet, it had at least given us a much clearer view of the Llactapata hillside.

This had also allowed me to see Machu Picchu afresh after the revelations of the recent epoch-making Yale exhibition, which had re-presented Bingham's 1912 findings to the world. One of the surprises of that show had been how playful were many of the artifacts recovered from Machu Picchu: musicians' instruments; beautiful plates with birds' heads for handles; another pair with butterflies; even a set of ceramic dice. People always approached Machu Picchu with such reverence − indeed over-reverence − that it was easy to forget that this was a place of pleasure, a royal estate. All too often archaeology sieved the playfulness out of daily life; what survived in the middens was the utilitarian and the prosaic. But Bingham's rich haul at Yale was a testament to the growing argument that Machu Picchu was not primarily a sacred centre, but a more secular and courtly retreat for the Inca emperor and his retinue away from the cares of state.

The Yale exhibition had been accompanied by the publication of a range of scholarly papers re-examining Bingham's findings with modern scientific techniques. Looking out over the empty buildings, I tried to imagine them as the cosmopolitan hive of activity that this recent scientific work showed they must have been. The analysis of the bone chemistry from burials showed that the population was an exceptionally diverse one, drawn from all over Peru, both coast and mountains, not just from the local population around Cuzco. The metalwork and jewellery were equally diverse, a showcase of styles and indeed of materials: obsidian from near Ayacucho, tin from the far south in what is present-day Bolivia and pottery from right across their realm.

We like to think of such ancient sites as being 'authentic' homogenous examples of just one culture – and of Machu Picchu as a showcase for the classic 'pure Inca' style – but in its heyday it would have been as cluttered with foreign objects as any department store in London or New York.

The food consumed would probably have been equally wide-ranging. Bingham was relatively uninterested in what types of animal remains he came across – he was more interested in human ones – but he did at least keep them. Modern osteologists have looked at these faunal remains and shown that a wide range of meat was consumed, from the familiar alpaca to more exotic wild deer and even an agouti, the large tailless rodent from the jungle, where it is still eaten by tribespeople as a delicacy. Guinea pig, famously the most sought-after delicacy for Andean Indians today, seems also to have been consumed, although it leaves such tiny bones that it is harder to find and analyse them.

The slender terraces to either side of Machu Picchu were used to grow exotic vegetables, similar to courgettes and peppers; other terraces might have contained ornamental flowers. More substantial food, like maize, the staple diet of the Andes, could have been brought over the hills from 'worker colonies' placed discreetly out of royal eyesight up the valley.

I had an image of a small, courtly community of less than a thousand people, who came seasonally and for pleasure – much as modern tourists do. As the sun slowly left the ruins, I followed it to the far side of the Sacred Plaza and watched it sink over the Llactapata slope, directly to the west. Earlier that day we had scanned that same Llactapata slope obsessively (and fruitlessly) with the thermal-imaging camera. Now I allowed myself a more leisurely scan with simple binoculars. I could clearly see the little *pampa* at 9,000 feet where we planned to camp, and I knew that not far above it were the ruins I had seen in 1982. 'Bingham's Llactapata' was somewhere above that, although even with the perspective of distance it was a dauntingly large area of forested hillside to comb. Still, his compass bearings gave a triangulation point at an altitude of some 300 feet above the lower site. I tried to get an approximation of it through the glasses, but it seemed to be where the vegetation was heaviest.

I noticed for the first time a semi-circular protrusion in the wall to the west of Machu Picchu's Sacred Plaza, which looked like a *mirador*, a deliberate 'viewing platform' from which to admire Llactapata and the setting sun. One of the most fascinating developments in Inca studies over the last few years had been the interest in the new discipline of 'archaeo-astronomy', which had focussed with considerable rigour on how the Incas observed the stars. One result had been a greater interest in the alignment of sites, both to the stars and to *huacas*, the shrines that spread out in complex spiritual patterns from Cuzco, the centre of the Inca dominions. Although not referring to Llactapata, Johan Reinhard had shown how carefully aligned on sacred peaks many of the buildings around Machu Picchu were – so this viewing platform was likely to have been for a purpose.

Above the Sacred Plaza, on the Intihuatana Hill, a woman in white was looking out over the empty city, rising and falling on the balls of her feet, as if letting the moment fill her. Machu Picchu drew many such spiritual pilgrims here. Indeed, it was a place that brought me considerable calm myself yet I had always been cautious about the dangers of transferring the spiritual feelings of many visitors on seeing Machu Picchu into an assumption that the Incas might have felt the same way. The whole move in recent archaeological thinking had been to reposition it as a more secular site.

That said, one detail in the Yale exhibition had particularly moved and intrigued me: the discovery by the Main Gate of a set of plain obsidian pebbles. These pebbles were natural and had not been worked in any way, unlike the obsidian tools found scattered elsewhere in Machu Picchu. Hiram Bingham's expedition had found them near the Main Gate in a cluster of thirty, as if deliberately placed together. Bingham had been so puzzled by this find that he had speculated they might be the chance result of a meteorite shower.

Obsidian is a rare commodity in the Andes; there is no source for it close to Cuzco. By using instrumental neutron activation and X-ray fluorescence, researchers had discovered that the pebbles came from a distant site some 250 miles from Cuzco, an obsidian flow in the Colca valley, near Arequipa. Jay Ague, a geologist at Yale, had gone further; he had shown that they were in fact river pebbles, small bits of obsidian that had been collected from the Colca river and had then been brought all the way to Machu Picchu. The river had washed them into natural, rounded shapes. As Ague pointed out, it would have been very easy to get larger, more impressive pieces of obsidian from deposits on the dry land near by. A decision had clearly been made to bring such river pebbles, bits of obsidian worked by water, and place them by the gate at Machu Picchu. Just as when I had circled over the ruin in a plane a few days before, it was a reminder of the intimate and intuitive connections the Incas made between water and stone.

And now I was lining up shots of *pisco* along the bar of the Orient Express hotel with the Canadian film crew and Patricio. The end of a perfect day. 'Try the *uña de gato*, the "nail of the cat",' suggested Patricio. 'It's superb.'

After downing his, Mike picked up where he'd left off: 'You guys are really something. You set off through the jungle, swing a machete and "wham, bam, thank you, ma'am", you've found a lost city!'

I winced. This was the first time Mike had been with us on an expedition, so he still harboured the illusion that there was some glamour attached. But he was also reminding me of the problems we had experienced with the media when our previous discoveries had been reported. Every sub-editor in the land had reached for a 'LOST CITY' headline, with an aside about 'real-life Indiana Jones' in the text. This would have been laughable if a few of the more po-faced archaeologists had not then used this as evidence of our lack of serious intent. Some of them were still inclined to the view that any such report of an Inca site should only be published in decent obscurity at the back of some little-read journal.

But along with Gary Ziegler, I had always disliked the elitism of the academic library; if we did find anything at Llactapata, while certainly writing a detailed specialist report for an academic magazine, we wanted to reach a wider audience as well. This was precisely what Hiram Bingham had done when he found Machu Picchu, publishing a scholarly account in a limited edition, *Machu Picchu: A Citadel of the Incas*, but also writing journalistic articles in *National Geographic Magazine* and his more populist account of the discovery for *Lost City of the Incas*.

The Yale exhibition had seen a substantial re-evaluation of Bingham's reputation. Once derided for not having brought an archaeologist along with him on his expedition, Richard Burger now praised him in the exhibition catalogue because of his multi-disciplinary approach, for while Bingham did not include an archaeologist in his team, he brought experts in many other fields – geologists, geographers and naturalists. Burger saw Bingham as foreshadowing today's equally multi-disciplinary approach, unlike the other more narrowly specialist archaeological investigations of his day.

I hoped that with Llactapata we would be able to build on the work Bingham had done there – and his expectation that there was more to find. And I also hoped, for his sake and mine, that those coordinates he had put down in his notebook had been right.

*

In a childish way, I've always wanted to catch a moving train. The next day I had the opportunity – indeed, necessity – to do so.

I'd spent the morning filming with the Canadian crew up at Machu Picchu, as they'd wanted the city lit up at dawn behind me as they did the interview. Unfortunately the city had been obscured with more of the cloud cover that had so frustrated us earlier with the thermal-imaging camera, and they had to make do with me emerging out of the mist, like some extra from *Highlander*. Nor, after the *pisco*-tasting the night before, were we all thinking lucidly.

'Maybe,' said Mike, 'you could, sort of, wave at the ruins behind you and ask the viewer to imagine the city behind the clouds?' It didn't work. We waited for the clouds to clear. We waited too long.

By the time I got back down to Aguas Calientes and the train line, our 'Tren Especial' arranged by Orient Express had just left. The film crew were catching up with us later, so I was on my own. The train was still moving through the built-up section of town and had not gathered much speed, although it had attracted crowds of onlookers curious as to why it was going the wrong way, for it was heading downriver, along a stretch of railway line seldom used since a disastrous landslide some years before had washed away the track to which it connected.

Already out of breath from running, I pushed through the crowd and, to the surprise of the onlookers (one of whom let out an ironic '¡Olé!'), launched myself onto the backplate, landing if not elegantly at least without dropping my pack. I rolled on unsteady legs into the carriage.

The sight that met my eyes was surreal. The only train that Orient Express had been able to loan us was the luxury coach being prepared for the inauguration of the new 'Hiram Bingham Express', an exclusive $150 round ticket to Machu Picchu, which included dinner on the train and all the opulence that Orient Express could provide: white linen tablecloths, comfortable club chairs, waiters in livery. And sitting among all this splendour were our motley group of hairy-arsed explorers, looking decidedly out of place.

There is something about a backpack that is inimical to style. Not for nothing were the cheapest sections of the other trains sold euphemistically as the 'backpacker' sections (that is, 'steerage'). And their owners in trekking gear and boots just lowered the tone further. Much as Oblonsky in *Anna Karenina* would not have been seen dead hunting in anything but his oldest and most worn clothing, so our team prided themselves on wearing clothes that had seen the world and were still covered in it.

The only person who seemed to the manner born was Nicholas Asheshov, the partially sighted British explorer, who was sipping the courtesy champagne and wearing a jaunty silk scarf knotted around his neck. Nick was a veteran of many such expeditions since his first in 1962 for National Geographic, and had spent a lifetime buccaneering around the South American continent, chasing either wars or business opportunities. He had lived in Peru for years.

He was holding forth with some vehemence on the absent Peter Frost, or 'Peter-von-bloody-Frost' as he called him, another explorer working in this area about whom Nick had strong views (the whole exploring and archaeological world was a minefield of animosities).

'Ah, is that you, Hugh?' Nick interrupted himself as he peered towards me. 'So you decided to join us after all?'

Nick had refused to let the degeneration of his vision, caused by a macular condition, prevent him from accompanying our various research trips. The previous year he had ridden with Gary and me for five days to get to the remote and hidden site of Cota Coca, with his horse led by a trusted helper. As an ex-journalist, he had a nose for getting to the heart of the matter when it came to archaeological investigation. Now he hardly let me get my breath back before buttonholing me: 'So this is the story. Bingham found one bit of this ruin ninety years ago. Then you were part of the team that found another bit twenty years ago. Now you want to find Bingham's bit properly, having cocked up the first time, and put them both together with anything else that's up there. I'm not sure what the hell any sub-editor will make of it for a headline, but I can see the point.'

I was having champagne as well. Any twinge of guilt at all this luxury was quickly alleviated by the thought that we were going to be living under canvas, with mosquitoes and mules our main companions. And Bingham would have approved – he had taken luxury hampers with him on his journeys into the Vilcabamba.

It wasn't long before we reached the end of the line, a literal petering out of the track, like a Buster Keaton movie where you can't progress further until you put down more rails. Chickens were picking their way over the remaining sleepers. *Huayno* music played from the scattering of shacks selling fruit and vegetables to the villagers who came up the valley to the railhead. They watched idly as we began the laborious business of transferring all our belongings to the bridge at the Aobamba river and the mules that were waiting for us on the other side. One plump señora was waving the flies away from her fruit with an Eminem baseball cap. A few kids played ring-a-ring-a-roses to the music.

While the others started off towards Llactapata, I took Kim Malville to show him the small Intihuatana site, which lay a little way back along the railway line. I hadn't talked much to Kim before the expedition. We had asked him to join us because of his experience in archaeo-astronomy. Now in his sixties, he had enjoyed a long and successful academic career as a professor at Colorado University, with a particular interest in how astronomy and mythology had combined to create the 'sacred landscapes' of Egypt and Tibet; he had set up a foundation to help the Dalai Lama's exiled Buddhist community at Dharamshala. With a shock of white hair, dark glasses and a black polo neck, Kim looked like a veteran Californian rock-star who had built a recording studio in Colorado and didn't need to try too hard.

The Intihuatana was so little visited that it took me a while to find again. This was embarrassing as I felt Kim would think me an unreliable guide. Lying just off the railway track, between the lines and the Urubamba river, it was unsignposted and unloved, with litter, overgrown vegetation and all the signs of neglect.

Yet this was a fine and substantial piece of pre-Columbian stone sculpture, carefully placed as the Incas positioned all such sculptures to harmonise with the setting by the river, again with that potent combination of rock and water they liked so much. The largest piece of rock had been partially worked and sculpted, the rest left natural, as was their practice – near by were other carved steps and niches.

I had brought Kim here for a reason. The previous year I had visited the Intihuatana and had been struck by its very precise position due west of Machu Picchu and due east of the highest-known sector at Llactapata, a small two-storeyed temple-building on the top of the ridge, with a distinctive tree growing beside it. I had just carried a compass with me. Now I wanted Kim to confirm my hunch and take more accurate readings with his inclinometer and more sophisticated instruments.

I realised as I did so that this was a significant departure for me. I had always resisted any over-mystical interpretation of the Incas. It smacked not just of New Age credulity, but of a desperation to credit the Incas with spiritual insights we might ourselves have lost. But recent work on what scholars sometimes described as the 'sacred landscape' of the Incas had been so persuasive and illuminating that I felt it was time to put away such prejudices and approach the subject with an open if rigorous objectivity. And given that Kim confirmed that the Intihuatana lay on a direct east–west line between the two sites, it could hardly be coincidence.

From the Intihuatana we also had a clear view of the path that ran south from Machu Picchu across a sheer rock face. The most celebrated feature of this path was that it contained a 'drawbridge', a point at which the Incas placed removable logs so that they could deny access to Machu Picchu. But I was interested in where the path would ultimately have led. While landslides had destroyed much of the route, it clearly seemed to be heading across the Aobamba – and so on to Llactapata.

Kim and I walked briskly to catch the others up in the Aobamba valley. I had remembered this small tributary of the Urubamba as one of the most beautiful in the region, lush with coffee plantations and with a charming small rope bridge across the river. But the recent landslide that had destroyed the railway had also ripped out the heart of the valley, leaving a raw gash across the centre, making the landscape so unrecognisable that for a moment I questioned whether I'd even been there before.

One consequence of this was that the new rope bridge over the savagely enlarged river bed was much longer and this caused us a problem with the mules; as it swayed far more than the old one, it was impossible to get them across. Instead we had been forced to bring them round in a long loop from the other side of the valley. I remembered an incident John Leivers had told me of, when he'd got halfway across a rope bridge and had turned to see some mules inadvertently following him across without their muleteers. The swaying of the bridge frightened them and they stampeded towards John. All he could do was crush himself against the wire supports and hang on as they passed. John survived with just some bruising; in the stampede several mules fell from the bridge onto the rocks below and had to be put down.

Beyond the bridge was a steep climb of 3,000 feet through the forest to the camp. We caught up with Mike and Eddy, the Canadian film crew. Mike in particular was struggling with the climb, perhaps after the assembled rows of *pisco* shots from the night before. At least the sun had left the mountainside and we could walk up in the shade.

Such a climb was usually a moment of humiliation for me. While Gary prepared for our trips by running up Pikes Peak and across half Colorado, I lacked the discipline to do more than jog around the local park and have a beer to recover. But this year I'd enrolled at the local gym for some aerobics classes, figuring that as I was the only man in a group of leotarded suburban mothers, sheer embarrassment would force me to 'keep with the programme'. It had worked. I had sweated profusely as a brisk instructor had 'burnt' our abdomens, thighs and legs in pitiless sequence; I was also exposed to more Phil Collins and Billy Joel than I had ever wanted in this lifetime, or the next. The compensation was that I now found I could head up the hill at a decent speed. The zigzagging steep forested path rose up through the handful of coffee plantations and smallholdings before crossing over to the broad shoulder of the campsite on the little clearing I had seen from Machu Picchu.

This was one of the oddest aspects of Llactapata – that it could be reached within a single day. The place was in sight of Machu Picchu. One might well ask why it had not been investigated more.

The answer lies partially in the inertia inherent to all arch-aeological enterprise. At the thought of wandering off the beaten track to look for new, uncleared sites, any investigator faces the problems of official permission, of organising the logistics – and, worse still, as I was all too aware, of total failure to find anything at all. Far easier to stick to the well-known and most accessible Inca sites, particularly as so little work has been done on even these.

Machu Picchu itself remains largely unexcavated and it was only recently that a whole tranche of terraces were discovered on its northern side.

There was another odd reason why Llactapata had not been investigated before. The Paul Fejos expeditions of 1940 and 1941 had been the largest and most significant to investigate the area since Hiram Bingham. Given that Fejos had combed the area with 300 men, discovering several interesting sites like Wiñay Wayna, I had always wondered why he had never gone back to Llactapata after Bingham had declared it to be so significant.

However, Llactapata is a commonplace name in the Andes. It simply means 'high town' in Quechua; like 'Newtown' in Britain, it is therefore the default name when no one can think of anything else to call a place. There happens to be a site of the same name at the start of the Inca trail, a fact I am continually reminded of by correspondents ('What's so special or new about Llactapata? Hundreds of people walk through it every day'). While Bingham had never returned to the Llactapata that we were now going to investigate in the Aobamba valley, he had excavated this other Llactapata in 1915.

The Paul Fejos team simply confused the two sites. They decided not to investigate our Aobamba site because they thought, erroneously, that Bingham had already done so. In his book, Fejos states: 'The expedition did not concern itself with the sites of Machu Picchu and Llactapata [in the Aobamba], where the Yale University–National Geographic Expedition [led by Bingham] had excavated.' A simple accident of nomenclature had left the site virtually untouched since Bingham's time, compounded by Bingham's failure to leave accurate maps of how to get there.

The tents were in shadow when I arrived at the campsite, but the sun was still catching the Quechua rainbow flag on the tall pole raised by David Espejo, one of the Peruvians on the team. It also lit up Machu Picchu in its cradle between two mountains to the east; the soft evening light burnished the granite of the distant city.

I remembered the view of Machu Picchu from here as being

spectacular, but only now did it become significant that it was so directly due east. The previous evening I had been looking at Llactapata from Machu Picchu – today I was returning that gaze. Kim Malville compared it to *darshan*, a concept I was familiar with from visits to the Hindu pilgrimage centres at the various sources of the Ganges, in which a devotee makes eye contact with a god who then returns the stare.

This valley was still a wild one. We had asked David Espejo to come up here before us and look at some ruins at the head of the valley. David was a tough and resilient guide who had travelled from one end to the other of the Vilcabamba. But he came back shocked from the reconnaissance with a report that he had been fired on by *campesinos* convinced he must be a cattle rustler. This had always been a rural backwater, well known as a smuggling route for coca from the jungle as it avoided the main – and policed – valley below. But the landslide and consequent shutting down of communications and access had made it more lawless.

That night we were all on a high. We expected that the next day would find us back at 'Bingham's Llactapata'. We broke open the vodka. By tradition we had a 'vodka mule' with us, loaded with a crate of Stolichnaya from the Cross Keys pub in Cuzco – for this trip, given the numbers, we had indulgently made it two crates, telling ourselves this would not then unbalance the mule. Given that we had seventeen explorers, eight muleteers and twelve horses with us, we already needed twenty-five mules to carry the other field supplies.

Crowded into the field-tent were a British contingent of six, mostly friends of mine from previous treks, five Americans who had joined Gary and Amy, several Peruvians and John Leivers as the token Australian. We had to choose the toughest person present to lead the small recce party that would next day cut its way through into the dense bush to look for the Bingham sector. Unanimously we chose John.

John Leivers had been with us to Cota Coca the previous year and had impressed Gary and me with his sturdiness and enthusiasm. Now in his early fifties, he had worked as a lifeguard on the beaches near Perth before getting the familiar Australian urge to travel; since then he had criss-crossed the world, driving Encounter Overland buses on the great transcontinental runs from Cairo to Cape Town or across South America. As almost every South American bus stopped in Cuzco, John had come to know Barry Walker, the genial host of the Cross Keys pub, Honorary British Consul and a good friend of Gary's and mine who had helped organise our various expeditions.

Eventually the bottom had dropped out of the long-distance bus market and Encounter Overland had gone bankrupt. Barry had suggested that we take John with us to Cota Coca. Gary and I had needed little persuading when we heard that he had crossed the supposedly 'impassable' Darien Gap between Panama and Colombia three times, solo, and on foot. He had also paddled a dugout canoe way down the Río Napo to Iquitos and had recently climbed two 7,000-metre peaks in Kyrgyzstan.

As such, he had been an impressive addition to the team. On trek he brought just one survival-issue set of clothes. To wash them, he would simply lie down in a mountain stream and then let the clothes dry on his body. But he was not just physically tough – he had an endless curiosity about the Incas and a determination to see everything for himself, which had taken him to some out-of-the-way corners of the Vilcabamba. Often, after doing a job for Barry, he would head into the hills on his own, tramping the high country for weeks at a time, only to re-emerge in Cuzco with hair-raising descriptions of getting held up by armed robbers or running out of food in the backend of nowhere, together with a list of intriguing leads he'd made about unreported ruins that he wanted to follow up further.

The attraction John felt for the mountain culture of the Quechua Indians was reciprocated – they liked his toughness, his occasional shyness and the directness of his aims. Often they would take him in when he tramped the hills and look after him ('I'd sleep by the door'), not least when he got ill – one occupational hazard of living rough, as John did, was that his stomach was quite often going 'to the cleaners', as he put it. He could list a formidable pharmacy of antibiotics he'd been through to get recurring giardia and gastro-enteritis out of his system.

Next day John went off with his small team, chosen either for toughness or because in their inexperience they didn't realise what they were letting themselves in for. As we waited for his return, Gary and I led a group in clearing the sector we already knew of, the building I had first seen in 1982 (and which our group then, I now realised retrospectively, had been the first to report). This was familiar, if overgrown territory. Erosion of the slope had taken one side of the sector right up to a steep drop over which some buildings may have been lost in the past, and it was not an easy place to work; although at 9,000 feet we were dealing with mountain cloud-forest rather than tropical rainforest vegetation, small trees and creepers had still inserted themselves into the crevices of buildings and had to be extracted with great care.

Pío and the team of muleteers were experienced at this. They had worked with us before, and all came from the same small village higher up in the Santa Teresa valley, so they had the slowness and methodical nature of country boys, not of the Cuzco *cholos* who sometimes accompanied tourists and would have been ripping out trees (and doubtless stones) with abandon.

I did notice them all stopping at one point and clustering around Pío, who was reading a magazine that had been brought to camp by one of the wives who arrived intermittently with fresh supplies of food. Curious as to what they were so interested in, I went over to join them. It was a tabloid piece on Saddam Hussein, still missing after the recent invasion of Iraq. '¿*Dónde se ha escondido*, where's he hidden himself?' Pío asked me. I could not really summon up much interest; I was more worried where the ruins had hidden themselves.

There is still a widely held fantasy, encouraged by the movies, that with a few slashes of a machete the vegetation falls away from the 'lost city' of an art director or sub-editor's imagination so that it can reveal itself, like a model shedding a bikini. The reality is more complex and considerably slower, more like a working party trying to clear a refuse dump. For a start, getting vegetation off and away from a site takes time – and there are inevitably layers of secondary vegetation to strip away. Anyone who has ever tried to remove anaglypta wallpaper will have some idea of the process. Even after considerable work, the shape of a site may still be unclear. In a movie, we would crane up above to see the 'pack-shot' of the whole site laid out below with all the neatness of an architect's maquette. On the ground there are no such viewpoints. After cumbersome surveying, the site had to be put together painstakingly on a grid-map, a job Gary did very capably.

After a day of this we were tired. John returned with his even more exhausted group at dusk. Many of them had long creeper weals down their backs. Roz Savage, our young sponsorship organiser, later said that she would have 'described the undergrowth as impenetrable, if it hadn't been for the fact that we were penetrating it'. One look at their faces told me the story. John spoke very deliberately and carefully: 'We went to the exact coordinates you gave us that Bingham had marked. There was nothing there.'

I felt that seventeen explorers, eight muleteers, twelve horses and twenty-five mules were all turning their heads to look at me. I had failed the expedition and brought everyone to the middle of the Peruvian jungle on a wild-goose chase.

THE INCAS AND THE ANDEAN LEGACY

CURSING BINGHAM FOR AN incompetent, I spent a bad night. I knew from his private journals that he had been plagued with difficulties on this particular expedition; his muleteers had been mutinous and had finally deserted him. It had been clear already that he had not been fully focussed – the loose sketches, the bad directions – and now he had failed even in the most elementary task, taking compass bearings.

And I cursed myself for being equally incompetent. Could I not have realised that the coordinates might be wrong? Perhaps that was precisely why Bingham hadn't published them – because he was doubtful as to their accuracy? What was the point of having spent many years fine-tuning my interest in literary criticism, both at university and in later life, when I then couldn't perform the most basic of literary operations: to detect whether a writer was lying or not.

I had let down myself and all the others, including the sponsors of what had been an expensive and ambitious expedition. People had backed me because they had believed in me.

Above all I questioned my own ambition. In some ways, it would have been much easier not to return to Llactapata at all. To do so was in a way an admission of a previous mistake – that when I had thought we had rediscovered 'Bingham's Llactapata' twenty years before, I had been wrong. The fact that this actually meant that we had been discovering a completely new sector of the site, rather than just refinding Bingham's, was irrelevant. As Nick Asheshov had pointed out, to explain that you were enlarging a known site was a far more complicated project than simply 'finding something'. Far easier to have left the issue undisturbed and not raise the inevitable sneers of 'Oh, I thought you had found it once already.' The archaeological critics would be waiting for me with their clasp-knives out.

As it was, I already felt as if I had been time-ramped. 'Time-ramping' is the effect used in documentaries when the camera accelerates through time and space, as pyramids come and civilisations go (sand and clouds whisking past the lens) to stop suddenly in the middle of an action frame.

For almost a year I had been planning this trip with Gary and the rest of the team. With single-minded obsessiveness, we had negotiated the complex security arrangements for exporting the infra-red camera from the States; we had worked with the Peruvian authorities to gain access to the site, liaised with the film crew who would help pay for the plane in return for footage, and done a myriad of financial planning and sponsorship raising. I had been to see the Royal Geographical Society and Mount Everest Foundation to get both their support and grants, for which a group of stern-faced men in a semi-circle at the RGS Library had asked me searching questions.

And then in an accelerated rush, I seemed to be already here, at Llactapata itself, having only arrived in Peru a few days beforehand. What with the excitement of flying over the cloud-forest, there had been little time to slip into my usual Peruvian mindset.

I remembered a conversation I'd had with the American critic Paul Fussell on the dangers of modern travel – that in the speed of arrival made possible by modern technology, the mind often got left behind, leaving the traveller dislocated and vulnerable. It was not just the luggage that could get lost in transit.

Fussell had written about how the mindset of the Edwardians had driven them to the First World War – and the mindset of the survivors of that war had driven many *Abroad*, as he had titled his book (quite where abroad didn't matter very much, but preferably a destination with sun). The travel writing of that period, as of any other, could only be understood in the context of the mental baggage the writers had packed to take with them.

Past explorers like Hiram Bingham and Eric Shipton had come prepared for the rigours of their expeditions after long ocean-going voyages, which had emptied their minds of all the pressures of home. Their modern successors had no such luxury of time; indeed if anything they had to bring their Palm organisers with them to catch up on unfinished e-mails.

I was also all too conscious that, as an explorer, 'you only ever find what you are looking for', a double-edged dictum, in that while you needed to prepare mentally, it was then all too easy to pass by something that didn't match your stated goals. Bingham himself had initially moved on from Machu Picchu after just a few hours at the site because he wasn't expecting to find anything there; it didn't fit in with his neat historical scheme of things and he had an ordered mind. Only much later, at the end of that archaeological season, did he send a team back to take a more considered look at this strange anomalous find.

What was required was not an open mind (too much like a vacuum) but an infinitely responsive one, alive to the possibilities of each discovery but not approaching with any preconceptions. But of course – and lying awake in my tent, I circled back to this – it didn't matter what your mental state was if you couldn't find the bloody ruin in the first place.

I stumbled out in the middle of the night to urinate; it was a completely clear sky and the stars of the Southern Hemisphere, disconcertingly twisted compared to those I was familiar with from the north, were as vivid and bright as if the lights had been left on outside. This high, with no light pollution at all, it was possible to see constellations like Pisces and Cancer, which could be very faint in England.

Peru had always seemed to have a clearer reality for me than my own cloud-covered home country. The night sky helped me to remember that, in South America, things come to you more readily if you do not go looking for them.

*

In *Lost City of the Incas*, Hiram Bingham had commented, ironically enough, on 'what should be done when one is confronted by a prehistoric site – take careful measurements and plenty of photographs and describe as accurately as possible all finds'.

I thought morosely of this as I hacked at the undergrowth the next day. The chances of coming across the ruin Bingham had so signally failed to 'describe accurately' were now slight. As soon as you ventured from the path, thick vegetation and a precipitate slope meant that you could pass within ten feet of a building and miss it. We had miles of densely covered hillside around us. Instead we consoled ourselves by carefully mapping what remained possible: the intriguing site that the Andeanist scholar Johan Reinhard had described finding some years earlier higher up the ridge.

Surrounded by giant tree ferns, it was a lengthy narrow building, an impressive 120 feet long, with twelve entranceways spaced along its sides. The building followed the slightly curved contour of the ridge-top. There were a number of equally spaced holes along the floor of the interior. Most had been opened by passing looters, *huaqueros*, looking for treasure. Some were stone-lined, similar to other sunken chambers we had seen elsewhere in the Vilcabamba. Three smaller, low-walled rectangular structures were near by. Gary and I agreed that the long central building might well have been a *qolqa*, a storehouse, for the main settlement below, placed high so as to be air-cooled and out of danger of any flooding.

Meanwhile Kim Malville and Amy Finger went up to take a look at the unnamed two-storeyed structure further along the ridge, which we had used as a marker from the Intihuatana below, so that Kim could get further readings. This was a finely worked, small building, set on its own with a dramatic view of the Urubamba as the river both approached and receded, and of Machu Picchu across the valley. It was on the edge of land that must once have been cultivated as a smallholding, and was now a tangle of wild strawberries, lupins and old calabash plants. One of the small pinnacles of the ridge rose up behind it. It was a classic position for a shrine, and while I use the term 'spiritual' with caution, it did seem to suggest either a ceremonial or astronomical function (or both), so we christened it 'the Overlook Temple'.

Here as elsewhere, Kim was continuing to find some new and

revealing alignments between the known sectors of Llactapata and Machu Picchu. So the day was not being wasted, although it would be fair to say that morale was low. Gary tried to cheer me by saying that the failure to find the missing 'Bingham sector' at least gave us 'the leisurely opportunity to reinterpret the rest of the site'.

Late in the day, one of the older members of the expedition, Bob Mrocek, who had worked with the Peace Corps in central America, wandered off to one side and headed into the cloud-forest. We assumed that he was just answering a call of nature, but he seemed to be getting further and further from the path. He could only just hear us when someone finally called out: 'Bob, are you all right?'

Just one word came faintly back, from far away: 'Ruins!'

*

When we caught up with Bob, he was standing next to a double-jamb doorway covered in brush. At one glance it was clear that this was Inca ceremonial architecture of a high order. And all around were other buildings stretching into the jungle. At the age of sixty-six, Bob Mrocek had just relocated 'Bingham's Llactapata' site, last reported ninety years ago.

I asked him how he'd done it. 'I just started to follow the light, and it led me here,' said Bob in his soft, southern States drawl: 'I figured the Incas would want to build on a flatter area of the hillside.'

It was an electrifying moment. For the rest of that day and much of the next, we slashed furiously with the machetes, which sparked against the rocks. As one female member of the team commented wryly: 'Give a man a machete and you can almost smell the testosterone levels rising.' Slowly the site began to clear to the point where Gary could survey it: walls, buildings, passageways, a plaza and the dark shadows of trapezoidal niches.

Gary and I checked the resulting plan against Bingham's original diagram. At first the two didn't seem to match, but I spotted a tiny detail I had never noticed before, partly because I had never been looking for it: a tiny nubbin on the entrance to one passageway, indicating that it was a double-jamb doorway. Suspecting that it might be the one Bob had first come across, we realigned our plan against Bingham's so that the doorways lay on top of one another. It was a perfect fit. We were without question standing in the middle of the Llactapata that Bingham had reported ninety years ago and which had been missing ever since.

Revelation followed revelation. Following one very long sunken passageway that ran some 150 feet, we emerged onto a plateau that faced directly onto Machu Picchu. The sight-line down the passageway to the famous city was remarkable, directly over the various valleys in between. Nor was it accidental: Kim's initial calculation suggested that it lay directly in line with sunrise at the June solstice, and with the rise of the Pleiades constellation, used in the Andes from time immemorial to tell the beginning of certain agricultural seasons. This would need more research to confirm.

We then discovered that there was yet another considerable and previously unreported sector above Bingham's, with an *usnu*, a ceremonial platform, and an unusual small, granite-lined building. The Incas had faced this with granite blocks that they had presumably dragged along the five-mile Inca 'drawbridge' trail from Machu Picchu, as the closest source of the stone.

Gary and I measured the *usnu* together at twilight. Striding long-leggedly through the undergrowth around the *usnu*, Gary advanced away from me with his tape measure. Our excitement levels fed off one another as we shouted out the measurements between us, like helmsmen plumbing the lead-line as they put out to sea: 'It's thirty feet long' – 'forty feet' – 'fifty feet' – 'sixty!' A ceremonial platform of such size was not something we had expected to find.

The *usnu* was a substantial raised, earth-filled platform, sixty feet by forty feet, enclosed by a five-foot-high retaining wall. A causeway wall connected it with another new group of buildings, and stone steps led onto the platform from the north-east side. The platform overlooked 'Bingham's Llactapata' sector, which was directly below it on the fall-line of the hillside.

Together with the success in refinding Bingham's site, it was almost too much. Like success for the England football team, true archaeological discoveries tend to happen rarely and at unexpected moments.

For having seen the other building that Johan Reinhard had investigated on the ridge above, again directly on the same fall-line, it was clear that this too was part of the 'greater Llactapata' complex that seemed to be emerging. Overall the site was turning out to be much, much larger than anyone had ever remotely suspected, with five sectors spread out over the hillside and the two-storey temple above.

As group after group had appeared, some uncovered after five centuries of concealment, it was now apparent that this was far more than the small compound of buildings described by Hiram Bingham in less than a paragraph. Llactapata, the supposedly insignificant ruin with the unassuming name, 'high town', was proving of considerably greater importance than had ever been thought.

*

That evening, I was the last to leave the Bingham sector. I wanted to be there when the constant clashing of the machete blades had stopped and I could just wander around on my own.

I followed the long passageways. The slashing had cleared long stretches of wall, although some still shaded off into undergrowth. Walking was treacherous, as there were cut bamboo shards under-foot. I remembered the famous etching by Frederick Catherwood that had so intrigued me when I first went to Mexico – the Maya ruins still half covered in vegetation, like romantic follies. Because the passageways were unusually sunken compared to the surrounding buildings, this effect was exacerbated, with shafts of light piercing through the dark undergrowth in places. Where the light fell on the passageway, what struck me was the good state of preservation of the walls, still over twelve feet high in places, despite abandonment such a long time ago; less well-built structures would long since have crumbled to the ground.

Off the passageways were the buildings themselves, still heavily overgrown; enough had been slashed away from the overhanging canopy to be able to see the Incaic niches at regular intervals along the walls. The Andean twilight, short but intense, made it easier to see the niches in the shadows, as the contrast was less strong than when the sun was out.

I was impressed by the extent of the sector. Bingham had only mapped the central element of it, again presumably due to shortage of time: one reason why it had taken a moment or two to match his plan to ours. It carried on for a considerable way. And I was under no illusions that we had necessarily found it all, let alone any other sectors that might be spread out over the hillside.

The Inca doorways were still intact, with their characteristic trapezoidal shape sloping inwards. Some had lost their lintels, which were lying near by. Lichen and small ferns were growing from them.

A flock of bright green parakeets swept overhead; they often flew over the cloud-forest in the late afternoon. I recalled having seen a flock on my previous visit to the area twenty years before.

I tried to photograph the site, but it resolutely refused to fall into the frame. There were none of the neat architectural alignments that could give perspective or distance – too much was still covered by the brush and shrub, the secondary vegetation under the creepers that we had removed. I felt more forgiving of Hiram Bingham for having just photographed his tent.

To be present at the uncovering of an Inca site such as this was a euphoric feeling. As I sat in a little clearing at the heart of the complex, I relished the moment. Way off in the forest I could hear the calls of the muleteers as they went down to the spring to get water for the camp. The site itself seemed tranquil, undisturbed despite all our activity earlier in the day.

But there was also a sense of sadness. The last occupiers of the site had probably left some five hundred years ago. Few had ever seen the place since the Spanish Conquest. It was impossible not to feel elegiac about the whole of Inca civilisation, which had left ruins such as these in wild parts of the Andes, but no written record of their achievements.

More than anything else, I wanted to understand, to decode the scant traces they had left, as well as those of their more shadowy forebears, the other Peruvian civilisations, which stretched all the way back to 3000 BC. It made me reflect how much more there was still to be done in the whole study of ancient Peru.

*

Part of the process of discovery was that every new emerging theory about a site had to be tested to destruction. This was why I enjoyed the evening sessions in camp so much, quite aside from the consumption of vodka martinis. After each day we spent at Llactapata, every possible interpretation of any new findings was ruthlessly challenged. It reminded me of my time in film school when you had to persuade sceptical and ambitious fellow students why they should be making your film rather than theirs, a process I had found terrifying but salutary.

It helped that not all those with us were experts – indeed, some were in Peru for the first time, so could ask deceptively simple questions that concentrated the mind: as for instance, why was Llactapata not a simple contained nuclear community, as one might expect?

In fact, it was a typical example of an Inca settlement; they liked to 'plan vertically', with different sectors of a site separated by different altitudes on the same slope, so that they could exploit the differences in height; the lowest sectors often for administration and dwellings, the higher sectors for storehouses and small religious buildings. Llactapata matched that pattern – as did the manner of its finding.

For there were parallels to one of Bingham's most important discoveries, Espíritu Pampa in the Vilcabamba, which he only partially uncovered in 1911. It was half a century later, in 1964, that further sectors were revealed and its true significance established, as Vilcabamba La Vieja, the last refuge of the Incas. Again, Bingham (and our own earlier expedition in 1982) had been misled by the gaps between the sectors of a settlement into thinking they had found the whole site when they had found only part of it.

One puzzle, which we discussed at length, was that there were many similarities in architectural style between 'Bingham's sector' of the site and the one below it that we had found previously. Both had the distinctive and curious long sunken passageways running between groups of buildings. As we compared the two, I began to suspect why they might be so similar. The Incas often divided their cities and settlements into matching upper (*hanan*) and lower (*hurin*) parts, as could be seen at Machu Picchu, Choquequirao and Cuzco itself, and Llactapata seemed to follow this pattern. Hence the confusion caused when subsequent expeditions, like the one I had been part of in 1982, had tried to relocate Bingham's site. Because the *hurin*, or lower site, contained architectural similarities to the *hanan*, or upper site, it was easy to assume that we had refound his site when we had in fact found the *hurin* or mirror version of it some one hundred metres below.

Overall, the Llactapata site could only be understood in relation to Machu Picchu, to which it was so closely aligned and whose function had been hotly debated in recent years. With its direct view of Machu Picchu across the valleys and with an Inca road leading from the great city in its direction across a cliff, Llactapata seemed designed to be both complimentary and complementary to Machu Picchu.

The Incas had built Llactapata as a place from which they could admire Machu Picchu and also use it to take astronomical readings. Indeed, the two combined, as they could have used the mountains to either side of Machu Picchu as exact calendrical marker points on the horizon, against which they could measure the rising of the sun and of certain stars.

The actual view of Machu Picchu from Llactapata was so striking that it was easy to ignore as a factor, as if this was a view that might matter to a modern-day tourist but not to a serious investigator or to the Incas themselves. However, given the Incas' predilection for sight-lines and *miradores*, I suspected that one prime purpose of Llactapata was simply as a viewpoint from which to admire Machu Picchu. After all if you had built such a magnificent creation, wouldn't you want to build an additional folly from which to admire your own work, in the same way that Shah Jahan reputedly wanted to be able to see his Taj Mahal from the Red Fort of Agra? And Llactapata was the only Inca settlement with a direct sight-line to Machu Picchu.

By comparison with that city, Llactapata was tiny – a folly, a parish church to Machu Picchu's cathedral. It also differed in one signal regard from its great neighbour. Machu Picchu was built from the granite that had been quarried on the site, so could achieve the polished look of fine-cut ashlar upon fine-cut ashlar. However, there was a geological shift between the two valleys; Llactapata was in an area of metamorphic stone, far harder to work than granite as it splits easily, so that the Incas had instead worked it more loosely with a view to plastering it smooth later. We had even found some small patches of surviving orange mortar on one of the more protected walls, around one of the niches.

Seen without the mortar, the walls of Llactapata, like those of other sites on the Vilcabamba side of the geological divide, were less impressive than the granite Machu Picchu walls and were easy to undervalue architecturally – perhaps one reason Bingham had done so little work here. However, one had only to see the great Inca walls at Machu Picchu's sister city of Choquequirao, recently restored, to realise that metamorphic rock could still be used to achieve the high, classic, Inca style.

One frequently asked question from the rest of the group was what, now that we had revealed the much fuller extent of Llactapata and its much greater significance than had ever been realised, was going to happen to it? It urgently needed conservation from the encroaching cloud-forest, and protection from looters.

The entrepreneurial Nicholas Asheshov had a startling answer to this: 'We could of course just buy it,' he suggested. 'It's outside the Machu Picchu Historical Sanctuary, so not government property. It'll be privately owned, probably by one of the little *canchas* below on the hill. We could form a consortium and make them an offer they can't refuse.'

As in the old advertisement where a man claimed he'd liked a razor so much that he'd bought the company that made it, I rather enjoyed the idea. But I also imagined that the Peruvians might, rightly, object to foreign ownership of an Inca ruin, however well meaning the intentions.

Nick was among other things a hotelier, so now, carried away, he sketched out for us a vision of how the whole hillside could be transformed into an eco-lodge: well-tended bougainvillea and honeysuckle would tumble over the paths leading up to the beautifully restored site above, from which pampered guests could no doubt sip their bellinis as they watched the sunset light up Machu Picchu, like latter-day Inca emperors.

So enticing was Nick's salesmanship that several of the wealthier members of the expedition were already reaching for their chequebooks. But whether it 'would fly', in Nick's phrase, was doubtful if entertaining. More desirable, it seemed to me, was for the Peruvian Government themselves to restore and develop Llactapata, as they had with the various 'tambo sites' along the Inca Trail. Including it in the boundaries of the National Park would divert tourists from Machu Picchu, which at the moment tended to monopolise their attention in a disproportionate way, distorting the local infrastructure and straining resources.

All this was for future discussion. More practically, we needed to do further research on our initial findings, particularly on the astronomical alignments, and publish a detailed academic report, to bring it to the authorities' attention. For the while, and particularly after a few vodkas, it was fun to speculate on a Llactapata Inc., co-owned by the team: 'We liked the ruin so much we bought it.'

*

We were heading out. Nor were we simply returning the quick way, back down the hill to the railroad. Instead we were making the more arduous six-day climb up the valleys behind Llactapata to cross the 15,000-foot pass beside Mount Salcantay, a chance to see the 20,500-foot giant up close.

It felt good to leave – both because we had been successful, but also because we had spent days working in a concentrated and claustrophobic area of cloud-forest just around the Llactapata site. When we reached the pass above and suddenly saw the wide expanse of the Vilcabamba mountain range stretch out in front of us, with the hook-nosed Mount Pumasillo at its centre and various Inca sites beyond, I felt a huge weight off my shoulders, the sort of relief that comes on completing a book or film. There had been a tremendous weight of expectation – and money – riding on the expedition. To fail would have been desperately disappointing.

As ever, the mere process of walking helped me assimilate what we had found. I have always liked to feel the ground under me as I think and looking at the landscape helped. And I was used to the way that there was often a process of delayed realisation as to the significance of any discovery.

Heading away from Machu Picchu, and seeing the rest of the Vilcabamba spread out ahead made me realise the extent to which Llactapata was a bridge between that city and the rest of the more distant Inca sites. There were Inca roads leading from the pass towards Choquequirao and Vitcos, roads that in the past I had traced.

A common assumption for many years has been that Machu Picchu was the 'end of the line' on the Inca trail from Cuzco, a final destination for the Inca emperor and his retinue, just as it is today for tourists. But it now seemed clear to me that it was just a stopping point on a much longer trail which would have continued on from Machu Picchu past Llactapata and into the heart of the Vilcabamba.

This would also have meant that Machu Picchu was accessible (via Llactapata itself) from the Apurímac river, 'the great roarer' as the Incas called it, so connected with the Inca royal road up to Ecuador and the northern half of the empire.

A further and welcome indication of this came almost immediately. I had remembered the path down from the pass on the other side descending to the Santa Teresa valley, as tough and unrelenting. But the loss of the railway line along the lower Urubamba had forced the locals to reopen old Inca trails and a fine one curled away from us at a gentle gradient traversing the slope, making for a much easier descent. It was six feet wide, with retaining walls both above and below it.

A team of local men were working on the restoration of the road at the top of the pass and were curious about what we had been doing. John in his usual amiable way gave them his name and address so that if they ever found anything they could contact him. It was an act he was later to regret.

As we descended along the beautifully contoured Inca path to Lucmabamba, an unexpected sight pulled me up short. For just above the village, the path widened to what could only be a full Inca royal road, some fifteen feet wide, heading down towards the bottom of the valley. It had just been restored and cleared by the INC (Peru's National Institute of Culture) as part of their Royal Inca Highway project and was an announcement by the Incas of how important the route was back up the hill via Llactapata to Machu Picchu.

The road's existence was not in any literature about the area, partly because it lay a little off the valley bottom and so would not have been seen by any archaeologists or explorers moving through the valley to other sites. Only the locals had been aware of it. Like much in Peru, it was uncharted.

I had last been in Lucmabamba twenty years before. It seemed another life when I had first passed through, suffering from toothache and carrying my own fifteen-kilo pack (and certainly not in any condition to enquire of locals whether there were any wide Inca roads in the vicinity). Quite why it had taken me so long to realise that for a few dollars more I could hire a mule I'm not sure – probably stubbornness and some purist conviction that one should carry one's own pack regardless.

Letting the mules take the strain meant that even after a full day's walking we had enough energy left to take the locals on at football. This was a much-anticipated match. Pío and the muleteers had been going on about the possible outcome since the start of the expedition, when they weren't feverishly speculating on the hiding place of Saddam Hussein ('Maybe he's in Venezuela, like Montesinos,' one suggested, referring to the recent spectacular discovery of the corrupt Peruvian politician who had been extradited from there, despite plastic surgery and the use of a much-derided toupee).

The Gringo Ramblers had played a few games before on previous expeditions to the Vilcabamba. As the pitch was always an uneven one, carved out of the mountain, subtle tactics never worked; for one memorable match played right on the main plaza at the Inca site of Choquequirao, Pío had been forced to terminate the game – we were losing – by kicking the ball over the edge of the parapet and down into the dense jungle canopy hundreds of feet below. The subsequent search by our opponents was so thorough that it might well have uncovered fresh ruins.

One of our muleteers' usual complaints was that we always had to accept an *arbitro*, referee, from the host village or Inca site, and they were invariably and unashamedly partisan. Or at least this is what we told ourselves when we lost.

But for this match the Gringo Ramblers had a few advantages: at over six feet and a half, my amiable cousin William Heath towered over the locals and even though gentle as a lamb in civilian life, his appearance after some time in the field was enough to frighten even the toughest Peruvian. He had proved adept at machete waving and had been fresh fodder for some of John Leivers' more extreme expeditions into the undergrowth, so had scars down his arms. Jeff Ford was a big lad as well. Moreover there were enough of us to field a few reserves.

The entire village had gathered at the football pitch. A women's match took place before ours; two sisters in smart Nike trainers powered up and down the wings to meet bone-crunching tackles from the solidly built opposition defenders. One particular stalwart was playing in a bowler hat, and her pigtails swirled around her head as she stomped on the ball or whoever was unlucky enough to be attached to it. Peruvian women took sport very seriously; their volleyball team was one of the best in the world.

Then it was the women's turn to line the pitch and watch as yet again the Gringo Ramblers, despite being an improved model, suffered humiliation at the hands of a local team. Pío was holding his head in his hands as he tried to marshal us into some sort of order. I retired early after clashing heads with a Peruvian who must have been made of adamantine, and watched ruefully from the side. A small boy asked me if I'd ever seen the Peruvian footballer Solano play for Newcastle back in England.

The late afternoon sun, with the assembled village gossiping and laughing as they watched the game, made for a jovial scene, even if we were losing. I felt a wave of affection for Peru and the resilience that small local communities like this one showed. They were slowly being depopulated as the young men headed for Cuzco and the bright city lights.

I also felt that the decision I had reached with my wife before coming was a good one – that she and our children would join me out here for a while and we would rent a house at Urubamba, in what was sometimes described as the 'Sacred Valley', with the children enrolled in the local school, and be part of such a community. I wanted a deeper and longer immersion than I usually got on my annual expeditions here. They had never been to Peru before. And this would give me the chance to explore all the many pre-Inca cultures, without which, I had increasingly realised, one could never possibly understand the Incas themselves, or for that matter their modern descendants.

*

After the match (score 6–3 to the home side), I made my way down to the river, just below the embankment of the village, and perched precariously on some midstream rocks to wash clothes and myself, while fighting off the sandflies. There was a rock pool with the sun still on it, where I could lie and look back up to the pass leading to Llactapata.

Having some time in the country would allow me to reflect on our findings there, and to work with Gary and Kim to present them to the world in such a way that the ruins' importance was highlighted and active steps taken to conserve and protect them. We would delay any announcement of our discoveries until we were absolutely ready.

For I was well aware of the problems that could ensue in trying to publicise such finds. The hint of a so-called 'lost city' story, and a red mist seemed to descend on journalists and sub-editors, who would reach for every hyperbole. The lure of a newly reported discovery also seemed to induce bad and obsessive behaviour even with professional archaeologists and organisations that ought to know better.

There had been a clear example of this just the year before. I had been shaving in my bathroom back in England when the morning radio had announced a big 'find' that had been made in Peru by a team led by Peter Frost. Peter was best known for having written an excellent short guidebook to Cuzco, where he was a long-term local resident. I had met him several times and liked him, but did not know him well. What puzzled me about the report was that it made no mention of Gary Ziegler, who, I knew, had co-led the expedition with Peter; it had been funded by the National Geographic Society.

A blizzard of angry e-mails circulated by my friend Barry Walker, the British Consul in Cuzco, clarified the situation. This was indeed the same expedition that Peter and Gary had co-led. However, they had argued in the field and so when it came to announcing their joint findings, it appeared that Peter had written Gary out of the story, or had at least put him in the smallest print. In the press release that had been issued, and which National Geographic had melodramatically headlined 'LOST' INCA CITY DISCOVERED IN PERU, Peter was clearly established as the leader and spokesperson, with Gary relegated to a small mention as a participant at the very end. In the accompanying website release, he had been written out completely.

Barry Walker, who knew both of them well, went ballistic. He e-mailed everyone he could think of to complain of Peter's seemingly cavalier behaviour. In the small world of Cuzco's expatriate community, lines were drawn and few fences mended as the town went to war over the issue. Such was the furore over both Peter's omission of Gary and of National Geographic's hyping of the site as a 'lost city' (it contained just a few buildings, and was no more a 'city' than any of the other small but perfectly formed Inca sites in the mountains) that National Geographic eventually were forced to issue a new statement clarifying Gary's involvement; they fell back on the technicality that what mattered was not who had actually led the expedition in the field, but who had applied for the National Geographic grant; this Peter had done, so he must be de facto leader.

In London, *The Times* ran an article headed INCA TRAIL OF HYPE? criticising both the National Geographic Society and Peter Frost: 'Even Peter Frost, 56, the British tour guide who says that he led the Geographic expedition to the Vilcabamba in June last year, admits that "with the benefit of hindsight, it would have been better to tone it down a bit".' In Peru also there were articles questioning what had happened. Edwin Benavente, the director of the National Institute of Culture in Cuzco, was quoted as saying: 'The National Geographic claims are very, very exaggerated.'

National Geographic wrote a letter to the Editor of *The Times*, defending themselves among other things on the grounds that their press release 'refers to the new find as a "city" only in the headline; the rest of the references were to a "settlement".' Quite why their headline was less important than the text was never explained. And in that text they had claimed, as *The Times* pointed out, that 'it was "one of the most important sites" discovered since the Incas had marched off into the sunset "more than 400 years ago".'

Luckily I had not played a part in any of this. Gary had originally asked me to join the expedition, but I had been unable to go. In the years since I had learnt more about what had caused the surprising rift between Peter and Gary in the first place, given that they were old friends.

The principal culprit seemed to be a mule. On their way to the site called Corihuayrachina (confusingly, as several Inca sites of that name already existed; the name means 'place of gold-threshing'), Peter had wandered close to a grazing mule, which had kicked him so hard he had been temporarily lamed. He had recently married and his wife was accompanying him on the expedition. Now Peter had to trail in a humiliating way long behind the rest of the party as they made for the site, which was scattered in small sectors near to a mountain-top. Worse still, Gary, not always the most tactful of people, was radioing back reports of the finds he was making up ahead. I could imagine the conversation, particularly given Gary's tendency to enthuse and Peter's more English, restrained character:

GARY: Peter, this is incredible, you've got to see this, we're finding more stuff everywhere.

PETER: Right.

GARY: I'm just going to head up to the next ridge, the muleteers tell me that there's more up there.

PETER: (mumble) Right.

GARY: Peter, this really is exciting, you've got to get up here.

PETER: (sharp) Well, I would if I could. (Walkie-talkie gives out in a blaze of interference and Gary's hyperbole.)

Archaeological camps are fertile territory for discord; the lack of clear objectives, or indeed of any certainty about the value of what is being found, along with potential stake-claiming, make for shifting ground on which even the firmest of friendships can founder, much like an old-time prospecting field. In this case, things seem to have gone from bad to terminal. By the end, while Corihuayrachina had been mapped and could be revealed to the world with a flourish by National Geographic, Gary's name was airbrushed from the report like some old Soviet picture of a fallen Politburo leader.

However, there had been one strange by-product of this, which had affected me. Gary, excluded after a while from the day-to-day running of the camp, had instead spent time talking with the muleteers, many of whom were old friends. One had a farm near by and told him that he had once gone down into the canyon of the Yanama river way below to see whether there was any arable land. There wasn't, but there had been what looked like ruins, very overgrown but far more substantial than the ones they were looking at in Corihuayrachina. Gary determined to return to investigate properly, with a full expedition – and without Peter Frost. So he had contacted me and we had gone back in the following year, 2002, with a new team that included John Leivers and Nicholas Asheshov.

*

It had been an exciting venture, not least because there was one simple reason why no one ever went down into the lower Yanama valley or used it as a route through to anywhere else: severe erosion by the Yanama river over the centuries since the time of the Incas had created such a steep canyon that it was impassable along the valley bottom. The only way our team could reach it was to descend directly, cutting a trail down a 5,000-foot mountain drop from the Corihuayrachina area above.

As the river had carved its course through the canyon, it had left some small isolated *mesas* or 'tablelands'. The ruins were on one of these, in an area now known locally as Cota Coca. Another reason the inhabitants of the upper Yanama valley avoided going there was that it was known for having ferocious midges; one early explorer, the Comte de Sartiges, who passed close by in 1834, although without seeing the site, referred to the area of 'Cotacoca' and 'the numerous and voracious mosquitoes that have taken possession of it. It was impossible to breathe, drink or eat without absorbing quantities of these insufferable creatures.' We found it equally unpleasant.

However, all thoughts of mosquitoes or the severe heat at the bottom of the canyon were dispelled when we first came to the buildings and, after clearing the vegetation away, could see that we had found something substantial.

What we had uncovered was a sizeable settlement of stone buildings grouped around a central plaza, with many more outlying buildings. One large building was in the characteristic shape and position of a *kallanka*, an Inca meeting hall. Fitted rectangular blocks of quartzite had been used in the construction of the windows, corners and trapezoidal doorways, while the walls were made of coursed stone. As at Llactapata, most of the structures would probably have been plastered over with a tan-coloured clay, giving the appearance of Santa Fe *pueblo* houses.

The functional rather than ceremonial nature of the architecture and its relatively low altitude of only 6,000 feet suggested it might have been a 'road town' or *tambo*, a stopping point along an important Inca route, which could also have served as an administrative centre for the local district (including the smaller ruins at Corihuayrachina high above) and just possibly for the storage of locally grown coca, hence the historical name of Cota Coca.

It was potentially the missing piece of a jigsaw that had been puzzling investigators for some time, as it lay on what, before the erosion of the valley walls, appeared to have been an Inca road along the river, linking central Inca strongholds in the mountains with their exit route to the south-west. This would have been of particular use after the Conquest when the remaining Incas had used the area as a guerrilla redoubt and had harassed the Spanish on the 'Royal Road' between Lima and Cuzco.

To be the first to report such a 'hidden place' had been a tremendously proud feeling for us all. When the Royal Geographical Society had released the story to the world's press, their reaction had been gratifying, even if inevitably one paper had taken as its headline: COTA COCA – IT'S THE REAL THING. And it had helped fund our subsequent expedition to Llactapata.

What I now had to keep pinching myself about was my luck in being involved in both the Cota Coca and the Llactapata finds. I had never expected to be the first to report any unknown Inca sites. For lightning to have struck twice in one lifetime was a great gift, and one that brought responsibilities.

I wanted to ensure that the interpretation of our Llactapata findings was done properly. Even if we had to wait until the end of the year to announce the new discoveries to the press or academic community, it was better to do so when we had fully analysed our results. Luckily my own relationship with Gary Ziegler was excellent – indeed, as one Mexican had put it to me of his *compadre*, he was a man I would trust with my life, my wife and my wallet. The only argument so far had been because I kept putting too much vermouth in the dry martinis.

*

A few days later we had reached the high valley just below Salcantay, at an altitude of 13,000 feet. It was drizzling with rain and I was enjoying being on a horse called Aventurero, 'Adventurer', a name that belied his placid nature. Water dripped over the brim of my wide hat and down the brown cattleman's poncho I'd wrapped around me as we plodded along. The landscape was the high desolate landscape of the *puna*, grey-green with only boulders giving any relief.

One of the horse wranglers, Goyo, walked beside me. I'd known him for some years. He was unmarried and in his early thirties. Earlier that day we had passed his family's hut, just below the village of Rayanpata, and I had been struck by the complete lack of any reaction from his parents when he had stopped to say hello, after an absence of almost a year. His father had not bothered to look up from his hand plough as he worked the smallholding of maize and potatoes behind their *cancha*.

This was not through any lack of affection or as a reproach – for Goyo was a model son – but just symptomatic of the lack of demonstrativeness shown by Quechua mountain Indians generally; they made the English look Italian by comparison.

The days we had spent trekking had combined all that I most enjoyed in the Andes: travelling up a small clean river that frothed grey and green beside the path; the cool turnings into the shade where butterflies gathered over streams as they trickled down to join that same river; the *curcurs*, the beautiful fringed bamboo that hang over the paths framing the view; and the sudden opening out of the mountains and the valley as we got higher, where I could see the rest of the party picking their way over the distant *puna* bowl as if they were in Wyoming.

Passing through the village at Rayanpata, where I had stayed in 1982, I found that Lucho, my friend and host from those days, had died and his widow Paulina had moved to a more comfortable village holding further below. When I asked one of the village boys what he wanted to do, he had dreamily replied: '*Quiero vivir en la ciudad*, I want to live in the city.' The slow, inexorable draining of the highlands was continuing.

All the rest of the party were ahead of me, aside from John Leivers who was lagging behind, uncharacteristically. I was concerned about John as he seemed to be suffering from one of his regular debilitating stomach illnesses, the result of years of tough living in the mountains. As he refused ever to ride on a horse, the result was that he just slowed down.

John and I had planned a trip up to the north of Peru after the expedition. So many new and exciting discoveries had been made recently in northern Peru along the coast that I had to see them for myself. And John, who had travelled backwards and forwards through that area, seemed to be the ideal companion. He had a seductive catchphrase when describing the allure of any new territory for us to explore together: 'There's just so much out there.'

Even as we had talked of the early pyramids and Moche *huacas* that we wanted to see, of route-maps and obscure trails that only John knew of, I sensed that he was still not well. 'I'm fine,' he protested. But as we shepherded some of the fieldworkers up to the pass, some of whom were not used to these altitudes, John had dropped behind.

I arrived at the camp ready to get out of my wet clothes and into a dry martini, as Robert Benchley once put it. Pío and I decided to send a muleteer back to accompany John over the pass, as clouds were coming in. The others were already huddled in the field-tent making a considerable impact on our vodka supplies.

Nick Asheshov was holding court. As the oldest member of the expedition and a veteran explorer, he had the licence to do so. Everyone had enormous respect for him; after forty years of venturing into the Vilcabamba, he had brought a depth of knowledge to the councils of war we had held each night in the field-tent at Llactapata, and he dealt courageously with his partially sighted condition. Nick suffered from macular degeneration, so had, in layman's terms, pinpoint vision. By swivelling his head carefully he could get a fix on things.

He had three favourite subjects: whether we could buy Llactapata; the supposed iniquities of Peter Frost; and his beloved railway. For Nick had with considerable initiative opened up a railway line. When I had first met him at his hotel in Urubamba, he had told me that the manager's house we were standing in had once been a railway station. He opened the curtains to show me the vestiges of an old track stretching away across a field – cows were now grazing on it. It was a spur line to the Machu Picchu railway and had been built in 1923 from Urubamba to Pacchar, but quickly abandoned. Nick informed me that he intended to open up the line again. I had treated this politely and with complete disbelief. The likelihood of reviving a railway after seventy years' disuse seemed remote.

And yet he had managed it. Indeed, he had even invited me on the inaugural journey when, top-hatted and jovial, he had taken his first train-load of passengers down the Urubamba valley to Machu Picchu. Fuelled by champagne and *pisco* sours, it had been a merry party, made memorable by the amazed reaction of the inhabitants of the valley as we passed, most of whom had never seen a train use the track. Children and pigs came tumbling out of the huts and the inaugural voyage was delayed by a cow that refused to budge off the line, perhaps because it felt it had long-standing grazing rights.

The train was now a daily service and a boon to the local Urubamba economy, as the local hotels could send tourists direct to Machu Picchu. As well as running the railway line and the hotel, Nick was still a practising journalist. He was already preparing a piece about Llactapata for a Peruvian magazine, which began: '*Encontrar una ciudad perdida no resulta sencillo aunque uno ya sepa donde está*, finding a lost city isn't always easy even if you know where it is.' He was a friend and ally.

John finally arrived, clearly exhausted but refusing with his usual toughness to let mere illness get in the way. Having put the world to rights with him and the others, and after more vodkas than is recommended at 13,000 feet, I emerged to find the rain clouds had lifted and revealed Mount Salcantay by night. It was the closest I had ever seen it, a great savage chunk of a mountain of over 20,000 feet, with its twin peaks. Johan Reinhard and others had written of the mountain's importance to the Incas, and of the way Machu Picchu was aligned to it. Reinhard noted that the name probably came from the Quechua word *sallca*, meaning 'wild', and along with Ausangate to the east, Salcantay was considered one of the fathers of all other mountains. I remembered the vision I'd had of it from the plane flying from Llactapata, swathed in cloud.

On the other side of the narrow high valley, Mount Tucarhuay towered over us, a perfect pyramid and not much lower than Salcantay, its shape mirrored by the tents in the moonlight, which was strong as the moon was reflecting off the snow around us on the high peaks. Off to one side the muleteers had lit a fire, and the smoke was rising and mixing with the wisps of cloud against the horizon. The Southern Cross was bright as a neon sign.

It was an accelerated rush of all that I liked in the Peruvian mountains. At that moment I felt on a tremendous high. And I knew that next day we would see a site that represented everything about ancient Peru that most intrigued me.

*

Called simply Piedra Labrada, which is the Spanish for 'carved rock', it was once one of the most extraordinary monoliths in South America. But within the past forty years it has been terribly mutilated. Remains of the animals and strange figures are still to be seen, but most of the heads have been destroyed either through superstition or caprice. Its present state is a glaring example of the necessity for preserving the ancient ruins of Peru, and for sending properly equipped expeditions to study these ancient ruins before the historical evidence they contain is lost owing to ignorance or greed.   (Hiram Bingham on the ruins of Sahuite, 1913.)

I was shocked by how small the Upper Stone of Sahuite was. In my mind it loomed monumental, as it did in the old photos Bingham had taken of it which I had found in his archive at Yale. The smooth rounded sides of the base gave no sense of scale; it might be a hundred feet high or thirty. In fact it was barely ten feet.

Perched at an odd angle, it looked as if it had landed awkwardly on the ground, like a meteorite shot from the past containing the Inca world in capsule form.

For this was the lodestone of Andean cosmology. Carved on the top of the rock was an elaborate network of channels, animals and buildings representing all that most interested the pre-Columbian mind. It had been sculpted by the Incas, but of all their monuments it was the one that seemed to draw most on the deep wellspring of Andean imagery from previous civilisations.

There were frogs, spiders, pumas, llamas – even a lobster. Channels ran down from small depressions in the rock, almost certainly divination channels like the ones that flowed down the carved stones at Qenko, just above Cuzco. All the channels leading to the edge of the stone were 'guarded' by one of the animals. Equally fascinating were the small sculptures of buildings that had been painstakingly carved like architects' maquettes out of the living rock. Nothing better illustrated the Andean people's almost organic sense of stone, and of an architecture that grew naturally out of it.

Little had been done to investigate or even preserve the site since Bingham's day, despite his strictures. The Upper Stone – which in some countries would have had a museum built around it or at the very least been covered – was open to the sky. Luckily it had been carved from hard andesite, so unlike the similar structure at Qenko, which was made from softer limestone, it had not been eroded by the weather. But it had been vandalised, probably by the Spanish when they tried 'to stamp out native idolatry'. Many of the heads of the animals had been broken off.

We know from Pedro Pizarro, young cousin and pageboy to the leader of the conquistadors Franciso Pizarro and one of my favourite chroniclers of the Conquest, that there was an oracle and shrine by this part of the Apurímac river. Pizarro gave an intriguing description of it in his vivid, direct prose style:

In the valley of the Apurímac there was an elaborately decorated building. A thick beam was set up inside it, thicker than a corpulent man, and many pieces had been hacked away from this beam. It was covered with the blood which had been offered to it. There was a girdle of gold bound around it and soldered on so as to resemble lace: on the front of this girdle were two large golden breasts, like those of a woman. The beam was dressed with the very fine garments of a woman, secured with the gold pins called *topos*, broad at the head and with many tiny bells of gold and silver hanging from them. The women use these pins to fasten their mantles over their shoulders.

Beside this main beam, there were others in a line from one side of the room to the other. These beams were also bathed with blood and robed in mantles to look like statues of women. They [the Peruvians] said that a demon used to speak to them through the largest beam. They called him Apurímac.

(Pedro Pizarro, Relation of the Discovery and Conquest
of the Kingdoms of Peru, 1571)

Pizarro went on to relate how Asarpay, the guardian priestess of this tomb and a royal princess, was so distraught by the removal of this oracle by the Spanish that she fled to 'the very high pass which lies down to the descent that approaches the bridge across the Apurímac. Covering up her head she threw herself into the river near this gully, more than two hundred *estados* deep, at the same time calling out to Apurímac, the idol whom she served.' (An *estado* was the rough height of a man, five to six feet, used for measuring vertical distances, so this would have been a drop of a thousand feet.)

While we cannot be sure that Sahuite is this same oracle-temple, it is in the right geographical position and has all the attributes of a place of worship.

We had the site to ourselves. The lonely custodian of the site told me that hardly anyone ever visited it. He dug around in a bag for the photos he had taken himself to sell to tourists – there was no point in making postcards.

The modern road from Cuzco to the distant sea looped just above Sahuite, with the unhappy result that the Upper Stone was the first feature of the site that visitors came across – indeed, often the only one, as most apparently didn't realise, or care, that most of the site lay below and that it was clearly designed so that one approached by walking up from the valley, past other carved stones and then ascending a great staircase, again with a divination channel beside it, before reaching what is likely to have been a temple. Beyond this temple (and presumably with restricted access through its labyrinthine corridors) lay the Upper Stone with its elaborate carvings.

By coming on the Upper Stone from behind and penetrating straight to the heart of the mystery so close to the car park, without any of this carefully calculated architectural preparation, the modern visitor experienced the more twenty-first-century experience of an instant but shallow gratification.

I walked down to the *usnu* some three hundred feet below, and was reminded of the *usnu* Gary and I had uncovered together at Llactapata: the same raised platform, standing isolated in a field of grass and yellow flowers. As at Vilcashuaman, where one of the most complete *usnus* survives, this would have been a place for the gathering of nobility and troops and even an occasional imperial display on the Inca emperor's travels. The ascent to the shrine and Upper Stone above may have been a privilege restricted to a few and observed by the rest from this large platform.

Near it lay a far smaller but to me even more interesting monument: a carved puma. The Incas rarely used figurative images – one reason why the Upper Stone was so remarkable was the profusion of them – but when they did the puma was a predominant one. It was hardly surprising that they should have been drawn to what was a creature of both power and of the mountains, as they saw themselves. The rock shrine at Qenko was guarded by a large upright one, much eroded.

This puma was smaller, but better preserved and with the clean simplified lines of an Epstein or modernist sculpture – the spine curved, dynamic, aquiline, with the legs and paws almost abstract buttresses supporting it in its sprung poise. The tensile line of the tail curled behind the stone.

I arrived just as sunlight lay on the puma, but with dark clouds covering the valley beyond, a shock of contrast that accentuated a constant of Inca sculpture: even more than for most rock carving, a sense of place was paramount to an understanding of the work – indeed, one could say that such work was not placed in the landscape, like the sculpture parks of the Western world, but could only be understood as an integral part of that landscape. Looking at the head of the puma, the mountain ridges beyond, covered in cloud, mirrored the shape of its curved and buttressed spine. The Incas had an elaborate system of *huacas*, natural shrines of rock, water or a combination of the two, which radiated out from Cuzco; this could have been one of them. Pizarro made the point explicitly, when explaining the death of the princess Asarpay and the idol that she served, adding that 'in this land there were idols which these Indians had and which they called *huacas*.'

On the hillside above the puma was a larger sculpture, the so-called 'Rumahuasi, house of stone', that had been dramatically cleft in two at some stage since being carved by the Incas; while doubtless something the Spanish would have liked to have done, the force needed to split the rock in this way was so extreme that it is more likely to have been the work of lightning. Although no figurative work was evident here, it exemplified the other strand in Inca sculpture and the one I had been fascinated by at Chuquipalta, the White Rock, some years before: the carving of small seats and steps into otherwise natural stone. The historian John Hemming had once described these non-representational carvings with a nice phrase: that 'they were made to mark the presence of man without depicting him'.

A large staircase cut into the hill ascended from Rumahuasi to the Upper Stone, with a divination channel running alongside it and high, unmanageable treads to encourage due respect. Having climbed this, the pilgrim visitor would enter a building with a labyrinthine arrangement of rooms, perhaps to emerge at the far side to have sight of the Upper Stone, if they were privileged.

Having breathlessly completed this climb, I was able to view the intricacies of the Upper Stone from above when the kind caretaker produced a ladder for me. As at the lines of Nasca, which I was determined to see later, it showed an intriguing mindset to make something viewed best, if not exclusively, from the air, without there being any easy way of doing so.

For what was much clearer from directly above was what the nineteenth-century French traveller Charles Wiener described as 'the topographical synthesis' of the carvings. Buildings were integrated into the landscape: three steps ascended to a pyramidal base, which rose to another pyramidal base, this time with a square depression in it; elsewhere two buildings side by side were divided by walls coming from alternate directions, creating an S-shaped corridor along each one; a series of steps rose up to a plaza whose dominant building had two trapezoidal niches, and in between these maquettes lay the natural stone, the carved stone, the divination channels and the representation of animals. One could not find a clearer example of the way that for the Andean mind every section of landscape was charged with significance – what we would call a sacred landscape.

But while the individual constituents of this 'topographical synthesis' were distinguishable, its overall meaning was still obscure, or, as the archaeologists liked to say, 'needed more research'. If ever one needed proof of the fecund complexity of the Andean mind, its otherness, it was here, in this rock, which could no more be properly read than if it had been in hieroglyphics.

As we drove towards Cuzco, with Mount Salcantay behind us in the distance and the low evening sun lighting up fields of ripening quinoa, maize and blue linseed flowers, I determined to penetrate far deeper into the Andean past than I had ever attempted before. The Incas had been only the last in a whole series of cultures predating the Spanish Conquest. To explain a phenomenon like Sahuite – or, indeed, some of the elements of urban planning we had uncovered at Llactapata – one needed to go back to the earliest origins of Andean civilisation.

*

Back in Cuzco, I had been hoping to return to my presidential suite at the Hotel Monasterio, but was demoted to a 'junior suite' by an influx of real presidents – the International Young Presidents Organisation (or YPO), who had flown into town and taken over every room and limo in sight. I was lucky to get a bed at all, although after our time in the field I'd have settled for anything that was flat and didn't have a mule munching grass outside the tent.

I knew all about the YPO. They had already booked me to give a lecture as soon as I got back to Cuzco. Their agent had explained that this was a group of high-achieving, 'asset-rich' individuals who were all presidents or chief executives of their companies. Every so often they liked to have high-powered conferences: 'For the one in South Africa, we flew in Nelson Mandela . . . and Richard Branson.' I wasn't sure that I was as impressed as I should have been by the mention of Branson. Indeed, I wasn't that sure that I was impressed at all. Did I want to lecture to them in Cuzco? My initial response was prejudiced. They sounded like the sort of people who wore blazers when they played golf.

The agent went on: 'You should know that to join the YPO you need to be under forty-five, employ fifty people and have at least US$8 million in gross annual sales or turnover.' He wasn't helping me to like them.

We established that our research expedition would be returning to Cuzco on the precise day that the YPO were in town, so in theory I was available. I named what I thought an absurdly high price as a polite way of saying 'no'. They accepted it.

So now I found myself in the back of a taxi, after only a few hours of sleep in Cuzco, driving over to the Sacred Valley to give a presentation to a group of international businessmen on 'Recent Discoveries in the Andes' and nursing the mother of all hangovers. The night before, having only just got back, we had hardly shaken the dust from our boots before heading for Barry Walker's Cross Keys pub with, in Gary Ziegler's words, 'its resident congregation of ex-patriots, treasure hunters and adventurers from far corners of the universe'. And Boddingtons on draught.

Despite the increasing fame and popularity of the place, it still managed to combine the rough edges of a travellers' bar with the early hours' tranquillity of a suburban British pub. We arrived during the weekly pub quiz and found ourselves, fresh from the Peruvian outback, in the incongruous position of answering questions on the composition of Take That and the manager of Derby County. As an international expedition, we had strength in depth and were able to get into the final play-offs. The hirsute barman managing the quiz leered as he produced his deciding and clearly killer question: 'Who led the Israelites into the Promised Land?' But we had Beth, who had taught Bible Studies in Colorado. Ignoring our sucker instinctual response of Moses, she told us to go for Joshua. And we won outright.

The succeeding celebrations were as exuberant as when we'd found the missing sectors of Llactapata. Where I had gone astray, I realised ruefully in the back of the taxi, was accepting John Leivers' suggestion that I wash back the strong *pisco* sours with some Cuzqueña Malt, a black beer as thick as Guinness but with fewer vitamins. It had left its mark. Following an Australian through the cloud-forest was hard enough work; trying to match his drinking was fatal.

But the drive was restorative. The taxi was taking a route that over that year I would come to know well – the high road from Cuzco to the Sacred Valley past the little village of Chinchero and the beautiful lakes of Huaypo and Piuray, before descending to the Urubamba river. As we wound down the road towards the town of Urubamba, where Nick Asheshov had his hotel and his railway station, I felt a warm glow towards the Young Presidents Organisation; the fee they were providing for an hour's lecture was enough to rent a house there for my family for the rest of the dry season. Nick had already helped me find the house.

The YPO were assembling in one of the grand old haciendas that had belonged to a landowning family before the communalisation of the 1960s. Scattered along the valley, alongside the many small rural communities and pockets of considerable poverty in the Urubamba, were these reminders of more feudal days, now often converted into hotels. This one was typical, with its large patio and verandas filled with pots of flowers. Inside there were old furniture and old retainers.

The Young Presidents looked at ease as they sipped their mimosas: they were an even more international group than I had anticipated, with representatives from Japan, India, Pakistan and many other countries, and gave off the genial self-centred glow that radiates from people who've made a great deal of money, so can relax with equally endowed peers. But even in this elect there were divisions, with a perceived difference between those who had inherited their wealth and their companies and those who had created their own. There was also a continual jockeying for position. I noticed this while signing books after my lecture; one purchaser paused and, in a voice that was louder than necessary, asked me to sign his copy with a special acid-free pen – as he told the others, 'It does increase any residual value substantially.' Later I heard another gentle put-down from one Young President to another: 'I see your Apple isn't a titanium special edition, like mine. Don't worry, if you want I can get you on the waiting list.'

Back at the hotel in Cuzco for their evening reception, the receptionist told me that my suit was waiting.

'What suit? I didn't realise the dinner was black tie.'

'It's not,' she said with an amused smile, which I only understood when I saw what was spread out for me on the bed in my room: a full 'Inca' costume, in the colours of the Quechua flag, with a bird's-head mask, a tasselled waistcoat, short stockings that ended halfway up the calf and a cane. The Young Presidents liked dressing up.

They had assembled in similar costumes in the lobby of the hotel. Some of the Young Presidents had enjoyed years of extensive corporate lunching as they built up their empires, and the tight stockings and waistcoats did nothing to flatter their profiles.

Their younger, slimmer wives or girlfriends were dressed in a high-fashion version of the Andean peasant look, with layered skirts in taffeta and chunky jewellery that looked more Oscar de la Renta than Cuzco market. I was embarrassed enough at my own appearance: the only footwear I had with me were a pair of trainers and some old walking boots, neither of which quite set off the quasi-historical Inca costume I was clearly going to have to wear for taking the YPO shilling. And I learnt that worse was to come: our one-hundred-strong group would process through the streets of Cuzco to the Museo Inka, the old museum, for a reception, with an accompanying brass band.

We set off across the cobbles of the Plaza Nazarenas, the ladies tottering on their high heels and me less elegantly clumping along in walking boots. I was not sure that Cuzco was any more ready for this than I was – and hoped that my companions from the expedition weren't around or I'd never live it down. At least I had the bird's-head mask to hide behind.

As one of my more politically minded friends used to complain, 'This was all very well, but where's the Marxist analysis, Hugh?' And ostensibly it did not look good: rich capitalists arrive, take over half Cuzco, appropriate the cultural hegemony for their own ideological ends and parade in triumph to the local population, like latter-day *conquistadores*.

But life can be richer than ideology, and as the wonderful sound of the brass band kicked in and the torches flared around us in the dark night sky, everyone started to enjoy themselves, including the watching Cuzquenos, who like any excuse for a party; the foreign visitors they dislike are the ones paranoid about being ripped off and consequently unable to risk a smile. The costumed marchers descended the streets swaying in pairs and with their canes waving in the air in time to the music, for all the world like a New Orleans procession. Several of the small boys selling postcards on the streets joined the procession at its end.

Cuzco was already *en fête*; an eclipse of the moon later that night meant that excitement was running high. The Incas had believed that an eclipse of the moon was caused by a serpent or mountain lion trying to devour her, and so made as much noise as possible to scare off the attackers, 'shouting at the top of their voices and whipping their dogs so they would bark and howl', according to one chronicler. For their Quechua descendants, it was still an excuse for letting off firecrackers. This was a good night for a party.

The old Museo Inka had been given a makeover for the Young

Presidents. The museum was a Cuzco institution which contained many pre-Columbian treasures but had always presented them in a dry and dusty way. It had been opened outside normal hours for this reception and was lit up to show off the colonial courtyard and stonework. Waiters handed out *bonnes bouches* on little silver spoons. The stone pre-Columbian artifacts were illuminated from below, casting great shadows across the walls.

I chatted to some of the Young Presidents group. Some had made impressive use of their fast-track access to Peruvian culture (shown around by one of the most knowledgeable of guides, Roger Valencia, and with every locked door opened for them) and demonstrated that quick ability to cut to the heart of an issue that made them powerful in the boardroom; I was struck by their acumen and their enthusiasm for what they had seen. My initial unfair prejudice about golfers in blazers started to slip away, mellowed as I was by fine wine and a cheque in my pocket. Not, it must be said, that they were all neophytes to the Inca cause; one wife, much younger than her husband, confided in me that she had spent the whole day shopping in Cuzco, so had missed Machu Picchu: 'I figure if I don't spend my husband's credit card, the next wife will!'

Unaccountably hidden away on a lower shelf in the museum were one of its great treasures: a set of forty miniature turquoise figures that had been found at the Huari site of Pikillacta in 1927. These had always intrigued me, both because of their beauty and because so little was known of the Huari people, despite having had an empire that lasted considerably longer than the Incas. The figures were just a few inches high, each one individually carved to emphasise very different individual features; some wore strange, protruding headdresses, or seemed to have masks on; many had cloaks with abstract patterns incised on the weaving.

Both the figurines and the canapés on their silver spoons were just appetisers for what was to come. The Young Presidents had arranged to take over the new museum of the Museo Arte Pre-colombino, which had not yet been opened to the public.

As we processed back up the hill to this new museum, the eclipse of the moon began. I could hear the amplified sound and feedback of the Santana-style rock band who had been flown in from Lima to entertain the YPO guests. The firecrackers were going off in the streets. And for me this was where the evening accelerated from strangeness to exhilaration, helped not just by the champagne cocktails and the chatter of the crowds assembled to see the eclipse, but the wonders of the new museum. I was already excited at the thought of it, but nothing of what I had heard had prepared me for the quality of what we were about to be the first to see.

The museum director, Edgar Casaverde, greeted us at the door and guided us through the new salons with their exhibits drawn from all over Peru. The significance of the museum's title was immediately borne in on me – this was a museum of pre-Columbian Art, not of pre-Columbian Archaeology or Anthropology. Rather than trying to give the objects context with maps, chronologies and historical apparatus, the museum largely let the objects speak for themselves and sometimes mixed artifacts from different cultures, so a fine Nasca pot might be next to a Moche one, or Chimú metalwork next to a Paracas weaving.

The insistence on the pieces as works of art, lit and presented as such, brought them alive in precisely the way the old Museo Inka had always failed to do. I was overwhelmed by their sheer opulence. It was a glittering selection, from the first pre-ceramic stone pestle and mortars, 5,000 years old, to the earplugs worn by the Inca nobility, at just 500 years old. What most impressed were the artistic vitality and energy of their creators – and of the museum's curators. They had taken as their benchmark Levi-Strauss's hope that 'one day collections from remote parts of the world will escape the ethnographic museums and occupy their deserved places in art museums.'

This had happened with ancient Greek and Egyptian art but far less so with native American art and perhaps for one simple reason: pre-Columbian artifacts had mostly come to light as the result of excavation, so had remained in the preserve of the archaeologists, whereas with the European and Mediterranean cultures it was the knowledge of literature and of the art already in galleries, so influential on the Renaissance, that had itself fuelled interest in the archaeology – the search for Troy or Mycenae.

There were necklaces of a thousand intricate pieces made from the shell of the spondylus, a sea-creature much prized by the Incas; a ceramic potato whose protuberances exploded in a riot of portraits and erotic images; three Moche ceramic portraits of the same individual; a pair of cormorant drinking vessels, embracing in the favourite Andean image of loving birds, and reciprocal so that the drinkers could toast each other; Nasca and Huari pots, with their austere restraint and abstract patterns, enlivened by a thin band of motifs around their rims; *ocarinas*, ceramic whistles in the shape of a shell. Throughout was evident the playfulness and enjoyment with which the artisans had handled every medium. One of the necklaces of seashells had been metamorphosed into something rich and rare – the pink shells cut in half and spiralled together so that they looked like a string of exploding flower petals.

The rich iconography of Peru with its figures of owls, llamas, cacti and pumas could be seen mutating over time into more abstract, almost formalised representations. There was an apposite quote from Kandinsky on the wall: that what drew him to so-called primitive artists, like many of his generation, was that 'they tried to express the truth from within'. He was not the only artist of his time to be fascinated by pre-Columbian art. There were other accompanying quotes from Picasso, Braque, Matisse and Gauguin (who had spent a considerable part of his childhood in Peru). Picasso and Braque had been to an exhibition of Huari art in Paris not long after the turn of the century and were fascinated by what has since been described as the 'Peruvian cubism' of Huari pots, with faces emerging from quadrants of colour.

But the best moment was still to come. We had settled down to dinner in the courtyard; I was with Arturo Zapata, a Mexican member of the Young Presidents whom I particularly liked, and Edgar, the museum director. Edgar leant towards us conspiratorially: 'Of course there is one final gallery that we are keeping for the opening by President Toledo in a few weeks' time. It is the gold room. I cannot allow a mass viewing. But if you come with me we can have a sneak preview.'

Everyone else was eating and listening to the Santana-style band in their bandannas, velvet jackets and flares ('Peru's best rock musicians' apparently, as I didn't need to be told – by now I'd realised that if you needed to ask how much anything cost, you weren't a Young President). Edgar led Arturo and me to the gold rooms and opened them up.

'You go first,' he instructed.

'*Pero es totalmente oscuro,* but it's completely dark,' protested Arturo.

'It won't be.'

As Arturo and I advanced into the gloom, it felt – deliberately, as Edgar told us later – as if we were entering a tomb. A set of intelligent lighting switches were triggered by our movements, and sheet after sheet of spondylus necklaces suddenly lit up behind the glass to either side of us, with a swish of noise. In the next chamber similar solid sheets of silver emerged out of the dark until in the final room we were met with a dazzling cascade of gold discs worked into a breastplate. It was the museum as theatre, as exploration in the fullest sense.

In the early hours of the morning, I wandered out into the square to absorb all that I'd seen. One of the Peruvian musicians, the tabla player, was taking a break and looking up at the eclipse of the moon which was almost complete. He discovered that I lived in Bristol. '*¡Hombre, increíble!* That's unbelievable, man! I played the first Glastonbury concert near there, in 1970.'

I stayed for a while, watching the last thin sliver of remaining moon. I determined that I would travel through the sites of ancient Peru in search of the places where this amazing art had come from, peeling back the layers like an onion to get at the earliest origins – and earliest impulses – of a culture that had grown up in such complete isolation from the rest of the world.

And this was not just to try to understand the origins of the Andean mindset, helpful as that was for work on Inca sites like Llactapata. Rather that if the civilisation of ancient Peru, beginning in 3000 BC, was the earliest in all the Americas, indeed one of the earliest in the world, and the most isolated, perhaps by understanding the impulses that led early man to form communal groups here might lead to a better understanding of why such groups ever formed at all. What was it that created a civilisation out of nothing?

The square had emptied as the revellers peeled off to the vibrant Cuzco nightclubs. In the middle of the plaza a solitary couple were left embracing. They were having an intense conversation, perhaps waiting for the moon to eclipse completely above them. A taxi driver slowly circled the square hooting at them as if to ask whether they had made up their minds which bed to go to. The sky darkened as the moon disappeared.

CARAL: THE BEGINNING OF
PERUVIAN CIVILISATION

A THOUSAND MILES AWAY and some weeks later, the *garúa*, the winter fog of the Peruvian coast, was blowing in from the sea, filling the streets. We were in Supe, a small town just north of Lima. Silhouettes of soldiers with sub-machine guns stood in ghostly outline at the corners of the main square and at the roadblock up ahead. This was not a surprise. We had been seeing soldiers all morning, in armoured cars, or marshalling traffic, or once a whole line of tanks parked casually beside the *autopista* on the hard shoulder.

Peru was in turmoil. The car radio was on as we drove and we kept hearing more and more frenzied reports about the *emergencia*. John Leivers just pulled his battered Australian hat down over his head, with an 'I've been in worse' attitude, but the exuberant Señora Flor, whose car we were in, had become more despondent as we drove along the coast: '*Ay, ay, ay, Hugo,*' she muttered: '*¿Que pasa con el Perú?* What's happening to Peru?'

The country's political problems, which had flickered away in the background on my many visits here in the previous few years, had suddenly and dramatically come to the fore. The issue was Peru's president, Alejandro Toledo.

Toledo had originally come to power the year before, helped by terrific popular support and revulsion against the corruption of his predecessor Fujimori's government. Toledo seemed the ideal candidate; the first Peruvian president to come from the Andes, he had chosen to be inaugurated at Machu Picchu rather than in Lima, to stress that Peru, like him, had indigenous blood. Famously he had once been a shoeshine boy, and had worked his way up in life. Not only was he 'a man of the people' but he had also been at the World Bank, so was in a position to win the approval of the international institutions in the way that all developing countries require. Yet after just one year into office, he had abysmal approval ratings.

Quite why was hard to pin down, but could be summed up in the sense that he didn't deliver. Whatever his faults, many Peruvians felt that Fujimori had at least built roads and hospitals when he said he would. Toledo, like many South American politicians before him, was a better demagogue than administrator. The economy had done well in terms of stability, exchange rates and all the usual indices – but none of this seemed to trickle down to Peru's desperate poor, or even the middle classes. The fact that Toledo had a foreign wife from Belgium, Eliane Karp, didn't help; although she had a strong interest in pre-Columbian culture and was doing much to help finance archaeological projects, she was seen as a big spender, out of touch with the woman in the street. Then Toledo was forced to admit, after an initial denial, that he had fathered an illegitimate daughter by another woman, and the Peruvian press, largely controlled by Toledo's enemies, wasted no time in pointing the moral finger at him.

But what had brought the current situation to the boil after months of simmering discontent was the realisation that Toledo was earning $18,000 a month ($216,000 per year, not far short of the US president or the UK prime minister) in a country where primary-school teachers were scraping by on just $200 a month. Toledo had chosen this moment to award himself a further spectacular pay rise. It was not surprising that this caused tremendous resentment, particularly as all the other ministerial salaries in his government were pegged to Toledo's, so were likewise sky-high and now going higher. Then it emerged that a large order had been placed for some MiG fighters, a continuation of a military policy most Peruvians thought unnecessary. The teachers went on strike. Farmworkers followed. A mayor was lynched near Puno. There was talk of a general strike. Tear-gas was being used to clear demonstrators from the streets. Toledo's approval rating was the lowest of any president since records began – indeed, once allowing for margins of error in the polling, was close to an almost impossible zero per cent.

While in Cuzco, what with the expedition and then the YPO festivities, I had largely missed all this, but now that we were searching out the earliest Peruvian civilisations along the coast, John and I had run straight into *la situación*; moreover, I had arranged for my family to fly out shortly and was concerned that I might have brought them to a country in meltdown.

Our drive along the coast had been a tense one, not helped by the fog and the constant roadblocks. Señora Flor, our landlady of the night before, had offered us a lift with her family as they were driving this way and she was intrigued to see our destination, Caral; like almost all Peruvians she had never been there. The start of the journey had seen her in a cheerful mood, teasing John about his need for a wife and how a *comadre* of hers who'd been recently widowed would fit the bill perfectly: 'She'd like a man with muscles like yours.' We'd stopped at a roadside stall for some home-made cheese, delicious mopped up with rough bread and sweetcorn. But at this moment Flor was having second thoughts on the wisdom of the journey, not least because she was accompanied by her teenage daughter, Nena; with the constant military presence and the road-blocks, they were feeding on each other's nerves.

Señora Flor's nephew, Rodrigo, was driving, and made John and me equally nervous; he was '*buen cabrón*, up for it' in the way of all testosterone-driven, twenty-year-old drivers the world over, des-perate to overtake every lorry, taxi and goat on the road. John, with his long experience driving overland trucks across the continent, had persuaded him to put new tyres on the worn-out old family jalopy, but this had just given Rodrigo added confidence to burn more rubber. I couldn't help wondering how the soldiers leaning casually on their sub-machine guns would respond if he started squealing away too precipitately.

We stopped to ask one of the town's taxi drivers how to drive inland to Caral: '*Es muy fea, la ruta*,' he grunted; 'the road's very rough.' Moreover, he went on, it not only took a long time to get there normally, but at the moment, with '*la situación*', it was completely impossible. 'You see, señora,' and he threw a dark look at Señora Flor and her daughter, 'the *agricultores* are coming down from the hills.' The *agricultores*, the farmworkers, were always a spectre that haunted the urban Peruvian mind. There was a deep-rooted fear, all the worse for occasionally having been substantiated, that the *agricultores* would rise up, block the roads with burning tyres and starve the cities by refusing to sell their merchandise. It was, after all, only a decade since the Sendero Luminoso, the Maoist 'Shining Path' movement, had been inspiring *agricultores* to do this and much more, almost bringing the country to its knees.

Señora Flor looked alarmed, while her daughter Nena murmured that perhaps she would stop and play in the video arcades in Supe while we went off into the wild badlands that the taxi driver was talking about. This was not helped a moment later when the same taxi driver flagged us down again, flashing his lights, and started to repeat exactly the same message, reiterating the words '*muertos*', '*agricultores*' and '*soldados*' in a circular chant, just in case he hadn't scared us enough already.

As a film-maker I was used to people telling me things were impossible and had a standard solution: to ask somebody else who might give me a different, more positive answer to the same question. The next taxi driver was indeed more sanguine and practical; yes, we could do it, and he could take us by a safe route, but only for an extortionately high fee.

We were saved by Rodrigo. 'These guys are pussies,' he said. 'Let's just go.' For once I was grateful for a bit of unreconstructed machismo.

So we headed inland from Supe along a dirt track to Caral. As we drove, we left the coastal fog behind and the sun revealed a beautiful and fertile valley, filled with sugar cane. There was no sign of rampantly hostile *agricultores*; the only danger was to the tyres, as the dirt track was bad. White cattle egrets stood out against the green fields, which themselves stood out against the faded brown of the hills beyond. This was one of the rich valleys that cut down from the Andes towards the Pacific, interrupting the otherwise desert coast – one of the green veins of Peru that had made civilisation here possible. Our spirits started to lift. I was beside myself with anticipation anyway, as Caral had been the site of a quite epoch-making discovery just a few years before.

To understand why this discovery had been so important, one needed to appreciate what a late developer ancient Peru had been in the world of archaeology. Along the Peruvian desert coast were whole clusters of pyramids, some still buried in the sands, like the Sechín pyramid, the largest structure of early man in the Americas, made up of two million cubic metres of material and the same size as the Great Pyramid in Egypt. Yet while the pyramids of Egypt had been studied for hundreds of years, it was really only in the last ten years that the other great pyramids of the world, those of Peru, had begun to give up their own extraordinary secrets.

Until quite recently Peruvian civilisation was thought to have started around 800 BC, with pre-Inca civilisations such as the Chavín culture based in the highlands. This was around the same time as civilisation had begun in central America. But then archaeologists turned their attention to these Peruvian pyramids, which had never been properly excavated because of their isolation and their huge size.

They made an unexpected discovery. A wooden prop found inside the Sechín pyramid was dated to 1500 BC, far earlier than had been conceived possible. It may seem odd that no one had investigated sites such as Sechín before, but in a region that has such fabulous archaeological riches – the Inca cities, the great lines across the desert at Nasca, the monoliths around Lake Titicaca – there had been plenty of more accessible sites, and excavating a pyramid calls for substantial resources.

The discovery of Sechín's antiquity sent the archaeological world into a feeding frenzy. As archaeologists started to examine and date some of the other great pyramids along the coast, they found the same thing: they were all far older than had previously been thought.

In the year 2000 came the most extraordinary discovery of all. A Peruvian archaeologist called Ruth Shady had for some time been investigating a large pyramidal mound in the valley we were driving into, at a place called Caral, which had never been excavated

Cloud forest beyond Machu Picchu.

Gary Ziegler in the plane flying over Llactapata.

John Leivers: '*not just physically tough –*
he had an endless curiosity about the Incas'.

Bridge over the Aobamba river, leading
towards Llactapata.

Llactapata: Tree ferns over the ruins.

Sunken corridor in rediscovered 'Bingham sector'.

Clearing Llactapata: *'group after group appeared, some uncovered after five centuries of concealment'*.

Heading out from Llactapata: *'I could see the rest of the party picking their way over the distant puna bowl.'*

The campsite below Mt Tucarhuay at night: *'an accelerated rush of all that I liked in the Peruvian mountains'.*

The Upper Stone of Sahuite: *'like a meteorite shot from the past containing the Inca world in capsule form'*.

Below The carved 'puma stone' at Sahuite.

The frieze at Cerro Sechín: *'two lines of "warrior-priests" advanced from either side of the platform walls'*. *Right* Decapitated heads.

Below Caral amphitheatre: *'There was no record of what was performed here, or of its history. This was an illiterate culture: the actors are mute.'*

before. One has to remember that a pyramidal mound is just that – a mound – and that clearance could reveal it to be no more than a man-made hill, without significant structures.

However, Ruth Shady was convinced the site would repay full excavation: 'When I first arrived in the valley I was overwhelmed,' she said. 'The place was somewhere between the seat of the gods and the home of man. It was a very strange place.'

I had met Ruth in Lima and had been impressed by her determination and charisma. She had full dark eyebrows similar to those Frida Kahlo accentuated on her self-portraits, which gave her gaze an added intensity. Sitting quietly in an office just off Lima's old colonial main square, Ruth had told me the whole story in a monologue that poured steadily out of her, partly from the sheer weight of time she had been working at Caral, partly from the bitterness she felt at the way she had sometimes been treated. Indeed, it impressed me that she had persevered in the face of obstacles that would have deterred most archaeologists.

In 1994, she had returned from a period at Dunbarton Oaks near Washington, where there was a centre for Andeanist studies. Her fieldwork had previously been in the mountains of the Sierra Norte but she had increasingly found this both difficult and dangerous, given the political instability of Peru, so she cast around for a site closer to Lima; she decided to simply drive north from the capital until she reached a valley that wasn't already being investigated. Caral was the first she came to.

What had discouraged previous investigators from looking at Caral was the lack of any ceramic artifacts near by. There was still a widely held belief that the capability to fire clay always preceded the building of monumental architecture. This certainly had always been 'the timeline' with other ancient civilisations. And there was also considerable opposition to the idea that a civilisation could have arisen based just on '*recursos maritimos*, maritime resources', rather than agriculture, as in other models. So there was a presumption, Ruth told me, that Caral was not worth investigating, given that considerable '*recursos modernos*, modern resources' were needed to clear the site.

For the next two years Ruth spent her weekends tramping the valley until she knew every last inch of it. National Geographic gave her a small grant for two months' work to see whether she could find any ceramic artifacts, but when she couldn't, '*me terminó la plata*, they cut off the money'.

Ruth turned to various commercial sponsors, but they all refused on the grounds that it was too low profile. She managed to persuade various university students to help her for their theses, although even for these students she had to provide food, which she did out of her own pocket, and drive them there in her own car; in this way she continued working the site over the next three years between 1996 and 1999.

Then came a stroke of luck. The mayor of one of the local townships had been born in Caral and was fascinated by the mounds. He loaned her two workers from the municipality. Another mayor matched his offer. Finally, having the sort of faith in her project that could literally move mountains, Ruth persuaded the Peruvian army to help her dismantle the surface of the hill. Under the rubble they had found a sophisticated building of a vast size; the largest platform mound was approximately the length of two football fields, nearly as wide, and five storeys high. Moreover the building was made out of stone, not adobe, a sign of civilised monumental architecture. And there were other such pyramids near by.

As it is impossible to carbon-date stone, at first it did not seem as if they would find any datable substances. But they later came across the most fragile of evidence – some woven bags of *shicra*, reed, which workers had used to carry the rocks up for the platform mounds. A few of the workers, perhaps exhausted by the climb, had simply placed the bags, rocks and all, inside the structures' retaining walls, instead of reusing them. Radiocarbon analysis is able to determine the ages of fibres from such woven reed bags extremely specifically, as reeds live for just one year.

Ruth did not have the resources to get the bags accurately dated. However, by 1999 she had achieved enough to persuade a French magazine to publish an article about her work. On the back of that she was able to give a presentation at the prestigious Field Museum of Chicago.

This was where the story got darker. I had been watching her as she told me the tale, in a quiet concentrated way that brooked few interruptions (like many archaeologists, Ruth was a better talker than listener). Her strong, dark eyebrows narrowed as she came to what happened next.

Jonathan Haas was the distinguished Professor at the Chicago Field Museum, who, together with his wife Winifred Creamer, had taken an interest in Ruth's work. Ruth was determined to show that there was 'a pre-ceramic context' to some of the structures she was uncovering, even though this went against precedent. So she sent a sample of a reed bag to Haas for dating: 'No one else at the time thought that Caral could possibly be pre-ceramic,' that is, that it could date from before 1700 BC when pottery was thought to have started in the Andes.

Haas rang her in some surprise to say that she was right. The dating, and subsequent ones, showed Caral to have been constructed from around 2700 to 2100 BC – over a thousand years earlier even than the other pyramids at Sechín, which had caused such amazement when they were dated to 1500 BC rather than 800 BC. Some other sites close to Caral, and part of the same 'cultural complex', were dated even earlier, to 3000 BC. In just a few years, the horizon of the birth of Peruvian civilisation had been rolled back by two millennia.

At a stroke it became clear that Peruvian civilisation was by far the most ancient in the Americas and one of the most ancient in the world, comparable to India, Egypt and China. This was important not only archaeologically but politically – for as Ruth put it to me, it showed that there was no such thing as the 'New World'. Civilisation, an emotive concept, had developed in the Americas at the same time as in the so-called 'Old World'. It had taken some time for the implications of this to sink in. Ruth was convinced that Caral would 'immeasurably improve Peruvians' self-esteem and become an important symbol of national identity', in much the same way as Machu Picchu had. She might well have added that it would be equally important for the whole continent.

Science magazine were alerted and ran a major article on the subject, with Ruth credited as an author, together with Haas and Winifred Creamer. According to Ruth, Haas had suggested that publishing the article on Caral in *Science*, with his and his wife's name attached – even though Haas and Creamer had never excavated at Caral – would subsequently make it easier to obtain funds for Caral if they submitted for a bi-national project in the United States.

The article naturally attracted a great deal of interest in what headlines worldwide heralded as 'the birthplace of civilisation in the Americas' and the 'mother city'. Newsweek reported breathlessly that 'this complex, pyramid-shaped structure built more than 4,000 years ago ... lies not in Egypt, but 120 miles north of Lima, Peru'. The BBC devoted a whole programme to the discovery, titled, equally breathlessly, *The Lost Pyramids of Caral*.

However, Ruth's uneasiness at giving co-authorship of the article to Haas and Creamer was compounded when she discovered that on Haas's Field Museum website the actual investigation of Caral was credited to Haas, while on his wife Winfred Creamer's site at the University of Illinois, the discovery of 'the oldest civilisation in America' was likewise credited to Creamer. Moreover the detail that really stuck in Ruth's throat was that Creamer was therefore nominated as the university's 'woman of the year'.

When Ruth remonstrated, Haas apparently told Ruth that it was all 'for presentation'. She sniffed dismissively: '*Son piratas, realmente*, the fact is they are pirates.' The word pirates carries a less jocular meaning in Spanish than it does in English – perhaps because the South American seaboard was terrorised by English ones.

Despite a public apology by Haas, the dispute remained a source of much bitterness and some controversy, which as of writing has yet to be resolved. I was conscious that I was only hearing Ruth's side of the story. University websites have a natural tendency to blow the trumpet for their own staff, not least because it helps attract more funding. But the mere fact that after years of solitary work on the site Ruth should be left feeling betrayed was at the very least a sign of insensitivity, if not outright bad faith.

Ruth had formally sent a *denuncia*, an open indictment, of Haas and Creamer's actions to the INC, the main Peruvian archaeological institute, in which she talked of '*su intento de apropiación ilícita de la investigación que venimos realizando sobre las orígenes de la civilización*, their attempt to appropriate illegally our investigation into the origins of civilisation' and of the affront to her 'intellectual rights'. After the fallout with Ruth, Haas and Creamer had started to work in other areas near Caral. Ruth suspected that they were attempting to find a rival site as old as or older than Caral, although she dismissed their methodology as poor: 'They leave their excavation trenches open after they have finished.'

All this had reopened old wounds. Peruvian archaeologists have always been vocal on the need for Peruvians to study their own riches rather than leave the work to foreigners – the memory of Hiram Bingham carrying all his findings at Machu Picchu back to Yale still rankles. The fact that American academics have more resources to excavate does not help. Even worse is the fact that they are so much better paid. Another of Ruth's justified points was that all too often foreign archaeologists did not bother to publish their findings in Peruvian publications. I was already intensely aware that we might get some criticism in Peru for our work at Llactapata (although in the event the head of the INC, Luis Lumbreras, was extremely warm about our research) – and that it would be important to publish our findings in the *Revista Andina*, the Peruvian academic magazine for Andeanist studies, as well as in an English language one.

As a general rule, I had noticed that archaeologists were spectacularly good at picking arguments, perhaps because they spent so long looking down the same hole. The only profession I could think of that was remotely as cantankerous and bad-tempered were minicab drivers, who spend too much time on their own listening to reports on the radio about how other drivers are picking up fares.

Despite having been left 'very depressed' by this experience with the Americans, Ruth persevered. In 2002 she invited Toledo's wife,

Eliane Karp, to see Caral, and the new First Lady supported the project. The site was proclaimed 'of national interest'. Commercial sponsorship came from a travel company, Lima Tours. But just as things were going well came '*un desastre*'.

One morning, at 9 a.m., as she drove along the very same dirt road to the site that we were now negotiating, four men waylaid her by blocking the way with stones; they then surrounded her car, two on either side. She was shot at and assaulted by the attackers; a bullet struck her breast-bone and was deflected. One of these '*delincuentes*' was captured later and confessed ('He only confessed when he was drunk,' added Ruth, 'but it was still a confession'). The judge set him free on a conditional release.

She was still shaken from all this when we met. Yet this was not stopping her from extending the work at Caral – she had yet to find the city's cemetery – and trying to get her remarkable findings, which I had seen, placed in a permanent exhibition space, either on site or in Lima.

Ruth was from the mould that seemed to have produced a whole swathe of indomitable and impressive female Andeanists: Catherine Allen, Adriana von Hagen, Sonia Guillén, Catherine Julien, Ann Kendall, Patricia Lyon, Dorothy Menzel, Susan Niles, Lucy Salazar, Katharina Schreiber, Helaine Silverman and the pioneering María Rostworowski, now in her nineties.

Nor was Ruth resting on her laurels (or those that had not been snatched away from her); she wanted to explore the trade routes between Caral and the jungle; indeed, she had proposed that I should help her do this, together with Gary Ziegler, whom she had a connection with as they had both been taught by the influential Peruvian archaeologist Jorge Muelle when students in Lima. It was a tantalising idea, if not perhaps for this lifetime.

*

After twelve miles along the dirt-track road we reached Caral. For such an epoch-making discovery, there was little to mark one's arrival at the site – a simple board pinned to a tree and an empty hammock swinging from the branches. It was still too early for any tourist infrastructure to have been put in place, hence the lack of a proper road (we had worried whether Rodrigo's low-slung car would make it over one ford), of any site information, indeed, of any guide. Excavations were still continuing and we came across some of the archaeologists later. But for now we could wander around the site completely on our own.

It was late afternoon and the sun was sweeping in low over the sands, for since its construction 5,000 years ago, Caral had been reclaimed by the desert. In its heyday there would have been a system of irrigation, which had long since collapsed. I walked up the Píramide Mayor (the 'Great Pyramid') to get my bearings; from the top I could see the size of the site. It was much more extensive than I had imagined. There were some thirty public buildings, of which the Great Pyramid was the largest, but there were several other pyramids in the complex. However, it was not just the scale but the detail that impressed – I had expected crude monoliths, but what I saw here was a civic architecture of considerable finesse. The Great Pyramid was façaded, with a monumental staircase some forty feet wide. At its base was a fine sunken circular plaza, linked to the pyramid by a walkway. On the summit stood a complex of buildings that included a circular altar. A frieze of interlaced serpents had been discovered on one wall by Ruth and her team, and there was evidence that the site had been painted in colours of red, white and yellow.

From the summit I could see the other pyramids. They shared common architectural features: the great staircases rose up past as many as nine layers of terraces in some cases before reaching the summits, where there were circular altars, often enclosed by square walls. I was interested to see that one pyramid had been built to project directly out of a large rock outcrop as if connecting with the living stone, a technique the Incas were still using at Machu Picchu four thousand years later. Right across the site I could make out another sunken, circular plaza called the 'Amphitheatre', even bigger than the one below the Great Pyramid. There were also many residential buildings, with benches, platforms and fireplaces, some quite elaborately designed with wooden supports and stone walls.

The view down from the summit also helped explain what had propelled Caral into a state of civilisation: just beyond the point where the city and the sands ended was the fertile valley of the Supe river, where around 2700 BC early Peruvian man had learnt to grow cotton, the traditional material for the Peruvian fishing net.

The people of Caral had mastered the technique of both growing and weaving cotton – as I wandered around the site I kept seeing little twists of woven cords that had been brought to the surface – and this was surely the beginnings of the facility for weaving that was to be such a hallmark of Andean life. It was the very fact that the *shicra* bag for carrying stones up to the pyramid had been woven that had allowed the first accurate dating of the site.

This skill enabled the people of Caral to barter with the simpler communities of fishermen on the coast. For the suggestion is that they grew cotton for the essential but easily perishable nets needed by the fishermen, who traded for them with fish. This theory is supported by coprolitic examination, the polite archaeological term for the examination of dried faeces, which shows that the inhabitants of Caral ate a great deal of protein-rich anchovies. The Pacific ocean off Peru's coast is one of the richest fishing grounds in the world, and there are anchovies in abundance.

Their intake of fish was supplemented with beans, peppers, guayaba and sweet potato, among other vegetables: an impressively balanced, nutritious diet. They also took *sauze*, a medicinal herb still used to provide one of the ingredients of aspirin, and *achiote*, a herb valued both for its red dye and its aphrodisiacal qualities; victims of human sacrifice in later Andean cultures were dosed with *achiote* before death. *Achiote* came from the Amazon, where it is still widely used by local tribes. Indeed, it is striking how many of the artifacts recovered show that, even this early, a substantial trade network had obviously sprung up all over the Peruvian region; as well as *achiote* from the jungle, there were camelid bones from llama or alpaca, animals of the highlands, and spondylus shells from further up the coast and its offshore islands.

The spondylus shells had been worked into jewellery, as had pieces of quartz and semi-precious stones; the simple implements of stone and bone that they used to work the jewellery have also been found, many in a building Ruth dubbed the 'Taller de Especialización Artesenal', the 'Specialised Workshop', one of the many smaller buildings that dotted the landscape between the pyramids. There was also a mortar in which minerals had been ground to obtain red pigment for dyes. Elsewhere in the complex, some of the most extraordinary of all Caral's artifacts had been recovered: eight seats cut from the vertebrae of whales, and then worked, polished and painted. I had seen one of these with Ruth in Lima; exotic, other-worldly pieces of furniture, the bones gleamed a soft matt white in the dark room where I had seen them stored.

In all this, there was one striking absence. It seems that unlike most early ancient civilisations in other parts of the world, there were no fortifications of any sort connected with Caral. Nor was there as yet any evidence of military activity or human sacrifice: no battlements, no weapons, no mutilated bodies. Instead, Ruth's findings suggest it was a gentle society, built on commerce and pleasure, with ritual activities celebrated on the pyramids that would have been visible from all over the valley. Many musical instruments had been discovered. Her team also found evidence of a culture that took coca recreationally (as well as seeds from the coca plant, they came across traces of lime in snail shells that had been used as dippers for the coca) alongside other aphrodisiac and hallucinogenic substances. The people of Caral fetishised the braiding of hair, and some of the clay figurines allude to this, as well as combs made from cacti.

What all Ruth's findings suggested was that the city of Caral arose not from the need to wage war or to group together for protection, but the need to trade. As archaeology has moved into hyperphase in Peru – for this is arguably the most exciting area of the world to be working in currently, with the greatest number of new discoveries and excavations being made – other early pyramids have emerged that support this new twenty-first-century view: the beginnings of Peruvian civilisation were essentially peaceful.

The common axis that drove the growth of the many different and exuberant Peruvian cultures of the next several millennia was trade, rather than warfare. The message that Caral and the early pyramids of Peru gives us is that early American man lived in a cooperative society, where people were driven together to form civilisations through the need for each others' goods in a relentlessly hostile landscape.

*

I thought of this as I explored the site, my boots dusty from the sand that had swept in to cover the lands that had once been irrigated. Some of the archaeologists working with and for Ruth showed me the recent work they had been doing, often in the smaller residential buildings lying scattered near the main pyramids. The domestic architecture was as impressive as the ceremonial. They showed me a variety of residential sectors, from high-status ones very close by the pyramids to smaller ones further afield. Indeed, there was what Ruth had described to me as 'an archipelago' of smaller buildings stretching away along the axis of the city. Overall, the site covered some 160 acres.

Having wandered all over Caral, I ended in the sector Ruth had described to me as 'the Amphitheatre'. This was the large circular sunken plaza I had seen in the distance from the Great Pyramid. There was a building set above it, but the relative proportion of plaza to building made clear that the plaza was the predominant focus. There were steps leading down into the plaza.

The Amphitheatre seems to have been designed to be reciprocal to the Great Pyramid – it lay right on the other side of the site and there was a suggestion that the city of Caral had been divided into an upper and lower half, *hanan* and *hurin*, as it was on two levels. The Great Pyramid was the focus of the upper half, the Amphitheatre of the lower. The division showed that the roots of Inca urban planning – the very duality that had so confused us at Llactapata with its two mirror-image sectors – was already present in the very beginnings of Andean civilisation; Caral was even divided on the same geographical axis, with one half to the west, the other to the east, as at Machu Picchu.

A set of thirty-two beautiful flutes had been recovered in the amphitheatre complex, which I had seen: made from the bones of pelicans and condors, they were finely crafted and elegant instruments, decorated with stylised drawings of monkeys, snakes, condors and human faces – the mouth of the face being the mouthpiece of the flute. Cruder, but also evidence of the considerable musical activity that seems to have taken place, were another set of thirty-eight pieces, shaped like cornets, which had been made from camelid bones.

As the last sunlight faded on the site and wind blew sand across it, the Amphitheatre was an emotive place. I thought of the flutes and cornets being played here, of the buildings coloured white, red and yellow, of bodies smeared with the red *achiote* dye; of the careful work on jewellery and woven nets, and of the pleasure taken in trade for such exotic commodities as feathers from the jungle and llamas from the highlands, or whale bones and shells from along the coast.

One must be wary of projecting an archaeological Eden, but Caral did seem to contain much of the most positive elements of Andean civilisation: the facility with monumental architecture and with stone; a feeling for music and for peaceful coexistence, fuelled by trade; a balance between domestic and political spaces.

With the backdrop of the fertile river and the mountains, the comparisons I immediately reached for were those most familiar to me: the Nilotic culture of ancient Egypt and the amphitheatres of Greece; but unlike those civilisations, there was no record of what was performed here, or of any of its history. This was an illiterate culture; there are no hieroglyphics waiting to be deciphered or Rosetta stones to be found, no fragments of surviving papyrus. The actors here are mute.

In one of the buildings, Ruth and her team had found the coloured outline of a child's hand pressed against a wall, whether in ritual or play. I found this strangely moving – an ephemeral snapshot impressed on such a monolithic site.

They had also found small figurines of women made from clay (but unfired, so not ceramic), often bundled together with spools of cotton and some fragments of semi-precious stones. Ruth speculated that the circular altars found both at the Amphitheatre and the other major pyramids might have contained an eternal flame that was always kept alight; there were hearths at the centre of each altar.

I found it tremendously exciting to be seeing the site so soon after the canvas had been restored; just a few years before one would have seen nothing here except a few mounds in the sands, virtually indistinguishable from the hills to either side. I felt sure that more such sites would be uncovered along the Peruvian coast in the years to follow. Haas and Creamer had recently dated several other sites near by as being of similar antiquity, so Caral was not an isolated example. Indeed, they had needed to formulate a whole new term for the millennium to take account of these various discoveries. It was now called, in snappy archaeological fashion, the 'Late Archaic or Cotton Pre-ceramic Period', accounting for the thousand years of civilisation before pottery began around 1700 BC.

Where had the people who built these pyramids come from? One theory suggests that humans first entered the Americas from Asia around 15000 BC when there was still a land-bridge across what is now the Bering Strait between Russia and Alaska, and when much of the rest of the world was already populated. Recent mitochondrial DNA analysis indicates that they slowly percolated their way down the Americas, reaching Peru around 12000 BC. But despite being almost the last area on the planet to be colonised by man, it now seemed to be one of the first to have achieved civilisation, which begged the question: why?

Caral's slow decline into a desert had given it a ghostly feel. When I'd been on the Tsavo plains of East Africa, with Mount Kilimanjaro looming in the distance, I could believe that this was the birthplace of humanity and that *Homo sapiens* had begun his migrations from Africa around 80,000 years ago. But the landscape of Caral did not immediately suggest a cradle for a civilisation, although its very harshness may suggest a reason for its emergence.

Or to put it another way, why Peru, not California? Early man, as he travelled down the length of the Americas, would have encountered numerous more hospitable terrains than this stretch of arid desert and harsh mountains. Why did civilisation not develop in California, or its climatic equivalent, in 15000 BC, on some fertile stretch of the American coast where all one had to do was reach out and pluck the low-hanging fruit from the vine?

The answer may have been that it was the very harshness of the land that forced cooperation between peoples and was the genesis for civilisation. The potential richness of the region – the fishing grounds, the mountain produce – could only be harnessed by working together, and by trade, by producing cotton fishing nets inland for fishermen on the coast.

As a traveller, I was inclined to speculate that perhaps natural selection had helped in this process – that only the boldest members of the human tribe would have been the ones to push continually onwards from Africa out to the rest of the world, over the thousands of generations after the first exodus, and that by the time they reached Peru, the furthest point, they were genetically predisposed to the creative solution of the challenges that confronted them.

However, this still does not explain the impulse to monumental architecture, so strong here that, uniquely among the world's ancient civilisations, the ancient Peruvians started to build with stone before they had even learnt to fire clay for cooking utensils. And the precise spark that ignited in a few isolated corners of the world and created civilisation is still a mystery, as is the way in which the human gene pool, separated for many thousands of years, should have simultaneously combusted into civilisation in both the 'Old' World and the 'New' at roughly the same time, around 3000 BC. It is one of those accelerations in human development remarkable for having happened once, let alone six times in different places.

As I watched the sands being whipped higher by the evening wind, I thought that the desert now covering Caral gave a clue to the real challenge faced by early man in Peru, the same challenge that faces twenty-first-century mankind: radical climate change.

For what destroyed many of the great civilisations of ancient Peru was the unpredictability of the weather. Peru lies in one of the most finely tuned ecosystems on the planet, as the well-known El Niño phenomenon demonstrates. Every six or seven years, a change in Pacific wind directions causes a build-up of much warmer water along Peru's coast; initially it is the fishing that suffers; then the whole climate gets thrown into reverse, with flooding in the deserts and drought in the mountains. The flooding in the deserts not only causes the *arroyos*, the river channels, to burst their banks, but brings a plague of mosquitoes and disease in its wake.

The phenomenon is called El Niño (the child) because it often occurs around Christmas and the infant Jesus in Spanish is 'El Niño Santo'. Some El Niños are far worse than others. My first visit to Peru had been just before the catastrophic 1982–3 El Niño, and as I left my Peruvian friends were all bracing themselves for the onslaught. The El Niño of 1997–8 had been even worse, with the sudden creation of Peru's second largest lake and vicious outbreaks of malaria. Such large El Niños have worldwide effect. In the 97–8 event, while Peru was flooded, across the Pacific, Indonesia and Malaysia were starved of rain and experienced terrible forest fires; the knock-on effects were felt as far away as Europe and Madagascar. Thousands of people were killed and over $30 billion of damage to property was caused.

El Niño is only the most dramatic expression of a Peruvian meteorology that has always been on a knife-edge. Small shifts in temperatures could have far-reaching effects, and the coast and the mountains were constantly alternating between drought and rainfall. The Andes are volatile mountains anyway, sitting on an area of intense seismic activity that is constantly producing earthquakes and landslides of the sort that engulfed 100 towns in the Callejón de Huaylas in 1970 and killed 70,000 people.

As Michael Moseley, the Andeanist who influenced a generation with his interpretation of climate change, has pointed out, so variable is the pattern that there is hardly such a thing as a 'normal year'. Recent studies on the ice-cores of Andean glaciers have shown that this random pattern has been repeating itself for millennia; the ice-cores clearly show that annual precipitation levels are constantly changing. In some centuries (around 500 BC, AD 600 and AD 1000), there was such dramatic climatic change that the landscape was permanently altered. What happened to the human populations who got in the way can only be inferred from the archaeological record. Certainly the demise of many of the later cultures of ancient Peru, such as the Moche, the Nasca and the Huari, coincided with particularly abrupt changes in the climate.

No wonder that the Incas and their predecessors were obsessed with storing vast quantities of goods in their *qolqas* 'for a rainy day', a phenomenon the conquistadors noted but were far less good at maintaining.

Nor is it surprising that after Caral, strategies for engaging with the gods of the weather, from building pyramids to hallucinogenic combat, should have begun endlessly to preoccupy the pre-Columbian mind; their courage and human ingenuity displayed in the face of adverse weather conditions was often admirable – a courage that we ourselves may similarly have to dig deep to find as our own climate worsens.

*

John and I were heading up the coast by local bus. Many of the sites we wanted to see were near small towns, so the air-conditioned coaches that thundered up the Pan-American Highway from city to big city, with their all-night karate DVDs, were no good to us anyway. The local buses suited our style, and John had a winning way with counter-girls in the ticket offices. In fact if given a dollar for every time they called him 'Crocodile Dundee' because of his hat and general all-round Australian-ness, I would have been able to hire us a limo.

I liked John's curiosity and enthusiasm. He was still using that favourite phrase of his when recounting the possibilities of some new area of discovery: 'There's just so much out there.' Like many of the autodidacts I'd met in Peru, he wanted to see everything at first-hand ('kick it with his own feet', as another explorer, Vince Lee, had once put it), and then record it in notebooks or on his digital camera.

In the local buses, a logbook was handed around for passengers to fill in their details, presumably in the event of one of the frequent accidents when buses went over cliffs or under each other. Many Western travellers filled in their occupation as 'Stripper' or 'US President'. John put down his details as 'Driver, 50' after years on the road taking long-distance buses across continents for companies like Encounter Overland. This had demanded extreme stamina and an ability to handle a disparate group of people thrown together in close proximity for many months through the roughest of terrains for no better reasons than that they had all bought tickets on the same bus. Some of his tales were hair-raising, as he'd dealt with psychotic passengers, trigger-happy African border-guards with guns and drug-runners on the Darien Gap.

Yet though he seemed hewn from rock, John had a questing, more worried side too. His constant journeying had left him financially insecure; like many of the drivers, he had invested in the Encounter Overland employee share-scheme, only for the company to go bust. He had no family, children or immediate responsibilities, so was free to travel at will, but as Janis Joplin used to sing, 'Freedom's just another word for nothing left to lose.'

He was obsessive about writing everything down in his notebooks, far more diligently than I was and almost to the point of logophilia. In his search for a system, for connections between the many places he had seen, there was something compulsive in John's quest for meaning. I sensed he had little interest in relationships or the lure of a pretty face, despite his considerable charm and the many temptations that had come his way when leading groups of clients.

As with many sites, given the journey times, it was late afternoon by the time we arrived at the Sechín complex, some one hundred miles up the coast from Caral, but now known to have been built a thousand years later, between 1800 and 1300 BC, so part of the next great wave of civilisations in Peru.

Sechín was as monolithic and overwhelming as an Andean site

could possibly be; not only did it contain one of the largest pyramids in the Americas, Sechín Alto, at 150 feet, as high as a nine-storeyed building, and faced with granite blocks, but near by was Cerro Sechín, a three-tiered platform decorated with an extraordinary frieze of around 350 monumental stone figures.

The late light was deceptively mellow as it fell on Cerro Sechín and the frieze, deceptive because the frieze was so shockingly violent. Two lines of 'warrior-priests' advanced from either side of the platform walls towards the steps that rose from its centre to the top, accompanied by the bodies of their victims. Most of the bodies had been decapitated or mutilated in some way; there were intestines piling out of stomachs; blood pouring from cuts to the head in great viscous streams; neatly truncated and stripped human vertebrae; even a 'skull rack' stacked high with a neat pile of trophies.

And this savagery was pictured with the greatest possible artistry, on granite slabs quarried from the hillside above. The designs had first been traced in charcoal and then hammered out laboriously from the hard granite, using even harder hammer-stones (the same technique the Incas used later at Machu Picchu), working with precision and artistic flair. For there was no doubt that this was a celebratory and fascinated art, which dwelt on the details of the pain, the mouths open in either surprise or horror, streams of blood ('chorros de sangre') spurting out like spaghetti. The style was fluid and expressive, almost cartoon-like, reminiscent of Maya glyphs or the graphic art of Keith Haring.

If the purpose of this frieze was, as some thought, to propitiate the deities that controlled the weather and the El Niño cycle, it did not help the people of Sechín. Around 1300 BC a tremendous flood seems to have buried the temple under mud and hidden it for some 3,300 years. It was only in 1937 that Julio Tello, the doyen of Peruvian archaeology, came upon the site and its existence was made known to the wider world.

Tello was in the middle of investigating the site of Chavín in the mountains, and looking for evidence that the influence of that intriguing temple-cult had spread further afield. When passing by Sechín, he had come across one of the stone sculptures incorporated into the wall of a house. The owner explained that it had originally been abandoned by a German who had somehow happened upon the sculpture and decided to take it with him in his merchant ship, with the casual approach to pre-Columbian antiquities typical of the time. Luckily the sheer weight of the stone had defeated the German seaman, and he had left it for the owner of the house to use on his building. Tello became excited by the similarities of the stone with Chavín iconography and so investigated further, finding its source at Cerro Sechín.

With the help of fifteen workmen, Tello uncovered the whole astonishing platform. Like many an archaeological discovery in Peru (Bingham's at Machu Picchu, for instance), it was made while searching for something completely different. We now know that far from showing the influence of the Chavín culture, Sechín pre-dates Chavín by a millennium and if anything is more likely to have been the mother not the child of that civilisation. But Tello's achievement in uncovering an obscure mound of mud in a neglected corner of Peru should not be underestimated.

Johan and I were shown around the frieze by César Leandro, the present archaeological custodian of the site, who detailed the slaughter with a professional dispassion, pointing out not only the stacks of removed eyeballs, but how the intact figures had lengthened index fingernails, the better to do the gouging.

I had an old-fashioned letter from the Peruvian Government, charging all those with whom I came into contact to render me 'due assistance', like the early passport letters that travellers used in the nineteenth century, but César was more than willing to help anyway; indeed, he was pleased to have visitors at all. Despite the provision of a new car park and a well-laid-out small museum, few ever came here, as it lay near no major city, so we had a site that in Greece or Egypt would have been packed to the gunwales gloriously to ourselves.

César led us around the back of the southern side of the platform, which was still being excavated and lay out of sight against the hillside, where yet more of the 'warrior frieze' was still being uncovered. He told us that so far 357 statues had been discovered.

Near by I couldn't help noticing a used condom that had been left in the passageway by a courting couple seeking the frisson of a liaison among the dead of a past civilisation. This was a phenomenon I had come across before, the widely held Peruvian belief that there was some aphrodisiacal benefit from having a tryst in the old ruins that lay conveniently close all around them.

There was an entranceway on the southern side and steps leading down into chambers below the platform. Much work remained to be done, both here and at the nearby pyramids of Sechín Alto and Sechín Bajo, and not for the first time I felt the excitement of all these early sites along Peru's coast – that work on them was really only just beginning to any great extent and that over the next generation more tremendous discoveries would be made.

César shared this excitement. In his late thirties, and fit and compact with the energy of an enthusiastic primary-school teacher, he had already created a football pitch so the children could play while their parents visited the site; beside the museum he showed us the small garden where he grew *algarrobo*, carob, and other pre-Columbian trees. Outside the museum he had positioned some of the outsize '*chicha* jars' uncovered locally as a reminder that by now the ancient Peruvians had mastered the art of firing ceramics as well as of more monumental building.

We took César off for a meal with us in the nearby small town of Casma where we were staying, sharing a $10-a-night room, which John thought recklessly extravagant. Over a few drinks, and then a few more drinks, César became voluble and forthcoming on his passion for archaeology. Much of it stemmed from his experiences during Peru's long night of the soul, the period in the nineties when the activities of the Sendero Luminoso had divided the country.

César had been the eldest of a large family, and from a very young age had need to support his brothers and sisters. He had joined the police, and when the Sendero Luminoso conflict started he had travelled the country with them, seeing, in his words, 'poverty and destruction that made me cry'. Families and communities had been torn apart amidst scenes of violence in what was, to all intents and purposes, a civil war.

All this came pouring out of him as we sat in a Chinese restaurant, drinking beers and waiting for our orders. John sat quietly, trying to understand César's fast Spanish, while I occasionally prompted him with a question. Like all who had worked in Peru, I was aware of excesses on both sides during the Sendero Luminoso years – and many of the muleteers on my expeditions had been scarred by the Sendero incursion up the Apurímac river – but César's tales had an immediacy about them, the sense of a man drawn into a conflict unwittingly, that brought it home to me more than any of the novels or films that had tried to do so. It was also a story that was easier for him to tell a foreigner like me than a fellow Peruvian.

The talk turned inevitably to Sechín. After leaving the police, and with the end of the Sendero conflict, César had thrown himself into archaeology. It had been a release after the violence he had seen, a way of trying to understand the country he had watched being ripped open. After completing his studies, he had joined the INC (Peru's Institute of National Culture) and had come to Sechín – ironically a site that seemed to embody conflict.

'There has always been the possibility of violence in Peru,' said César. 'There always has been. It is in the geography of the land.'

Certainly if Caral had given all the impression of a peaceful birth to Peruvian civilisation, by a thousand years later Sechín was showing all the signs of some strain of violence. Yet to presume that this necessarily implied actual warfare might be precipitate. Just as at Caral, nowhere in the Sechín complex do there seem to be any signs of fortifications, as one would expect if there was fighting between different polities in the area.

Indeed, there are several alternative explanations for the 'warrior frieze', and this term may itself be misleading. The simplest is that it is an actual depiction of historical events, of some great battle. The next, put forward among others by Richard Burger, the Andeanist at Yale who had been so helpful to me in getting access to Bingham's papers, is that it is more literary than literal, a metaphorical or allegorical recounting of some pivotal story for the Sechín culture. This is supported by earlier versions of the same story, which seem to be retold in simpler clay friezes on the walls of earlier phases of the site. While this theory is attractive in some ways, there are immediate questions. The struggles of Homer's epic may likewise be allegorical but they are thought to have their origin in historical events, or at the very least in a knowledge and experience of ancient warfare. If the Sechín frieze tells a story, it is hardly one told by a peaceable civilisation.

But there is another hypothesis: that what we are seeing is the beginning of the tradition of human sacrifice that was to continue for millennia in the Andes, right up to its very occasional use by the Incas, often to propitiate the fickle deities of the weather that could cause such havoc. Living as they must have done in a state of abject dependence on the whims of climatic variance, the impulse to make dramatic declarations of faith and of offerings must have been strong. And what could have been stronger than the offering of a human heart? The line of figures with their attendant body parts all seem to be processing towards the central stairways, leading up to the platform's top, a natural place for any such offerings.

Before coming to Sechín I had talked to Henning Bischof, the distinguished German archaeologist now in his late sixties who had done pioneering work at Cerro Sechín between 1979 and 1984. Together with Peruvian colleagues, he had been the first to establish an accurate radiocarbon figure for the site, when they had found a wooden post supporting one wall and dated it to around 1500 BC. I asked him about the intense debate on the meaning of the frieze.

'What you have to remember', said Henning in slightly accented but perfect grammatical English, 'is what was happening to Peru when all these different interpretations were being made.' He argued that Peruvian archaeology reflected political events far more than has ever been acknowledged. While the military governments of the sixties and seventies held sway, they welcomed a purely military interpretation of the frieze – Peru's great military past, so to speak, which they were inheriting – 'and that interpretation is precisely what the archaeologists gave them'.

But as Henning pointed out, there was a real problem with any interpretation of the frieze as military: without iron, the weapons available for actual warfare to the people of Sechín would never have been able to achieve such clean-cut savagery. Speaking in his precise German accent, Henning said: 'It would have been impossible to cut off limbs in combat. You must remember that it is time-consuming work to disassemble a human body.' Any warfare would have been a far cruder process of slings and battering stones.

Equally political was the later urge to interpret the frieze as metaphorical (or as a vision induced by hallucinogenic drugs) for this arose during the virtual civil war of the Sendero Luminoso period, when archaeologists turned with anguish from such early images of conflict among Peruvians and sought reassurances that they were not intrinsically violent. One essay was even entitled 'The Cerro Sechín Massacre: Did it Happen?', echoing similar works about more contemporary dirty wars, the implied answer being 'no'. While Henning could see why such an interpretation might arise, his view on it was succinct: 'It's bullshit,' he said, using a technical term that I noticed archaeologists often used to describe each other's work.

Henning favoured the interpretation of the frieze as showing some sort of ritual human sacrifice, with the figures being priests rather than warriors, therefore able to secure their victims before ritually dismembering them. In some ways this was the least 'politically acceptable' interpretation of all (only recently a huge furore had been caused in the States by the suggestion of similar practices among early Native American cultures), but the one that seemed closest to what we know of subsequent Andean civilisations.

The riddle of precisely what the frieze represented may never be solved. However, I wanted to investigate a fascinating lead from a little-known article Henning had written about Sechín in a Peruvian magazine ('Los relieves de barro de Cerro Sechín, evidencias de un culto marino en el antiguo Perú', 'The clay friezes at Cerro Sechín, evidence of a marine cult in Ancient Peru').

The great 'warrior-priest' frieze of the stone statues that Julio Tello had found had naturally drawn the most attention as the most visible and extensive remains, but having worked on the earlier clay frieze at the heart of the platform, Henning drew attention to the relief images of two large carnivorous fish at the bottom of a stairway, with bodies tumbling towards them.

Sechín lies some six miles from the sea; on the coast was another much smaller site called Las Aldas, which Henning thought might hold the key to the meaning of the Sechín frieze.

*

To get around John and I were supplementing the local buses with taxis when all else failed. But with Las Aldas we hit a problem. No one, least of all the local taxi drivers, seemed to know where it was.

'Apparently it's at Km 345 on the Pan-American,' I told the local taxi driver in Casma. 'I was given directions which say you turn in from the filling station and it's near a bungalow resort by the sea.'

'I can promise you there's nothing there,' said the driver. 'But if you pay me, I'll take you anyway.'

Standing at Las Aldas, I could see why he'd been puzzled. To all intents and purposes, there was indeed 'nothing there' – or no walls of any height, just their foundations. Some stone gateways remained, and low terracing, but the casual observer could easily walk straight through the site without noticing it.

As we stood at the top of the headland, with the full light of midday on the dirt brown of the desert coast, the outlines of the site were revealed to John and me like magic writing on the landscape as the ghostly image of a city, its succession of terraced plazas peeling away towards the horizon, with circular depressions showing the same sort of sunken plazas we had seen at Caral.

Sketched out on the sands like a blueprint, Las Aldas, like Caral, had all the constituents of monumental architecture: the sunken plazas, the forecourts, the staircases, the stone entranceways and above all the empathic placing in the landscape that was to be such a feature of Andean urban planning. The site was laid out towards the distant hills as if it was a landing strip. It reminded me of some children's toys I had seen in the Yucatan – plastic moulds in the shapes of Maya pyramids, which you could press into the sand on the beaches.

There were other tracks in the sand too – the marks of four-wheel-drive vehicles that had swung off the Pan-American Highway and driven into the dunes around the ruins. The taxi driver, Carlos, nodded at these: '*de novios*, of lovers,' he murmured. 'They must come here for the "*ambiente romántica*", the romantic atmosphere. And to be private.' He made an unnecessary and graphic thrusting movement with his hips before relapsing into a more thoughtful pose: 'So how much do you think I could charge passengers if I brought them here on regular tours?'

My mind was on other things. I was trying to visualise the site as Henning Bischof had suggested, following his work at Sechín. For Henning had speculated that Las Aldas was linked to Sechín directly and viscerally – that the older clay frieze at Sechín of, in his words, 'fish approaching bloody human remains, as if receiving an offering' represented one purpose of Las Aldas and that this was clearly a place with its own 'ritual dramaturgy'.

To understand what he meant, I needed to approach Las Aldas along his proposed 'pilgrimage route' from Sechín. The ruins lay on the slope of a large headland. Walking up to them from the landward side, with the desert and the distant hills behind me, I passed up through a series of stepped terraces, including the sunken circular plazas, before reaching the stairs leading to the very top. Taking this route bore out Henning's contention – that in what he maintained was a deliberate and controlled way, the pilgrim, supplicant or victim would not see or even hear the Pacific until they reached the very topmost terrace. From there, a curious set of steps led on further up the northern side of the headland, ending abruptly above the rocks far below, where the sea suddenly appeared, breaking in a tumult of frothing turbulence.

The suggestion from the iconography of Sechín was that victims were led here from the inland site, brought up the steps until the Pacific dramatically revealed itself, and then sacrificed to the sea and the 'carnivorous fish', such as the *mero*, the grouper fish, which inhabit the waters along the coast. As evidence, he pointed to the way the body falls down towards the fishes in the early Sechín clay frieze, and the unusual way, much remarked upon by commentators, that the body parts in all the friezes are arranged at strange angles, as if viewed from above. He also speculated that the *chorros de sangre*, the streams of blood, which are represented in such a stylised form flowing from the heads, are separate and viscous to match the way in which blood would seem to float away from a body underwater.

Henning would be the first to see his interpretation as extremely speculative, on slender evidence – and there is no accurate dating for Las Aldas to make it necessarily even contemporary with Sechín, although a similar rough dating is usually given for it. But it was an attractive and imaginative idea, which fitted in with much of what we knew of the Andean mindset. Certainly when I saw the site, it made sense, for the ceremonial way the terraces slowly rose up out of the desert towards the headland had the formality of a controlled event. This was an architecture of purpose and power. It was certainly not a mere fishing settlement.

The links between inland Peruvian sites and the sea were intense and binding. Much later, the desert lines at Nasca would include images of whales and of seabirds. Julio Tello, the discoverer of Sechín, had heard the following story from a contemporary shaman:

Wari is the God of force; according to a legend common to almost the whole Andean region it was he who constructed the irrigation dams and channels that remain from the prosperous agricultural past. When in former times the local shaman went to visit him in his mountain range, at the lake formed at the mountain's foot by the melting ice, they would always take human blood mixed with maize flour as an offering; and his successors today still take offerings of animal blood and flour, and throw them into the lake.

If the air is turbulent in the mountains, or if the waves of the lake or the sea are stirred up, it is Wari asking for human blood. When it does not rain in the mountainous areas and a bad year for agriculture is threatened, the shaman will descend to the coast, having first fasted and prepared himself, and gather a small amount of water from the most agitated and turbulent part of the sea: this water will then be carefully guarded in a canteen flask; through certain ceremonies the shaman identifies himself with the spirit of the water he is carrying up into the mountains. As he ascends, he will from time to time let loose roars that imitate a feline beast; these cries are heard echoing around the Andes by the Indian population, and are seen as a portent of rain.

The shaman leaves some of the water in the wells that he passes and on finally arriving at the lake, tips out the rest, little by little. A cloud is then said to come out of the canteen flask and darken the air, setting loose the storm which will inaugurate the rainy season. (Tello, 1923)

The idea that the sea needed to be propitiated in order for the seasons to flow normally made meteorological sense. It was, as we have seen, an alteration in the sea's temperature that precipitated the alarming El Niño phenomenon, while the wellspring of coastal prosperity was derived from fishing. The literal translation of the name of Viracocha, the principal Inca deity, meant Espuma del Mar, 'Foam of the Sea', according to Pedro Cieza de León, one of the most reliable of Inca chroniclers; the Augustinian priest Antonio de la Calancha described him as the god of *'aguas, ríos y fuentes,* waters, rivers and their sources'. The worship of such a deity stretched right back to the beginning of Andean culture.

How had the more peaceful civilisation of Caral given way to the troubled violence of Sechín? Living with a perpetual and corrosive fear can do unpleasant things to the human psyche. An inexplicable and fickle environment, which could suddenly shift in temperature and destroy crops, communities and whole civilisations, would have led to just such a perpetual anxiety, with ugly results.

In recent years our own fear of a nuclear winter has been replaced by fear of a perpetual global summer as the world heats up – for reasons that we understand, even if we seem incapable of acting to prevent it. How much worse for the ancient Peruvians, who likewise were at the mercy of climatic variation, but had no way of understanding why, nor means to ameliorate it.

The solution they seem to have reached at Sechín – human sacrifice, possibly to a deity of the sea – was relatively simple compared to the more extreme stratagems of the later cultures that lay ahead of me on my journey: the Moche to the north; the temple-cult of Chavín, buried in the mountains; and the lines of Nasca.

The first of these that I wanted to see was that of the Moche, perhaps the most splendid and extraordinary of all the coastal civilisations of ancient Peru.

THE PYRAMIDS OF THE MOCHE

More and more I think that pyramids are like mountains.

Anthony Aveni,
Andeanist and archaeo-astronomer

IT IS CURIOUS THAT the Moche remain so little known to the wider public (books still have to include a strapline like 'the Moche, a Culture of Peru' to identify them), given that they were such an exuberant and colourful civilisation. They flourished on the north coast of Peru in the first millennium, from around AD 50 to 700. While many of their textiles have perished in the humid northern deserts, their wildly imaginative and often sexually explicit ceramics have been drawing attention and have been placed in locked basements since the German archaeologist Max Uhle first identified the civilisation at the very end of the nineteenth century. Before that, their ruins had been assumed to have been left by the Incas.

The Pyramids of the Sun and the Moon are the best-known and most desolate of the great Moche monuments, despite being so close to the bustling city of Trujillo – indeed, just as the suburbs of Cairo have subsumed the Great Pyramids of Giza, so the Moche pyramids are now virtually on Trujillo's outer city ring road. But they still lie on a planetary landscape of dirt-brown baked clay that somehow excludes all human activity, despite the pock-marking of the desert by the numerous looters' pits that from a distance look like crab-holes on a beach.

The larger of the two, the Pyramid of the Sun, rises up by the Moche river – and it is very large indeed, a monster of a pyramid that sprawl over some twelve acres. Over 130 million adobe bricks were used to create the biggest man-made structure in the Americas before the arrival of Columbus. The Spanish, in an audacious if brutal bit of adventuring, redirected the river in the early seventeenth century to wash away much of its side so they could expose the inner chambers. It was common practice to 'mine' such old *huacas* – indeed, the colonial government issued licences to people to do just that. A local Trujillo scholar has shown how quarter-shares in the misnamed 'Huaca del Inca' were bought and sold at regular intervals during the sixteenth and seventeenth centuries – a successful business, as in just one year three tons of gold were extracted.

Despite the depredations of time and looters, the Pyramid of the Sun still stands huge above the desert, a time-thrashed hulk of a building whose brown adobe walls rise up some 100 feet, like an old tanker tied up in the desert and left to rot.

The Pyramid of the Moon faces it across the desert floor and is built into the side of Cerro Blanco, a striking mountain with a band of black andesite running across it, whose shape it may have been designed to replicate. A rock outcrop from Cerro Blanco was deliberately incorporated into the structure of the pyramid, with a plaza built around it, to make clear the connection of the building to the rock, just as the Pyramid of the Sun was clearly sited by the river: 'rock and water', the classic combination of spiritual forces in ancient Peru.

The names are modern superimpositions – we have no idea as to their true ones – but it does seem that the Pyramid of the Sun had a more administrative role, while that of the Moon was more ritual. The magnificent façades of each of the tiered layers that make up the latter pyramid have been uncovered and restored in just the last few years. Despite this long delay in revealing the artwork, it is perhaps to be welcomed. The few friezes that were uncovered in the early twentieth century were not adequately protected once exposed, so have since perished; much better pre-servation is now possible.

The more recently found platform walls have friezes as vivid as a restored set of paintings. Approaching the summit of the pyramid, one rises up past a succession of images: first a line of prisoners, naked and tied together with a rope; then another line of dancers holding hands, seemingly watching; a spider or octopus figure holding a *tumi*, a sacrificial knife; the so-called fisher-king or 'god of the fishes'; then an anthropomorphised fox-figure holding a trophy-head; an undulating snake; and on the topmost platform, a demon figure with staring eyes, sometimes referred to as 'the god with fixed eyebrows'. The iconography is complex but for archaeologists the inference is clear: this was a ceremonial site where human sacrifices were made.

Just as at Sechín 2,000 years before, the imagery seems savage – the prisoners appear to have been mutilated before being roped and bound – but in the intervening millennia a far more elaborate mythology has evolved to accompany the ritualised and stylised process of execution. The spidery 'decapitator figure' is an ominous presence. And there can be no question as to whether the scenes portrayed are mythological or literal.

In 1996 the Canadian archaeologist Steve Bourget dug around the outcrop of rock that had been enclosed in the upper plaza, on the intuitive hunch that if sacrifices were made it would be to just such a focal *huaca* or stone shrine. His instincts proved correct. He found many dismembered body parts, from over seventy individuals. Moreover from the deposits of clay, it seemed that some of these sacrifices were carried out during a period of rare heavy rains, disastrous in this part of the world as they cause flash floods. Prisoners were 'killed, decapitated and dismembered' over an area of sixty square metres, with increasing intensity as weather conditions worsened. The link between human sacrifice and an attempt to propitiate the weather could not be more explicit.

For one such sacrifice, clay statues of prisoners, all naked and bound with a rope, were thrown down among the actual bodies. The statues were either broken beforehand or in situ, as if representative of the real broken prisoners. Bourget also found the tombs of the officiating priests, men who had died in old age. Although looters had taken anything of commercial value, in one of these tombs they had left an old wooden mace of the sort we are familiar with from representations on pots, where priests grasp it in their hands like a club. Just such a pot was found near the actual mace. There was a black residue on the head and handle of the mace, which, when analysed, showed in Bourget's words that it was 'literally caked in human blood'.

As with the Sechín culture, there had for some years previously been an academic debate as to whether the human sacrifice rituals on Moche drinking vessels were literal or literary, depicting actual practice or some Andean mythic battle, a Peruvian Troy.

By analysing many fine-line drawings on Moche ceramics, as part of his comprehensive cataloguing of Moche iconography, Christopher Donnan at UCLA had built up a clear picture of 'the story of human sacrifice', or as he described it somewhat euphemistically, the 'Presentation Ceremony'. The drawings often show a prisoner being taken in combat – whether in ritualised combat within a Moche community, or in actual combat with another Moche city-state, is unclear. The prisoner would not be killed outright, but struck on the head to incapacitate him. He would then be stripped naked and his arms tied behind his back. His victor would carry his weapons and lead him on a rope to officiating priests, who cut his throat and offered his blood in a drinking goblet to a senior 'warrior priest'. The victim's body was then dismembered and the head used as a trophy.

All this was depicted in a stylised and almost light-hearted way, which encouraged a fictional interpretation. Some of the events seemed to take place in a nether-world; the warriors battled in a disengaged way, just as they would if seeking to stun, not kill; birds seemed to carry messages between the participants: strange fruit hung over the goblets of blood; and some of the players in the ceremony, by their greater size and dominance, with their feathered headdresses and zoomorphic appearance, could be thought of as deities partaking in human affairs.

However, Steve Bourget reached the graphic conclusion, both from discoveries made at the Pyramid of the Moon and elsewhere, that this was not some constant retelling of a shared myth, but a literal account of 'extensive and complex sacrificial practices' among the Moche.

Further striking proof of this came when actual vessels were found resembling the drinking goblets depicted in the sacrifice ceremony. On analysis, some were discovered to contain residues of dried human blood. More representations of the 'strange fruit' hanging over the goblets of blood in pictures have also been discovered in the tombs of those associated with the sacrifice ceremony, which give a clearer depiction of the fruit than the stylised paisley shape used in the fine-line drawings. The plant has been identified as the *ulluchu* fruit, part of the papaya family and with one distinguishing characteristic: it has anticoagulant properties, so can be used to keep human blood fresh for drinking.

All this came as a shock to some academics working in the field; here, as elsewhere in Andeanist studies, there was a desperate wish to ignore the violence and sexuality of Moche society and interpret it as somehow symbolic, when it was horrifyingly actual.

Forensic anthropologist John Verano, a specialist in bone analysis, was brought in to look at the skeletons Bourget had uncovered near the sacred rock in the plaza behind the Pyramid of the Moon. Verano wrote a report that reads like one of those issued by tough pathologists in movies about serial killers when they have to list the physical evidence in a detached and professional way. He found that many of the prisoners were killed by cuts to the neck (as with a *tumi*, the ceremonial knife), but that their flesh may also have been severed from the bone, either alive or dead, and that they were dismembered. He also notes that, here as elsewhere, 'the bodies were not promptly buried, but were left exposed on the surface', often for some time. This would accord with the idea that vultures could then pick at the bones, as evidenced in some Moche ceramics.

The Pyramid of the Moon is just four miles inland – the Pacific is clearly visible from the summit on a clear day, and even more so from the summit of Cerro Blanco above. The pyramid seems to have been built to make a connection between the mountain and the sea; in Steve Bourget's description, this was a *'teatro de sacrificio, a theatre of sacrifice'*, which celebrated the link between them.

One of the very first travellers to report on the site, the American

E. G. Squier, who thought it the 'most impressive monument' he had seen in Peru, commented in 1877:

> [The Pyramid of the Moon] stands on the edge of the desert slope, at the base of Cerro Blanco, just where irrigation begins – a kind of gigantic landmark between luxuriant verdure and arid sands, between life and death.

Squier knew nothing of the tradition of human sacrifice, as the friezes had yet to be uncovered, so his remark is a useful reminder that, like so many other important pre-Columbian monuments, the Pyramid of the Moon is built on what would otherwise be waste ground, as if trying to impose meaning and order in a landscape 'between life and death'.

Although the pyramids have been restored with the help of the brewery company Backus, few tourists have yet become aware of the pyramids on the so-called 'Northern Circuit' of Peru and again, as so often on our journey, John and I had the place to ourselves. Gazing out with my binoculars across to the nearby Pyramid of the Sun, which had yet to be restored in a similar fashion but will undoubtedly yield its own revelations, I remembered Squier's attempts to poke around inside its chambers, using one of the looters' passages to gain access:

> Having brought candles with us, we followed the passage to its extremity. It was fetid and slippery with the excrement of bats, which whirred past us when disturbed, dashing out our lights, as if they were the sinister guardians of the treasure.

I noticed a taxi driver heading straight across the desert towards the shadow side of the pyramid, driving erratically across the plain. The driver stopped, slipped round to the back seat and began what was obviously a clandestine session with his lady passenger, the car rocking very slightly in the heat-haze, like a pantomime, before they both emerged.

The only other sign of life in the desert between the two pyramids was the endless looters' holes, a phenomenon that was often referred to dismissively as if it were some sort of social disease, but which I wanted to find out about at first-hand.

*

Near the Pyramids of the Sun and Moon is the little hamlet of the Campiña de Moche. The inhabitants maintain a set of *sequias*, irrigation canals, which give the soil an incredible fecundity – some indication of how the Moche were able to flourish here. There are roses, leeks and immaculate market gardens to match those of any English shire. And just as many an English village has a long underground tradition of poaching, so the inhabitants of Campiña de Moche have from time immemorial looted the nearby pyramids.

I was able to talk to one of the best-known families of *huaqueros*, looters, by catching father and son when they were taking a rest from stacking adobe bricks in the burning sun and welcomed an excuse not to get back to work. And it was clear that the looting was also work: 'I'm a professional *huaquero*,' said Enrique, with some pride. 'So was my father, and his father before him. I don't remember my grandfather talking about it a lot, but my father showed me the ropes.' Enrique was in his fifties, burly, with a cheerful disposition. He was halfway through building a house with one of his sons, Lucho, who in trainers, casuals and baseball hat had all the insouciance and joviality of a jobbing burglar.

'I work at nights from nine to one,' Enrique told me. 'Sometimes the lads help, sometimes I go with friends from the village. It's a job and you have to be professional about it.' His son nodded in agreement. 'But on Saturday night we have a rest and go to the *cantina*.'

Enrique warmed to his description. 'Of course in the old days things were different. You got a better price for your pieces, for a start. And the money meant more. *Un agricultor*, a labourer, used to earn $2 a day if he was lucky; but if he looted a few pieces out of the ground, he could feed his family for months. Now you get less money because there are so many fakes around.' He sniffed moodily. 'Fucking forgers. I hate them. *No tienen respeto*, they have no respect.

The police snoop around too, although they're all on backhanders.'

Lucho tried to lighten his father's mood. 'We did get a lot from that Chimú tomb the other day [the Chimú were a later coastal culture]. We filled two rice sacks.'

Enrique spoke as authoritatively as a university lecturer: 'You always get more pieces from a Chimú tomb. A Moche one might have twenty or thirty pieces. From a good Chimú one you can get 130. Easy. Not that we make a lot of money,' he added hastily. 'I know we're building a new house, but most of the money comes from my wife's job.'

Enrique described the methods they employed to find tombs. Using a *vaqueta*, a metal spike three feet long, they would systematically probe a chosen area centimetre by centimetre until either they felt the ground give – a tell-tale indicator of lighter, disturbed soil around a tomb – or the tip of the *vaqueta*'s spike showed white from hitting bone.

Descending into the tombs had its risks; popular superstition held that, quite apart from the risk of disturbing ancestors who might then haunt you, the tombs *malodoró*, gave off gases of ammonia and cinnabar, the red mercury sulphide that the Moche used on their dead. Enrique knew of one looter from the village who had got stuck in a tomb for longer than intended: 'His belly swelled up and his legs shrivelled away, like a fat bird, from the *vapores*, the gases. Then he died.'

To prevent this, they went *coqueado*, having chewed coca leaves and smoked constantly – by preference, I was amused to hear, a brand of cigarettes called Inca. They also worked in small teams and never alone, as the villager who died had been: 'He shouldn't have been on his own. That's Rule One. It's what I keep saying – you have to be professional.'

He paused in his story to add, a trifle melodramatically: 'Whatever you do, the dead may come back at you in the night later. There's not much you can do to prevent that.' As an attempt to avoid such vengeance, when they found a skeleton, they often detached the skull and threw it to one side.

Their most effective recent find had been an entire Moche

ceramics workshop, a *taller*, complete with firing oven and sets of moulds. The Moche were the first pre-Columbian culture to mass-produce ceramics with such moulds and they had proved invaluable for Enrique and Lucho, as they could make their own copies and sell them as originals.

'We wrap them in newspaper, leave them in damp ground for a week and they come up nicely, *hongeado*, with mushrooms growing on them. The tourists can't get enough. We wait by the gates to the pyramid, until one wanders by and then,' Enrique mimed taking off his cap and standing shyly, with his legs crossed, 'we say: "Excuse me, sir, we found this digging our fields, is it something that might interest you?" What's even better is that they think it's real, so they go to all this effort to smuggle it out of the country hidden in their luggage.' He laughed. It didn't seem the right moment to remind Enrique of any inconsistency with his earlier comments about 'fucking forgers'.

But they reserved their greatest scorn for the archaeologists and the *coleccionistas*, the dealers. When Enrique and Lucho had discovered the Moche workshop, they had been impressed and wanted the archaeologists to preserve it, so had left it 'all neat and *bien arreglado*, well organised'. The archaeologists had indeed seen the workshop – but according to their workmen (many of whom also came from the village) had not realised what it was and promptly ordered that it be covered up again.

Perhaps to justify his looting, Enrique claimed that the Peruvian archaeologists, like the police, were involved in the *contrabanda*, and often sold pieces to the *coleccionistas*, many of whom were only interested in sending pieces to the States or Europe – and made far more from the looted pieces than the looters themselves.

His son Lucho described how carefully they had to break open the decayed textiles they sometimes found around the corpse, knowing that often the beads of a necklace would still be there. Lucho had become expert at rethreading these semi-precious stone beads, work of great delicacy.

I have no wish to romanticise looters, yet equally it would be too easy to view all *huaqueros* as mindless and destructive. Of course they eliminate all sense of archaeological provenance, of the significance of context – how the belongings might be arranged around a body, implying status. However some, like Enrique, were as knowledgeable as the archaeologists – if not more so, not least because they had probably been in far more tombs. The sheer quantity of Moche ceramics in circulation as a result has enabled scholars like Christopher Donnan to compile detailed catalogues of their art and iconography.

There is a difference – similar to poachers using lines or dynamite in rivers – between local families doing some individual looting and the systematic and wholesale organised stripping of antiquities that has sometimes occurred, when landowners with an interest in building up a collection have employed whole teams of labourers to work the land. In areas like Lambayeque to the north, close to the pre-Columbian gold mines, an insatiable greed for antiquities seems to have seized some powerful local families, who would pay their *agricultores* an additional fee if they were assigned to the *huaquero* teams.

The German anthropologist Réna Gündüz, having spent many months talking to looters in Lambayeque, divided them into two types: the *huaquero tradicional*, the local looter, often carrying on a family tradition, who would sometimes keep pieces they liked and took a great deal of pride in their knowledge and skill at looting; and the more audacious modern looter, completely uninterested in the culture they are digging into but keen to make a fast buck, often from the city and working in organised teams.

While the original Spanish conquistadors were no slouches when it came to looting, at least they took only the gold out of a tomb and left the ceramics, textiles and bones behind, all of which they considered worthless. The modern wholesale looter will take everything and probably smash even the bones to pieces in the process.

The issue is also complicated by racial politics – the local, more Indian *huaqueros* feel that they are just liberating their inheritance from pre-Columbian ancestors. Who are the descendants of the Spanish conquerors, the archaeologists and administrators from

Lima, to tell them that they can't? There is also a widely held suspicion that the Limeños just pass work on to the *coleccionistas* under the table and get the money anyway.

Local families traditionally initiate young sons into the finer arts of looting on *El Día de Todos los Santos*, All Saints' Day, more familiarly known as the Day of the Dead, when they head off to cemeteries and have a picnic beside the tombs before getting out the *vaquetas* and the spades. Father-and-son teams treat their looting sprees as if they were going on a hunting trip, with many of the same accoutrements – flasks of alcohol, coca leaves and cigarettes to kept them going, and in some of the wilder areas, guns, to protect themselves from police and other looters. Some even refer to the looting as a form of *deporte*, sport.

The whole ambivalence about looting was summed up for me by a Peruvian friend: 'It's like cheating on your wife – we know we shouldn't do it, but it's considered a "soft" sin. As long as you get away with it, who cares?'

*

A striking example of how museums colluded with the looters could be seen in nearby Trujillo. The Museo Cassinelli was one of the most eccentric I have ever seen. It was in a basement under a garage on the city's outskirts. The owner of both the garage and the museum, José Cassinelli, was in his eighties and had been collecting 'local pieces' for fifty years; he now had no less than 6,000 items, many of which were on display.

It was not a prepossessing entrance, off the garage forecourt and through a bare reception area with just a desk. I was led down concrete steps into a fluorescent-lit, low-ceilinged single room where a veritable treasure trove lay.

Of all the pre-Columbian cultures, the Moche had poured their creativity into their ceramics; their vases and stirrup-spout bottles were decorated with a quite staggering fecundity and range. Never had illiteracy seemed so unimportant or writing less necessary.

There were pots showing every aspect of the Moche universe:

lobsters, *viringo* dogs, toads, llamas, sea lions, crabs, snails, owls, foxes, iguanas, pelicans; pots with human portraits of striking realism, men with their heads thrown back – so realistic and detailed that the Moche scholar Christopher Donnan is said by colleagues to be able to recognise individuals when he comes across them portrayed elsewhere. A series of pots showed the same man as he aged. One could even see the range of illnesses from which the Moche suffered: hemiplegia, elephantiasis, syphilis, thyroid complaints, *uta* or leish-maniasis – the disease caused by river sandflies which often attacks the nose. Other ceramics played with the motif of the skeleton, with skulls laughing or copulating with humans. Elaborate 'maquette-pots' showed a range of architectural styles from the domestic to large temples (it is one of the only ways in which we know how the Moche gabled their roofs, as no originals have survived).

Behind the locked door of a cabinet was a panoply of 'explicit' ceramics with sexual options to make today's internet sites look impoverished; women masturbating men; men masturbating them-selves; anal sex, fellatio, male (but not female) homosexual couples.

Academics have tied themselves in knots trying to argue that this did not reflect actual practice. Christopher Donnan, for instance, has stated: 'I am confident that the erotic activities shown in the art were part of religious rituals and not the sexual activity of ordinary life,' basing his view partly on the grounds that the ceramics do not all show straightforward procreative sex. This seems a curiously white-bread approach to human sexual appetite – and it is interesting that Alfred Kinsey, America's leading crusader against such 'nor-mative' values, travelled to Peru in 1954 to examine Moche pottery, which he described as 'the most frank and detailed document of sexual customs ever left by an ancient people'. Peruvian scholars have always found the male homosexual activity the most difficult to accept; some still continue to argue that it must celebrate 'ritual warrior activity' rather than the hedonistic coupling it so clearly was.

The erotic and other pottery was so startling because of the level of detail that not only delineated orifices in pulsating close-up, but could tell narrative stories in sculptural detail. In one piece a shaman laid his hands on the belly of a woman in an attempt to cure her – both he and the woman had the wide staring eyes associated with the drug extracted from the San Pedro cactus. In another, even more detailed piece, a young adolescent boy peeks through a hole in the wall to see a couple making love in the next house, while a dog sleeps on the floor outside.

The playfulness and mastery of the ceramic craft was outstanding. The Moche artisans experimented with outrageous tricks of trompe l'oeil and of high relief: a woman combed her hair by the spout of a jar as the fleas dropped and settled down the sides. They could also produce pots of rigorous, tactile simplicity, the waves of one side of a pot giving way to the fine-grained sand of the other.

Beautiful flared bowls, with their wide expanse around the brim, used fine-line drawings to tell more sequential stories; of sea-lion hunts, of implements rising up to chase their masters, like magician's brooms, and above all of human sacrifice; for the figures that often recurred were of a prisoner bound with his hands behind him, while beside him a priest in a ceremonial headdress wielded the wide-bladed knife, the *tumi*.

As I was the day's sole visitor, Mr Cassinelli came over to talk to me; at eighty-four he was still vigorous, with a firm handshake. In a florid, rhetorical style he declaimed, looking over his lifetime's collecting: 'Yes, you can see here how the Moche could communicate sadness, tenderness, fear, pain, happiness and the most sublime human emotions.' I could only agree. Perhaps unfairly, I then asked him how he had built up his collection. He looked into the middle distance, as Peruvians do when following an official line: 'Ah well, you know, sometimes *campesinos*, fieldworkers, come upon these items when they are digging their irrigation canals, or trying to find a well.'

Having talked to *huaqueros* who supplied the museum, I knew that this was far from the case. Like other *coleccionistas*, Cassinelli actively encouraged looters to come to him – indeed, he made it clear that he would blackball anyone in future who did not offer him first refusal on any stolen artifacts.

But this was not unusual in the context of looting, given that at almost every level it was accommodated within the antiquities business. The Museo Cassinelli just happened to lie close to the source of its holdings and so had direct unmediated contact with looters. Behind the more immaculate displays of pre-Columbian items in many museums lay plenty of artifacts that had originally been stolen, if since 'laundered' by dealers, and there were many grey areas in the provenance of the pieces that had started to fetch higher and higher prices at the auction houses.

I felt a certain admiration for Cassinelli – he had at least set up a startlingly good private museum in the area of archaeological origin and made accessible a range of pre-Columbian work that would almost certainly otherwise have ended up abroad or in Lima. And the fact is that if we had to wait for archaeologists to find Moche ceramics, we would have very few to see.

*

After my comfortable stay at the Orient Express hotels, I had now gone back to more Spartan accommodation, particularly when travelling with John, who considered paying anything over $4 a night an insult – and was doubtless thinking that I had grown soft on luxury. As a result we had been getting that familiar landladies' look when asked whether they had hot water: a mixture of optimism, willingness but not total certainty as to whether any would actually materialise.

So it was a relief to discover that John had friends in Trujillo, Michael White and Clara Bravo, who ran a guiding service from their large rambling lodging house off a small park, which became our comfortable base for an exploration of the Moche ruins.

They were a striking couple. Michael was slightly built, with a wave of white hair and intense blue eyes; Scottish by origin, he had been the smallest in his class when it came to playing football, but with a wiriness and intensity that had probably made him combative on the pitch. He had ended up in Peru because of Clara; they had met in Australia and Michael had accompanied her back to her native Trujillo. Clara was a dark-skinned Peruvian, impulsive, occasionally forgetful and always warm-hearted. Since childhood she had been intrigued by archaeology and had observed digs whenever she could – 'I like to watch' – considered unusual behaviour for a girl by strait-laced Trujillo society. Both Michael and she could talk the hind leg off a donkey. In just a few days I had heard both their life stories (Clara's twice).

Their house was a mecca for travelling *estudiosos*, 'studious types', the polite Peruvian word for those who are interested in archaeology but are not archaeologists: autodidacts, as so many researchers here have been. Michael himself was just such a self-taught *estudioso*; he ran a sort of free-form university on the Moche, and was an assiduous collector of obscure articles on them. This was fortunate, for just as with so many of the Incas' predecessors, reliable and accessible sources were hard to come by and the only general book on their civilisation, by Garth Bawden, was generally agreed to be about as readable as a tractor manual.

The house had previously been a nursery and there was still a mural of children walking to school, which looked down on the communal dining table of travellers and *estudiosos* as they read Michael's photocopied articles, or listened to his thoughts on the various sites. Michael had an excellent memory, and could recite details of past excavations of Moche sites at great length; his knowledge of the Moche ran in parallel with an equally encyclo-paedic knowledge of British football, which he kept track of through cable TV. He was inclined to switch between the two in mid-flow, if he happened to catch sight of a particularly arresting moment, in a deft pass between Moche funerary art and the inadequacies of the English long-ball.

Staying at Michael and Clara's was delightful but occasionally overwhelming; the constant coming and going of *estudiosos* and travellers, though it could be stimulating, was also exhausting; the cable TV was always on, with a mixture of English football and local news; Clara was a young grandmother, and her teenage daughter and grandson were a lively part of the household.

John and I would occasionally take off into Trujillo town centre in buses run by the Cesar Vallejo company. It amused and impressed me that they had named the bus company after Vallejo, the melancholic and impoverished poet who had been born there – you would hardly find a Philip Larkin bus in Hull, or a Robert Lowell one in Boston.

In most Peruvian cities, the cheapest and most reliable restaurants served fried chicken and chips, and there was just such a *pollería* by the main plaza. John was in an unusually expansive mood, perhaps because he had heard by e-mail that he had recently been elected into the Western Australian Surf Life Saving Hall of Fame. He had a habit of eating any food left uneaten on other people's plates, so had finished my remaining chicken as well as his own.

As we relaxed over chilled Trujillo Pilsners, he talked to me about a friend of his who, like John, had become obsessed with travelling to the most remote sites and had spent months on his own, searching the world. So desperate to find a true wilderness had this friend become that he had lost contact with his home and relatives. The friend had finally travelled to the Tasmanian wilderness and had gone missing, presumed dead.

The story left me feeling melancholy. The need constantly to travel, such endless questing, seemed to have become an unreflecting modern obsession, to which I was also subject, if not more so than most. Many of my friends seemed to measure out their time between trips; travel was supposedly more real and exciting than anything in cotidian Britain. But was there not something to be said for the old Islamic model under which a man was happy to spend his whole life at home, apart from one transcendental Haj to Mecca?

The most recent instalment of *La Guerra de las Galaxias (Star Wars)*, was showing in the local cinema. Tickets were dirt cheap in an attempt to beat the pirate DVDs that had flooded Peru. This was the last cinema left in town as all the others had closed. It made for a good place to end the evening – there is nothing like being in a packed cinema with 300 Peruvians chorusing, '*¡Que la Fuerza avanza!* May the Force be with you!' to lift the spirits. A helpful middle-aged Peruvian lady beside me glossed the film aloud as we went through: 'That nice young man is going to become Darth Vader later, *no lo piensas ahora*, you'd never think so, would you?'

But nothing in the *Star Wars* galaxy was quite as strange as the Moche were turning out to be.

One of the more disturbing ceramics at the Cassinelli Museum had shown a young man engaged in an act of self-circumcision; the mutilation of the penis seems to have held a fascination for the Moche. Another of their *chicha* jars was in the shape of a giant phallus, so that whoever drank from it would seem to be indulging in fellatio. Although archaeologists were too polite to mention it, the Moche were also prone to showing naked prisoners in the sacrifice ceremonies with erections, as if the prospect of approaching death were in some way erotically exciting.

There has been some suggestion too that they were intrigued and even attracted by physical deformity. Many individuals were portrayed with amputated limbs, and I had already noticed how at the Cassinelli Museum the ceramics showed an intense interest in disease. There may have been a suggestion, as in some other ancient societies, that illness was a sign of the seer. At one burial site investigators were surprised to find a series of high-status tombs, all containing individuals of the same family who were a full foot taller than the average Moche man and seem to have suffered from gigantism.

But I now wanted to investigate the most famous of the Moche burial sites that had been discovered, and about which I had heard many tantalising reports; the next day John and I left the house at dawn with Clara to see the treasures of Sipán.

*

The relationship between archaeologists and looters had been thrown into high drama with the discovery of the famous Sipán tombs in 1987. Peruvian archaeologist Walter Alva had first been alerted to the possibility of a Moche tomb in a previously unsuspected site for such a burial, Huaca Rajada, by the flooding onto the market of some unusually fine artifacts. These had come from a group of local *huaqueros* led by a man called Emilio Bernal. When Alva investigated further, he found that Bernal was openly boasting of the enormous wealth he had liberated for his community and which, Robin Hood-style, he was returning to them.

Alva participated in a dawn raid on the family farmhouse, which resulted in Emilio Bernal being shot dead. Predictably Bernal became a martyred folk-hero to the villagers near Huaca Racada or, to use its original Moche name, Sipán, which means 'place of the moon'.

Clara, who had witnessed many of these events, told us how with great personal courage, and at the risk of being lynched, Alva and his assistants had gone back to Sipán, convinced that further tombs might be uncovered near by. Helped by the influential Christopher Donnan, Alva had managed to raise immediate funding to excavate further, before the looters got it all – and had shrewdly employed some of the local looters to work with him, to the alarm of other archaeologists and his bosses in Lima.

Yet the time-honoured tradition of using 'poachers turned game-keepers' proved a triumphant success. With the looters' local intuition and his own archaeological knowledge, Alva made what, after Machu Picchu, must be considered the Peruvian find of the century: not just one but three intact high-status Moche tombs, of two rulers and a high priest, wrapped in textile shrouds stained with cochineal red and with quite fabulous ornaments of turquoise and gold around them. Just as important for archaeologists, beside the burials they also found sets of ceramics carefully arranged to tell a story, with the rare 'provenance' that ceramics ripped from the ground by looters could never give.

Moreover the tombs were of different ages. One, the so-called 'Old Lord of Sipán', dated from the first century AD, at a time of Moche expansionism, and was the last to be found, right at the bottom of the pyramid, when construction on it began. From the evidence of the surrounding artifacts, it seemed that the main 'Lord' was both ruler and priest, in that he may have carried out human sacrifices himself.

By AD 250, some two hundred years later, the roles of leader and priest had become divided, as could clearly be seen when the other two tombs were examined. 'The Lord of Sipán' was found buried on the same platform level as 'the Priest of Sipán', in the last, topmost phase of the pyramid's construction. Judging from the Moche iconography that accompanied the burial and was carefully decoded by Christopher Donnan, it was apparently now the priest who conducted the sacrifice, and then ritually offered his ruler a goblet full of the resultant blood to drink. There were elaborate headdresses to differentiate warriors from priests, and the sacrifice ceremony seemed to be more complex and elaborate.

Such details – of fascination to archaeologists as they show how Moche society stratified over time – were lost in the open-mouthed astonishment of the general public at the wealth of treasures uncovered. Even after Bernal and the early looters had taken their portion – and some of this resurfaced anyway in museums in Lima or was recovered by the FBI from dealers in the States – there remained a treasure trove unparalleled since Tutankhamen: gold pectorals, turquoise statues, spondylus shells, all worked with ingenuity and skill.

They were now on display at a magnificent museum near by that received shamefully few visitors. One Lima *coleccionista* had told me dismissively: 'Why did they go and build it up there in the sand, just because it was closer to where the tombs were found? They should have built it here.' As he had accumulated many of the remaining looted objects from Sipán for his own collection, he was perhaps not the right person to comment objectively.

The museum's display was worth more than a king's ransom – just one piece alone, a pectoral, had been offered on the American black market for $1,600,000 before being seized by the FBI, which had only become interested in the burgeoning trade in illegal pre-Columbian artifacts because the same people often trafficked in another Peruvian export, cocaine.

Such metalwork was a royal prerogative. The same moulds that Enrique had been so delighted to find on one of his looting trips had enabled the Moche to mass-produce ceramics and make them accessible to the wider population (although, oddly, not for use as tableware – the Moche ate off carved gourds). But jewellery remained a luxury item, and the goldsmiths evolved some complicated techniques with alloys and the fine hammering of materials to match the best of the Western world. Because the nobility were buried with all their jewellery, rather than bequeathing it to their successors, there was a constant need for more to be created.

At a more basic level, what stunned both the Peruvian and international public was the sheer amount of gold. One item alone, a beaten gold backflap, to be worn attached to a costume, was a solid kilogram in weight. Despite expectations to the contrary, the conquistadors had not found much gold in the Inca heartland around Cuzco for one simple reason: it would all have been imported. The southern–central Andes near Cuzco and into Bolivia are fabulously rich in silver (Potosí being the largest silver mine in the world), but not gold.

By contrast, Sipán was in the heart of a gold-producing region. An estimated 85 per cent of the objects at the Gold Museum in Lima hailed from the area. The Moche lords had therefore been able to produce treasure beyond the dreams of even the most hardened looter.

The burials had been skilfully recreated in the museum, both with photographs of the process of the dig and with replicas of the tombs, so that the visitor could look down into them as if making the discovery themselves. The rulers and the priest had attendants who were sacrificed with them; in one, a sacrificial dog also lay at his master's feet.

The tomb that intrigued me most was the last to be discovered, right towards the bottom of the pyramid: the Moche 'Old Lord of Sipán' from the first century AD, when the culture was just beginning. The artwork had a freshness and virility to it; there was a necklace of jaguar heads, their teeth grimacing with inlaid shell; another made up of spiders that had the portrait of a man on the back of its head, its web a net of fine filigree gold; a silver nose-piece with waves of birds crossing it, their eyes picked out in turquoise; a gilt warrior holding a club against his chest, with gold and silver sceptres beside him, the silver one with miniature human heads suspended from its finial; the gilt statue of a man shaped like a crab, with a necklace of owls; a mask in the shape of a fox; silver bells, which would have been attached to staffs and carried in procession; a giant pectoral with tentacles that, in the words of an excited Walter Alva, would have turned the wearer into 'an anthropomorphised octopus'; nose-pieces made from gold, silver and turquoise, one of a warrior holding a war club and wearing a full owl headdress twice as long as his body; backflaps with images of the Decapitator God; a pectoral made of shell, inlaid with images of catfish; bracelets of lapis lazuli. All this to enclose the skeleton of a middle-aged man five feet three inches tall.

When Walter Alva and his team carefully unpicked the remains of one banner of gilded copper, which had oxidised green over the centuries but which they restored to a brilliant glittering gold, they found that its edge was decorated with tiny embossed representations of the paisley-shaped *ulluchu* fruit – and that underneath each metal fruit were the remains of a real *ulluchu* fruit, hidden in the cavity. It reminded me of Steve Bourget's striking finding at the Pyramid of the Moon: that alongside the real sacrificial victims, the Moche had placed small clay models of them.

Sad to think that the one element that had not survived in the tomb was the elaborate weavings that would have covered the body as a shroud, only small fragments of which remain due to the humidity. Given the richness of their ceramics and metalwork, we can only imagine the fineness of Moche textiles, or their original colours. Yet there are some clues: soaked into the floor of the burial chamber, underneath the fine jewellery and the skeleton, was a red dye, and while for the Western eye it is the surviving gold that glitters, for those that buried their rulers the weavings with which they draped them may have been more important.

*

Despite the interest aroused by Sipán, many pyramids of the Moche and the other northern cultures of Peru remain unexcavated, at least by archaeologists if not by looters. As John and I travelled around with Clara in her battered old VW Beetle ('You need a sturdy frame for these roads,' John noted professionally), my predominant impression was of the untapped potential and the sheer scale of the task. Seeing Huaja Rajada in the flesh, or what was left of it after the Sipán excavations, was a reminder that there were two even larger pyramids beside it. At Tucume we had seen some of the numerous pyramids that Thor Heyerdahl had begun to investigate towards the end of his long life. And as we headed up the coast from Trujillo to see new excavations at a site called El Brujo ('The Wizard'), we passed countless smaller mounds and potential archaeological sites. In a way, the delay in excavating so much of Peru may be of long-term advantage, as much can be learnt from the techniques painstakingly developed in Egypt, and just as crucially some of the mistakes made there can be avoided.

Clara was talking non-stop as we drove. She was describing to us what it was like to see the treasures of Sipán at moonlight, just a few days after they were found, together with tales from her own adventurous life. Clara had met some of the best-known Andeanists; as well as Walter Alva and his wife Susana Meneses, who had worked together at Sipán, she had come across the explorer Gene Savoy, and eminent archaeologists like Michael Moseley who had excavated at nearby Chan Chan. Indeed, Clara could remember a time when the locals still used to hold motocross rallies around the ruins there. She was scared of *huaqueros*, looters, and claimed you could always tell them because they had yellow faces from inhaling the gases of tombs.

It was midday and the overhead desert sun was intense. On the otherwise empty Pan-American Highway ahead, an oncoming truck pulled onto our side of the road and headed straight for us. This was not that unusual as, despite being the continent's trunk road, the 'Panamericana' was as pock-marked with holes as if it had been looted. However, the truck kept on coming, even when we could clearly see that there were no holes for it to avoid. It was also weaving slightly from side to side. I wondered for a moment whether the heat haze on the road had confused the driver. Then, at the same moment as Clara, I realised he must be blind drunk. She pulled onto the hard shoulder as the truck screeched through where we had been.

We pulled off the Panamericana and drove past villages with ancient Moche names: Mocollope, Chocope, Cao. Their meaning has been lost as Moche is now a dead language; the last speaker died in the 1940s and there is no dictionary.

The El Brujo complex lay even closer to the sea than the Pyramids of the Sun and Moon; while there was likewise a pair of Moche pyramids here, only one of them was being excavated, Cao Viejo. It loomed up as we approached along a rough dirt road, past fields full of sugar cane. The site was not yet open to the public, so one of the foremen took us around. The murals were protected by canvas awnings from the constant humidity and the sea-mists that came in. To show us each mural, the foreman and his assistants rolled up each awning, an effect that was both dramatic and useful, as it concentrated the mind on each piece before it was 'put away' again.

Just as at the Pyramid of the Moon, but in far better condition, there was a long frieze showing naked prisoners being led on a long, heavy rope by a man carrying their weapons, their legs and penises slashed; above, a line of watching men, holding hands, their eyes distended slightly, as if by the San Pedro drug. Above them was the 'Octopus God', associated with the *tumi*, the ceremonial knife, and in a temple at the top, just to make explicit the preceding friezes, the so-called 'Decapitator God', half man, half spider, holding a trophy-head by its hair, a traditional symbol of conquest, so well preserved that the red mineral dye on his body and on the bloody head stood out against the yellow of the background.

To see these as a 'private show' conducted by the site workers felt both intimate and almost prurient, a casual violation of a ritual that was so savage and intense for the participants. Human bones had been incorporated into some of the reliefs, like the feet of the watching men holding hands, and sacrificial victims had been found elsewhere on the site. When the first reliefs were uncovered and the excavations made, *National Geographic* ran an article on it with the headline PERU'S TEMPLE OF DOOM (sub-editors being incapable of not referring to Indiana Jones in some way). There was an excitable graphic reconstruction of what the sacrifices might have looked like:

a priest swung a ceremonial *tumi* and blood spurted from a prisoner's throat, as other waiting prisoners watched. The strapline went: 'Perhaps they heard the Pacific surf rolling into the beach in the distance; perhaps all they heard was the pounding of their own hearts.'

In such beautifully restored Moche friezes, just as in the associated ceramics, the hair of prisoners is important: they are sometimes shown having it cut shorter, while the priest or Decapitator God often holds heads by their shorn locks. And many representations of the sacrifice ceremony show prisoners with erect penises, either when being led or when sat and bound with their hands behind their backs, whether to show the virility of the sacrificial victims or to make the connection between sex and death that their sculptures of grinning skeletons copulating might indicate.

Yet the savagery of the sacrificial act was celebrated in art of startling virtuosity. Alongside the image of the Decapitator God in his temple was a frieze of elegant beauty, showing stylised representations of catfish and stingrays in high relief. Aside from the continual focus on the sea that I had seen throughout this exploration of the coastal cultures, the choice of these fish was not accidental. The catfish appears in the rivers after rain in the mountains, while the stingray is likewise more prominent when the coastal waters heat up during the El Niño phenomenon, so both are climatic indices.

El Brujo has a similar small panel-frieze to that of the Pyramid of the Moon, in which images from the sea – lobsters, carnivorous fish, seabirds and a 'fisher-king' with a five-pointed crown – combine in a kaleidoscopic swirl very different from the usual ordered repetition on the long friezes decorating each platform level. There has been a suggestion that these smaller panel-friezes were attached to the priests' quarters at each pyramid, and so might be visionary representations of their religious world, particularly as experienced with the San Pedro drug.

These rich pictorial texts have yet to be decoded, but it seems clear that for the Moche there was an inextricable link at both pyramids between the sacrificial ceremonies in which they invested so much and propitiation of the sea, the wellspring of their maritime riches but whose volatility could bring climatic disaster.

Just climbing the pyramid at El Brujo was a reminder of this. The approach, as at Las Aldas, was from the landward side; there was a long forecourt against the face of the pyramid where prisoners may have been gathered before the sacrifice (the site archaeologists told me they had found strange, unexplained markings on the floor, and ramps leading from the forecourt to lower chambers). Only on climbing up to the top platform would they see the Pacific below. The sacrifice could have been conducted in sight of the waves.

The pyramid was continually heightened over time. The Moche technique, here as elsewhere, was to fill in the existing temples on the current platform and build a new one on top. This could be done in a relatively short period, if necessary, by teams of *adoberos*, bricklayers, working together, and we know from their large-scale agricultural works that the Moche had a great deal of available labour. That this was an effort made by different communities pooling resources can be seen from their charming habit of 'branding' each adobe brick with a sign – some scratches, a drawing or even a hand-print – to show which group had provided it. In the event of some climatic change that might need appeasing, a new layer could be added to the pyramid relatively quickly and more sacrifices made. They were, in effect, building a mountain by the sea.

Looking out over the fog-meadows from the top of the deserted pyramid, having had my private viewing of these rituals of human sacrifice, I felt a chill. The Moche, as evidenced by their pots and their art, were a warm sensual people, who embraced life in all its zoomorphic and sexual diversity, with humour and often love; but fear of extreme climate change seems to have driven them to construct these elaborate, eroticised rituals of death, in a desperate attempt to appease the gods that controlled the capricious weather.

Yet their efforts were in vain. The climatic record, as evidenced by ice-core samples taken in the Andes, shows there to have been extreme El Niño phenomena in the years following AD 650 – first a sustained period of flooding, then of drought, enough to bring any civilisation to its knees. Some of their administrative centres, like that at Pampa Grande near Sipán, were burnt, as if by a revolt. The Moche left the unprotected cities of the plain and began to build more fortified hilltops. There is some evidence of civil war. By AD 700, the Moche were in decline. By AD 800 they had disappeared and sand-dunes started to cover over some of their sites; others were reused by later cultures.

Whether their decline came from climate change or from a political rebellion stirred by the resources needed to maintain such an elaborate theocracy, we do not know. Although anthropologists would never stray from their moral relativism, one would like to speculate that perhaps the Moche people, from whom the sacrificial victims were largely drawn, finally rebelled at such pointless and unproductive slaughter. There is such a thing as the heart of man.

CHAVÍN: AT THE HEART
OF THE LABYRINTH

I arrived at the pueblo of Chavín to see the important ruins called
el Castillo, 'the castle': I penetrated into *sus obscuros subterráneos*, its
darkest depths.

Antonio Raimondi,
El Perú (1874)

THE SETTING SUN STRETCHED the shadows low across the path
in front of us as John Leivers and I approached Chavín from the
west at the end of the day, along a high mountain ridge latticed by
the greys and greens of young eucalyptus trees and lupins. Turning
downhill, I started at the sudden shadow of my own boots sliding
away down the slope.

I had wanted to come here, to Chavín de Huantar, the old
temple town and wellspring of Andean culture, in order to see
another, less savage way of trying to appease capricious climate
changes than that practised by coastal cultures like the Moche. It
was good to be back in the mountains.

Two thousand feet below, we could see the ruins for the first
time, side by side with the modern village of Chavín, the two
only separated by the Huachesa river. From an illuminated cross
high above the town, a cross whose memorial significance only
became apparent later, we had a clear view down to the sunken
plaza, the high platforms to either side, the great temple in the
foreground. The modern village oddly paralleled the ancient site,
laid out in similar blocks of plaza and surrounding buildings, if
in much-reduced scale; by the time we reached it, the light had
melted to give a soft, calcineous effect, woodsmoke mixing with

dust from the track to create a pink wash over the houses.

The laughter of the children was carried by the still evening air long before we came across them playing hide-and-seek around the bandstand of the main plaza, which had been built as a mock-up of the ruins, with jaguar heads protruding from the walls and a similar portico of alternating black and white stones, albeit in breeze-block and plasterboard. One enterprising boy had climbed right up onto the lintel of the mock-stone doorway, so that by lying completely flat he was hidden from his friends below.

Apart from the children, the village was quiet, preternaturally quiet. Men's comatose bodies were propped up in doorways, as if in a zombie movie; one man staggered past so drunk that he urinated ahead of him as he walked, a hard trick to pull off even when sober. We learnt later from our disapproving landlady that the road through the village was being upgraded from a dirt to a tarmac one, in an attempt to make Chavín more accessible; the men of the village had knocked off at noon to spend the rest of the day drinking their unaccustomed wages.

This was an isolated valley some way off from the departmental and now tourist centre of Huaraz. If it were not for the ruins, Chavín would be one of those many forgotten villages in Peru, ignored by central government and living close to the poverty line. Even as it was, despite having one of the most important and atmospheric sites of the Andes – one often described as being the 'mother-culture' – it was comparatively little visited. But there was a tragic reason for the slowness of the way Chavín had been restored and recognised for its value.

*

Julio C. Tello first came here in 1919. For the doyen of Peruvian archaeologists, this was to be the centrepiece of his interpretation of Andean man. The ruins were known of, but slenderly; one traveller had already suggested that they might pre-date the Incas, but the reality – that they were some two thousand years older than Machu Picchu and built between 1200 and 200 BC – was unimaginable.

Tello began excavating. He found the jaguar heads on the side of the main temple, the so-called Castillo (Castle). He found stairways. He uncovered friezes with some of Chavín's complex iconography. He recognised Chavín's great antiquity. And he also immediately realised the central paradox of the site – that here in a remote mountain village, in the heart of the Andes, the images were all from the jungle: caimans, snakes and the jaguar heads themselves. Could it be that it had been founded by peoples from the Amazon, who had brought their belief systems with them? Could Peruvian civilisation have begun in the jungle? Was this the only visible manifestation of some great culture that had rotted away in the rainforest since?

This was not just of archaeological interest. At the beginning of the century, Peru was trying to define itself anew as a nation after losing the War of the Pacific with Chile, and suffering economic contraction as a result. Tello, who was a pure-blooded Indian, promoted Chavín as the cradle of Andean civilisation and the Amazon as the dominant influence on Chavín – an orientation that turned the country away from the coast and Lima. The coast was seen by Tello as '*una cosa aparte*, a thing apart', to be populated later by offshoot cultures from Chavín. (We now know, as I had seen at Caral and Sechín, that in fact some coastal civilisations were even earlier than Chavín, but this discovery was still to come.) And the coast, above all Lima, 'the City of the Kings', was where the Spanish had settled principally after the Conquest, and from where they had ruled the country. For Tello and his generation, defining Peru by its interior was a political statement that grew out of the *indigenismo* of the time, the growing celebration of Peru's pre-Columbian roots and rejection of its colonial past.

A small five-year-old boy living in Chavín called Marino Gonsalez was fascinated by Tello and his work on the monument. Marino had little education. His father wove and sold woollen hats while his mother ran the village bakery. Most of the villagers were, to say the least, uninterested in the ruins; they grazed their animals around its slopes and occasionally took loose stones for their own houses. But Marino was small enough to fit down some of the narrow ventilation shafts and entrances before they were cleared, so he proved invaluable to Tello in his initial investigation. During the years that followed, Marino became his chief assistant.

By early 1945, after twenty-five years of intermittent investigation of the ruins, Tello had completed most of the restoration work. He had even built a small site museum on top of the old temple to house many of the *cabezas claves*, the jaguar heads. The work had proceeded at much the same time as Machu Picchu was being cleared for tourists by Luis Valcárcel, who had similar *indigenista* intentions. Yet Chavín was never to receive the same amount of attention as that Inca site.

Tello invited the prefect of the area, who was based in Huaraz, to visit Chavín in his absence and see how the area could be opened up to tourism, as the roads into the valley were bad. Tello himself remained in Lima, but asked Marino Gonsalez to go to Huaraz and accompany the prefect on his mission. Early on the morning of 17 January 1945, the prefect of Huaraz set off with his delegation. Marino was supposed to meet them on the bus at three in the morning, but he overslept and the prefect left without him, reasoning that he could perfectly well get to Chavín of his own accord.

With the prefect was his eighteen-year-old daughter, who, as it happened, had been studying archaeology and wanted to visit Chavín to help with a dissertation. The party descended into one of the numerous labyrinthine galleries that honeycomb the temple. Inside they heard a distant roar. One by one (as the passageway only allowed single file) they emerged back on top of the temple.

What happened next was described to me by one of the few survivors of that day still to live in Chavín, Edgardo García Colcas, whom after some considerable searching I found in one of the back streets, where he had a small grocery store.

'In those days I had some land just above *las ruinas*, on the far side of the bridge. I was there early, and when the roaring began I could see right up the ravine where it was coming from.

'I could see uprooted eucalyptus trees flying through the air, as if they were nothing. At first I thought it was an earthquake, as I felt a shuddering. But when I saw the waters of the river run dirty,

I realised it must be something up above. I was the far side of the river from the town. I ran back shouting to all the people that they had to escape. They all thought I was mad, as I was waving my hat in the air. And I was too late anyway to save many of them.'

What had happened above was that a block of ice had fallen from a glacier into a lake, damming it temporarily and creating offshoots of floodwater that were finally followed by a complete inundation as the water rose high enough to flow past the block of ice.

The roar as the water breached the ice-block was what the prefect, his daughter and the delegation of thirty visitors heard as they came back out of the galleries. None of them survived the torrential deluge of mud and water, as the floodwaters caused a landslide. The restored ruins were covered in tons of mud. The museum, with its collection of jaguar heads, was swept into the river. The whole south-west side of the town was destroyed. The army had to be brought in to shoot the wild dogs that came to eat the corpses of the dead.

Edgardo told me that the worst of it was that many inhabitants were carried along in the mud and initially survived, but as the mud was deep and impassable ('*como gelatina*, like jelly') they could not then be reached, so died from exposure the following night. January is the middle of the rainy season in the Andes, one factor that may have precipitated the ice-fall and exacerbated the landslides, so conditions were bad. 'There was one man I always remember and whose voice I will hear until my dying day. He had got stuck in the mud near our house, and I could hear him calling until two in the morning. There was nothing we could do to help him. Then he died.'

*

What one now sees of the ruins is what has painstakingly been restored since then. At the time of the disaster, Tello was already sixty-four. Although he began the heartbreaking process of restoring his own restoration, he died two years later in 1947. Much of the work was then overseen by Marino Gonsalez, who continued his involvement with the site until his own death; he took part in the clearing of the main plaza in the 1960s and of a newly discovered circular plaza in the 1970s. Another museum finally opened in 2001, over fifty years after the destruction of the previous one. Marino lived to see this and died in 2002, aged eighty-seven. Meanwhile archaeologists such as Luis Lumbreras, Richard Burger and most recently John Rick have continued the interpretative work.

But there is no doubt that the landslide set back Chavín's investigation and restoration by decades. Only now were the better access roads being built that the prefect of Huaraz had come to prospect in 1945. The memorial cross above the town, which I had passed on my walk in, was just one of the symbols of loss. The old pre-Columbian stone bridge that had stood for millennia over the Huachesa river had been swept away, to be replaced by a modern one. As we approached the ruins the next day, kids were cheerfully throwing bottles and rubbish from the bridge into the river.

A combination of the landslide and long-term subsidence had piled some fifteen feet of soil against the walls, so the buildings were not as tall as they would originally have been, but they were still imposing; as so often with an Andean site, it was not size that mattered but the very precise placing of buildings within a landscape. Like Cuzco, Chavín was sited at the confluence of two rivers, high up at 10,000 feet. Spur valleys led off both west and east, so that it was on a natural travel route between the Amazon and the coast, as well as up and down the Andes. As a crossroads, it allowed – and potentially controlled – access to some of the few passes across the nearby Cordillera Blanca (called 'the white mountains' because of the daunting amount of snow and glaciation on them).

The approach to Chavín was important. For the original pilgrims and travellers, the temple would have seemed an impregnable castle, as it presented an apparently unbreakable façade with no entrance. The only way in was through the 'blind side' of the site at the back, along the narrow strip between the ruins and the river.

Yet this was not for defensive reasons and the term 'El Castillo, the castle', very much in use when the Italian geographer Raimondi passed this way in the nineteenth century, is a misnomer. Chavín was primarily a temple, and the tortuous route needed to enter the grounds is mirrored by the labyrinthine passages within the buildings. This was an architecture of disorientation and intimidation. Travellers on their approach would have first seen the *cabezas claves*, the huge jaguar heads, weighing up to two tons each, which would have looked down at them from thirty feet above, seemingly cantilevered against the wall with no visible means of support (in fact they are tenoned; a mass of unworked stone behind them anchors them into the structure).

Only one has been left in place, but it is easy to imagine what an intimidating impression they would have made. Although often described as jaguar heads, the figures show other animals, like river eagles, and have anthropomorphic features as well, some more so than others, with wide staring human eyes and flaring nostrils.

Inside the temple complex, the jaguar theme is continued; the early pilgrim would have come to a sunken circular plaza with some of the finest stonework of any at the site. A frieze of jaguars links each side of the plaza with the white granite steps that lead up toward the temple; above them march an accompanying series of costumed figures, some holding musical instruments, some a staff made from the San Pedro cactus. Whatever Tello may have thought of Chavín's jungle origins, John and I were reminded more of architectural elements we had seen at the coast: Caral's circular plaza of *c.*2700–2100 BC and Sechín's frieze of warriors, likewise advancing on steps, from *c.*1800–1300 BC. Chavín's main period of construction and influence has recently been dated from 1200 to 200 BC, although it may have started as early as 1400 BC.

Astonishingly this circular and central plaza was found only in 1972, when the eminent Peruvian archaeologist Luis Lumbreras and Marino Gonsalez dug down through the mud of the landslides. Many pilgrims would have probably got no further than here; the theocratic nature of later Andean shrines suggests that only a few people, or possibly just the priesthood themselves, would have been allowed to make the ascent of the white granite stairway to the Old Temple at the centre of the complex.

No one else was at the site as we climbed. The Old Temple faced east and the hard early morning sun picked out the granite walls against the mountains; from this line of approach, the temple seemed almost an outlying forerunner peak of the hills beyond.

The shock of entering the principal gallery was extreme. It was lit by just a few low-voltage bulbs (there was talk of installing a proper lighting system, sponsored by Telefónica, the multinational phone company). From small ledges in many of the interior galleries, it seemed that torches could have been lit by the priests, but the chief effect, then as now, would have been of darkness.

That was as nothing to what lay ahead – for this first and central gallery was the site of the Lanzón, the extraordinary statue carved from white granite that lay at the centre of the cruciform gallery formed by two crossed passageways. For its protection, it was usually kept behind a locked grill, but the INC curator had kindly given us the keys, so we could walk around it from all sides.

With the Lanzón, position was everything; the carved replica on display in the museum forecourt, however faithful to scale, could do nothing to give the sense of power of the original.

It was the figure of a god compressed as if into a blade – and this 'blade figure' dominated the narrow cruciform gallery to such an extent that it protruded up into the ceiling above. Because the walls were narrow, one was forced extremely close in order to view it, in an intriguing reversal of the usual principle by which godhead is reinforced by remoteness. The experience was like seeing a shark up close through an observation port.

The figure was made up of many elements – fangs, claws, some features that were human, many that were not – but it was the shocking, outsize scale that overwhelmed the supplicant, a scale that can only have been achieved by building the temple and galleries around the statue when in situ. The impression was of an object that was too big for its own space, that had broken free from its constraints and pushed up into the galleried room above, like a vertebra that had been forced back and out of someone's skull.

In his writings, Richard Burger has suggested that the gallery with the Lanzón may have interconnected with the other galleries through a now lost passage – certainly the whole temple is honey-combed by galleries, not all of which have been properly investigated. The indefatigable Marino Gonsalez had opened up some of these: the Gallery of the Snails, the Field Camp Gallery and the Gallery of the Offerings. The last-named of these proved important, showing the range of offerings brought to Chavín from across the Andean world as its power and influence grew.

That we still do not understand the full complexity of all the galleries and passages between them puts us into much the same position as the original pilgrims, for whom much of the power of this building, and its capacity to induce offerings, must have come from the architecture of concealment and disorientation.

Despite the predominantly jungle motifs on the Lanzón and the other principal statuary of Chavín (like the 'Tello Obelisk' that is thought to have originally been placed in the centre of the circular plaza), Tello's theory that the Chavín culture originated in the Amazon now seems to have been simplistic.

When I had visited Richard Burger at Yale, while researching Hiram Bingham, he had talked to me about his views on the culture. A clue lay in the jaguar heads surrounding the temple. Precisely how they were originally arranged is uncertain, but following his investigations at Chavín, Richard speculated that as some have more anthropomorphic features than others, they could have been ordered to show a gradual transformation of men into felines. An indication of how the priests might have achieved such psychological shape-shifting is hinted at by the gaping nostrils and staring eyes of the jaguar heads, and the presence of the San Pedro cactus throughout the site, both in the imagery on the walls and growing freely in the valley, as well as implements for different hallucinogenic snuffs from the jungle. The San Pedro cactus produces mescaline and is well known for giving intense psychotropic visions. The intensity of these visions would account for the staring eyes of the jaguar heads; the side effects include nausea. Meanwhile streaming mucus from the nose is a common side effect of jungle hallucino-genic snuffs such as anadenanthera, which contains DMT (dimethyltryptamine).

In Richard's view, the priests who ran the temple would have taken such hallucinogenic substances in order to be able to consult the oracle. The Chavín cult would have centred around the idea that its priests could transform themselves into jaguars and other animals of the jungle world in order to contact and affect the behaviour of supernatural forces (in particular, those relating to water and climate, a key consideration in meteorologically vulnerable Peru).

Academics, whose knowledge of drug-taking can be just that – academic – are inclined to lump all psychotropic drugs together as much of a muchness. However, there are some fine distinctions, as Mike Jay, who has written widely on drug cultures, investigated in a recent essay.

Jay has teased out the implications of Burger's findings that both mescaline and DMT were consumed. They are very different drugs, the equivalent of mixing strong beer with a tequila chaser and with similarly striking results: stand well back.

The mescaline of the San Pedro cactus is obtained by boiling the plant and then drinking the liquid; it is slow-acting, with long-lasting effects that Jay describes as 'euphoric, languid, expansive. The effect on consciousness is fluid and oceanic, including visual trails and a heightened sense of presence.'

By contrast the hallucinogenic snuffs from jungle plants like anadenanthera, which produce DMT, have an intense and immediate effect. Such snuffs are still taken by the Yanomani Indians, who blow it up each other's noses, creating brief and startling hallucinatory moments.

The two taken together would have had a potent and explosive effect, a snakebite of a drug cocktail that even such hardened narco-travellers as Jim Morrison or Hunter S. Thompson would have thought twice about ingesting, particularly before entering a dark, labyrinthine and subterranean complex with anatropic figures leering from the walls.

DMT is today most often taken as *ayahuasca*, which has become popular in the West (in New Mexico, for instance, 'shamanic groups' take it as a sort of psychic depth-charge). It is very much a jungle drug, unlike the San Pedro cactus, which grows in the mountains, so their blending continues the mix of selvatic and montane influences so characteristic of Chavín.

Jay's thoughts on anadenanthera and DMT are worth quoting in full:

> *Anadenanthera*, by contrast [to San Pedro], is a short sharp shock, and one that's powerfully potentiated by a prior dose of San Pedro. About a gramme of powdered seed needs to be snuffed, enough to pack both nostrils. This process rapidly elicits a burning sensation, extreme nausea and often convulsive vomiting, the production of gouts of nasal mucus and perhaps half an hour of exquisite visions, often accompanied by physical contortions, growls and grimaces which are typically understood in Amazon cultures as feline transformations. Unlike San Pedro, which can be taken communally, the physical ordeal of *Anadenanthera* tends to make it a solitary one, the subject hunched in a ball, eyes closed, absorbed in an interior world.

The San Pedro cactus is usually consumed as a drink, while the seeds of plants such as anadenanthera, which contain DMT, are taken as snuff. Many implements suggestive of snuff-taking have been found at Chavín and associated sites – tiny pestles and mortars for grinding the seeds, as well as finely worked bone tubes for sniffing it (reminiscent of the silver spoons used by today's narcocracy to snort cocaine).

To get such hallucinogenic snuffs, modern Peruvian shamen travel down to the jungle and visit the Indian tribes who specialise in these substances. The presumption is that the Chavín priests of the first millennium BC did just that, or that they obtained it as offerings from the travellers who passed through the funnel-neck of the Chavín site on their way backwards and forwards across the Andes and from the Amazon.

Many of the figures on the Chavín statuary are anatropic; that is, they can be viewed as if upside down, or as mirror images. We are familiar with this illusion from the joke faces in which one man's chin becomes another's head when the image is inverted. As Burger

Juan Manuel Castro *Eisein en los papayales*
(Eisein in the papaya groves)

Juan Manuel Castro *Manta de peces (Cloak with fishes):*
'Textiles in Andean societies are carriers of meaning and power.'

Facing page Juan Manuel Castro *Hombre de
Callacancha (Man from Callacancha).*

The Moche: *'Of all the pre-Columbian cultures, the Moche had poured their creativity into their ceramics: their vases and stirrup-spout bottles were decorated with a quite staggering fecundity and range. Never had illiteracy seemed so unimportant or writing less necessary.'*
Above Moche portrait head. *Top right* Scene with captive. *Right* A pair of llamas.

Drawing of 'The Arraignment of Prisoners', showing the sacrifice ceremony, taken from a Moche fineline ceramic (Donna McClelland).

Chavín: entrance to the temple.

The 'jaguar heads' which were originally
supported on the walls of the temple.

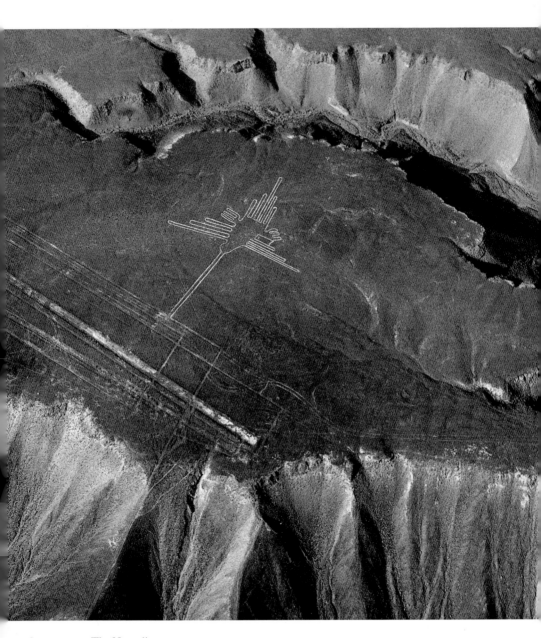

The Nasca lines:
Juan Manuel Castro *Colibrí de Nasca (Nasca hummingbird):*
'One way of looking at the lines arose directly from the topography.
The Andean peoples liked to create meaning out of landscape.'

Maria Reiche studying the
Nasca lines: *'the patron saint of
autodidacts the world over'*.

Hiram Bingham in front of his
tent at Machu Picchu in 1912.

Hugh Thomson and Gary Ziegler on the 2002
Cota Coca research expedition.

Machete-wielding team discover Inca fastness lost for four centuries

By ROGER HIGHFIELD,
SCIENCE EDITOR

ONE OF the last Inca strongholds against the conquering Spanish has been uncovered in cloud-forest by a British and American expedition investigating a rumour of lost ruins, the Royal Geographical Society will announce today.

Called Cota Coca, after the coca grown there, the site is more than 8,000ft up in a valley near the junction of the Yanama and Blanco rivers in Vilcabamba, one of the least understood and most significant areas in the history of the Incas, rulers of the last great empire in the Americas.

The Spanish went there in search of gold, plundering the region and waging war against the Inca. Their leader, Manco Inca, led a rebellion in 1536 that nearly overthrew the Spanish before he and his followers fled to Vilcabamba.

At Cota Coca, which provided a strategic link between the interior and the coast, they fought a guerrilla campaign and defied the invaders for almost four decades.

Valley walls cut off the riverside plateau that holds a settlement of almost 40 structures, including a 75ft-long *kallanka* (meeting hall) grouped around a major plaza, low walls that might have supported wooden-sided houses, a *huaca* (small shrine) and walled enclosures.

The layout appears functional rather than ceremonial: the inner part is thought to have provided lodgings for high-status visitors to the exiled Inca court, and the outlying parts may have housed bureaucrats and imported workers.

The discovery of Cota Coca comes just months after the *National Geographic* announced another "lost city", consisting of scattered settlements. However, the constructed area of this new site is more than twice as big and far better preserved, though it has yet to be excavated.

John Hemming, author of *The Conquest of the Incas* and the Director of the Royal Geographical Society from 1975 to 1996, said: "This is an important discovery because it is a sizeable centre of good quality late-Inca masonry."

Gary Ziegler, an American

Hugh Thomson, left, and Gary Ziegler led the Peruvian expedition

The 75ft-long meeting hall is the largest of 40 buildings on the site

archaeologist, and Hugh Thomson, a British writer and explorer, led a team of specialists, field helpers, eight mule handlers, 16 mules and seven horses into the Peruvian Vilcabamba beyond Machu Picchu.

Acting on a rumour from a previous trip, they made the difficult journey into some of the most remote territory in this part of the Andes, where the mountains slope down towards the Amazon cloud-forest.

"We did not know what we would find. It could have been a 20-year-old corrugated shack," said Mr Thomson.

Instead, what emerged was a substantial and completely unknown site, covered by dense vegetation.

"It was an amazing feeling to cut our way through the cloud-forest to suddenly see this site," said Mr Thomson.

The team used machetes to clear the many stone buildings arranged around a central plaza, so that they could be mapped and studied.

The isolated location has kept the Inca site at Cota Coca concealed for hundreds of years. Erosion by the Yanama river over the centuries since the time of the Incas has created a steep river canyon, which is impassable along the valley bottom; the only way that tourists could reach it was to descend from the mountain above, cutting a trail down through the dense cloud-forest with their machetes.

"It is some of the most difficult terrain anywhere in the world," said Mr Thomson.

The site is on an isolated bench

or mesa just over a mile long, an eroded remnant left after the Rio Yanama river cut a chasm near its intersection with the Rio Blanco. The valley bottom is hot and semi-tropical, with a micro-climate environment.

Before the erosion of the valley walls, it appears that there may have been an Inca road along the river linking the settlement with another of the great Inca cities, Choquequirao. It is likely that the Incas would have used the site in their period of unrest from the Spanish after the Conquest of Peru in 1532, when they were hiding in the mountains until their capitulation in 1572.

"There are no records of the Spanish ever having found this site," said Mr Thomson.

He added: "It's only once in a lifetime that one's likely to be present at the discovery of a genuine new Inca site — with so much of the world discovered and mapped, it's reassuring to feel that there are still places we don't know about.

"The physical geography of South-east Peru is so wild that it is possible that there are even more ruins waiting to be found."

It is unlikely that the site was visited or known of following the fall of the last Inca emperor, Tupac Amaru, in 1572.

However, one early explorer, the Comte de Sartiges, passed nearby in order to reach Choquequirao in 1834. He refers in his writing to the lower Yanama Valley "being known as Cotacoca", although he did not find the ruins.

He commented at the time that he thought it "unlikely anyone could have inhabited this narrow valley because of the tremendous and voracious mosquitoes that have taken possession of it. It was impossible to breathe, drink or eat without absorbing quantities of these insufferable creatures".

It is unlikely that any of the early visitors to Choquequirao found Cota Coca. Although the sites are only a few miles apart, they are across a deep canyon whose connecting Inca routes have long been lost and severed. The new site of Cota Coca has never been documented, reported or known to the outside world until the present investigation.

Mr Ziegler and Mr Thomson are planning to return to the Vilcabamba area next year to look for further ruins.

Pictures: HUGH THOMSON

Hugh Thomson above the Cota Coca canyon. The team are thought to be the first to set foot in the city since 1572

How the sub-editors treated it. Other headlines included 'Cota Coca: The Real Thing'.

points out: 'the use of anatropic design requires extra eyes, noses, and other details which are meaningless when viewed under normal circumstances and add further to the perceptual confusion,' and he has described the Chavín style as 'intentionally inaccessible' to the uninitiated. These sculpted figures, upside down, zoomorphic, distorted, would similarly match an altered psychotropic state.

A further disorientating factor was noted by the Peruvian archae-ologist Luis Lumbreras when looking at the many air ducts and water channels running through the site, which seem surplus to practical requirements. Lumbreras has suggested that these could have been used to create strange acoustical effects, by controlling the intakes like the valves of a trumpet, which would have been heard both inside the temple and outside in the plaza where many supplicants waited. He conducted an experiment with one water channel to show that this worked and compared the result to 'the sound of applause'.

More recently, in 2001, John Rick of Stanford University dis-covered a set of twelve trumpets made from large sea-snail shells in one newly opened gallery, which would have produced 'a quite substantial throaty roar', as he found when they were played again, so adding to the repertoire of synaesthetic effects going on in the temple.

As I wandered from narrow gallery to narrow gallery with their cul-de-sacs, their sudden openings and reversals, even at the full sobriety of ten o'clock in the morning, and without the aid of psychotropic drugs of any sort, I could sense the intense, internalised world of the Chavín cult: a world in which priests battled with the deities who controlled the unpredictable climate. Rather than doing so from the tops of pyramids, in front of admiring or cowed multitudes and by ripping the throats out of human sacrifices, they engaged in hand-to-hand psychic combat, sitting in some darkened chamber, their guts hanging out, senses distorted with drugs, and to the sound of echoing, distorted water, of music playing on sea-snail shells.

I could sense how the whole Peruvian world would have pressed down with an intense gravitational pull on a man, as his nostrils expelled mucus and he lost track of whether it was day or night outside, whether the drugs were coming or going. To encounter the Lanzón under those circumstances would have been to feel that here was a deity who was, like you, trapped in the earth.

And just as the whole Peruvian culture zoomed down into these small black cells with tremendous compression, so it was projected back outwards again with equal force, like a slingshot; for such was the psychic power of the Chavín vision, its connection to something elemental in the Peruvian mind, that its influence had swept right across the Andes by the time of its demise around 200 BC. Chavín pottery and design motifs could be found in every quarter, from the area in the north around the incipient Moche pyramids to the desert plains of Paracas and the Nasca cultures in the south. There is even evidence that what eventually became the lingua franca of the Incas, Quechua, originated at Chavín. For the first time, one can talk of a truly pan-Andean, shared culture, what the archaeologists call a 'horizon'.

The spirit-world of ancient Peru was now in place. I emerged blinking back into the sunlight.

THE SACRED VALLEY

I WANTED TO SEE my family. They were flying into Lima soon and I went there ahead of time to meet them.

I still had my Orient Express 'gold card'. This time I was not in the presidential suite, but in one the size of a generous yacht rather than the full ocean liner. It could still have accommodated every occupant of Michael and Clara's guesthouse. The bellboy discreetly asked whether I wanted to keep my mule-bags hidden away in storage.

At dawn the first morning, a *New York Times* digest was slipped under my door with a helpful sun sticker on it, so that I didn't have to open the curtains to see that it was shining. I swam in the rooftop pool, with its infinity horizon; a hang-glider peeled up from below and circled above me, before spiralling past the smoked black windows of the nearby Marriott and on towards the beachfront.

The seaward districts of Lima had become prosperous only recently. After years of ignoring the Pacific and building inland, the Limeños had finally built a long and meandering ocean promenade, the Malecón, along which the power joggers and fast-walkers threaded past ice-cream vendors and luxury apartments with expensive views. The first surfers were already sitting out beyond the breakers. In the low dawn light, their heads looked like black seals against the water. Alongside them stood the pier of the Rosa Náutica, Lima's best-known and most expensive restaurant, from where power-breakfasters could see the occasional surfer detach himself from the pack and essay a few elegant lines on a wave before regrouping. Near by too was the Larcomar Shopping Mall, with its Radio Shack and multiplex cinema, its Tony Roma's restaurant – 'Famous for Ribs!' – and bowling alleys, where rich Limeño kids met to flirt over ice creams.

Strolling (not power jogging) along the beachfront, I chanced across a girl asking the gardener watering the park plants why her boyfriend never called her – the gardener was giving advice; three clipped poodles were being exercised by a large woman in Lycra; down by the sea, a white-haired leonine man, stripped to the waist and wearing just a posing pouch and trainers with white socks, was playing football by himself, kicking the ball to one end of his beach strip, then loping over with his impressively bronzed paunch and kicking it back again. I passed an inland lighthouse that had been stranded by the changing coastline and no longer marked the headland; in the 'lovers' walk' section of the Malecón was a mosaic that said, 'Lovers are like birds passing in the night.'

Lima was a city of dreams lived to the rhythm of individual lives, often oblivious to those of others, like the power-walkers with their headphones on.

Back in front of my hotel, chauffeurs were polishing imaginary bits of dirt from the windscreens of black limousines. Some prosperous bits of the city were increasingly like showbiz LA, with valet-parking, personal trainers, designer dogs and people being recognised because they were in a soap opera. The big news that day in *El Comercio*, the daily paper, was 'Elton John to marry David Furniss'. At breakfast, one of the models at a nearby table was wearing stack-heeled wedges with gold straps, Police dark glasses, gold bangles and a transparent blouse with a black mesh bra. Through her make-up I could see she had once had a Latina complexion. And this was at nine in the morning. Her male companion had waist-long hair and a shoulder bag.

I didn't let this distract me from the job in hand. Is there any greater pleasure for the traveller returning from the desert than the delights of a five-star buffet-bar breakfast, particularly when it's free? Even St Anthony would have had a hard time resisting the temptations: smoked river trout, silver salvers full of bacon (almost as rare in Peru as it is in India), tamales and scrambled eggs; freshly squeezed tropical fruits, iced berries; pancakes with maple syrup;

all on that clean white fine linen which is a true luxury in a country where the humidity made even my notebook damp. Thank God John (who had returned to Cuzco) couldn't see me, or it would have confirmed him in all his suspicions about my incipient Pommie tendency for soft living.

A family next to me were looking tense, despite these banqueting opportunities. It seemed to be a family reunion of some sort, with American-accented parents who had just flown in from Miami and two Lima-based sons in their early twenties. They began a speakerphone conference with a third, absent son, which is why I knew so much about them. Indeed, the whole restaurant did, as the speakerphone broadcast the views of the disaffected, absent son after the mother had put it to him, forcefully, that he should have shown up to see them: 'Mom, I know I should be there for you, but I just want to say that I've tried really hard and I feel you've never listened to me, or wanted me to be who I really am, or helped me with my dependencies.' As he continued with the nature of those 'dependencies', mostly cocaine, a freely available local produce for rich Limeños, it was clear that he did not realise his words were being relayed to the rest of his family, let alone to the audience of breakfasting businessmen and models, trying, like me, to ignore the amplified conversation. His father was taking notes as he spoke, while his brothers sat there with the truculence of those who have heard it all before and resent the attention paid to a prodigal son. One pointedly got up and headed over to the breakfast bar.

A waiter remembered me as he refilled my cup with the finest Blue Mountain coffee from Jamaica. I asked what was new in town. A taxi driver had already given me the rundown – disappointing performances by the Peruvian football team, by President Toledo, by El Beckham for Real Madrid and gasoline going up a sol – so I knew what to expect. But he disconcerted me. 'There may be an El Niño coming,' he said, talking softly, as if not to alarm the neighbouring tables. 'It should be winter now. But it's still hot. Can't you feel it? It's wrong.'

And it was true, I had noticed the unseasonable sun although, it must be said, with some enjoyment. He continued: 'The moon is very full and the nights are too cold.' For a moment I felt like an ethno-historian – but that was before I spent the morning with a real one.

*

She was sitting in a hard chair, at a desk whose only ornament was a silver quilled pen, pointing towards her. A simple grey filing cabinet was in the corner. Otherwise the room was completely bare, narrow but high, giving the effect, rather like the small woman herself, of an immense mental projection upwards.

This was María Rostworowski de Diez Canseco, the legendary anthropologist and ethno-historian. More than any intellectual in Peru, she had reconfigured our understanding of the Incas and of the Andean mind. Now in her eighties, she continued to come in every day to her office here in Lima at the Instituto de Estudios Peruanos, the Institute of Peruvian Studies, which she had helped to found.

Small as a bird, she had precise, permed hair and a silk scarf tied around her neck in the style of the 1920s. Despite the many decades she had lived in Peru, she still spoke English with the meticulous upper-class accent of Roedean, where she had learnt it as a girl. She sat very still and told me her life story, wearing a knee-length brown coat that she kept on throughout as it was so cold in the office.

María had been born in 1915, in Lima, to a Peruvian mother and an aristocratic Polish father who, she told me, had 'the wandering habits of a hippy before his time'. Her family had moved to France when she was young, but after the death of her sister, aged eight, her parents had become protective of her, and she spent a lonely childhood with few friends. Then at thirteen she went to Roedean, characteristically not because she was sent there by her parents but after choosing it herself and writing to the school: 'My father took no interest in these things.'

The loneliness seems to have continued there. María had not foreseen the English regime of school sports, which she disliked;

however, she learnt to précis books, an invaluable tool for her later work. As she had no family or friends in England, she had to remain at the otherwise empty school for half-terms. This lasted for a few years until her father lost much of his fortune and she was taken in by a convent school in Belgium.

Meanwhile her eccentric father, who spoke eight languages, became a Buddhist and left his family behind while he went to India on a spiritual pilgrimage. Later he took María back with him to Poland, at her request, as 'I wanted to find where my ancestors came from.' She was intoxicated by the romance of Warsaw's high-society balls: 'I married a Polish noble because he sang and danced well.'

Then she also wanted to explore the Peruvian roots of her mother's family, so travelled there with her new husband, had a daughter, and divorced (she later remarried, to a Peruvian). 'The first time I went to Cuzco I was struck by its *luminosidad*, its luminosity,' she told me. She had already read Clements Markham's influential book on the Incas of 1911. Now she set to teach herself everything she could about her refound land of origin, particularly as it was in the excited grip of the *indigenismo* movement, which celebrated pre-Columbian history. 'I am an autodidact. I have always been very curious. I dedicated ten years to reading all the early Spanish chroniclers. I made index card entries of them all' (she gestured at the filing cabinet), 'and that was one of the most useful things I ever did.'

'And was that when you decided to write your biography of Pachacuti?' I asked.

It was the one time in her conversation that she reacted sharply. 'It's not "Pachacuti". It's "Pachacútec". That's John Rowe's fault. He would insist on calling him Pachacuti, which is a *disaster*.'

Her biography of that Inca emperor (as an agnostic on the issue of his name, I have used 'Pachacuti' as being the more common version) had paved the way for the more extensive and ground-breaking *Historia del Tahuantinsuyu*, translated as *History of the Inca Realm*, which deconstructed the suppositions made by Spanish colonial historians about pre-Columbian history – including even the very European idea that the Incas had 'an empire' at all in the Roman, imperial sense. She argued it could be seen as more of a trade confederation. She also showed how the Andean principles of kinship wove a complicated thread through Inca politics, which did not observe the strict European principles of primogeniture but instead depended far more on a matrilineal line of influence; nobody had taken much notice previously of who an Inca emperor's mother was.

But it was for her work on the pre-Inca cultures that I had come to see her. She had initiated many studies of what had previously been an under-researched area, partly because the Spanish chroniclers immediately after the Conquest were not particularly interested, and neither were the historians who followed them.

María looked for documents that had never been studied before: the bureaucratic records of the courts and of tax registers, of censuses and of government inquiries. Some of the most interesting material was in the lawsuits to do with the inheritance of chieftainships brought by claimants just after the Conquest. She found a wealth of material and, over eleven books and countless articles, had built up a picture of the Andean world in which the central element of reciprocity was stressed.

We are familiar with this from Japanese and to a lesser extent Western customs ('We must invite them to our wedding as they invited us to theirs'), but in the Andes reciprocity developed into such a dominating cultural influence that it became more important than even military considerations. Some of the large regional centres that the Incas built, like Huánuco Pampa, were built not so much to impose military order on the local population, the European model, but to allow festivals of reciprocity to be held between themselves and the local tribes – toasts would be drunk in matching drinking vessels, known as *qeros*, and allegiances confirmed. And it was clear that this was a pattern the Incas had adopted from their predecessors, like the Huari and the Nasca, who likewise built ritual centres that I was determined to travel and see.

María smiled when she heard this. She had always insisted, as she put it, 'on walking over and over again the ground I am writing about', like the Río Chillón valley for instance, or the *ceque* lines of Cuzco. She lapsed into silence, thinking about all the places she had been to: 'You realise that the study of Peru takes a lifetime. You need your whole life to do it. The best thing I ever did was spend ten years at the beginning just reading the chronicles and making notes. My second husband bought all the books for me.'

After he died suddenly, in 1961, María gave up her studies for a while and went to the jungle, to a leprosy hospital (just as Che Guevara had done in Peru) where she worked as a nurse: 'The lepers gave me more and taught me more than I could ever give them.'

She was a remarkable woman. Just short of her ninetieth birthday, she was still avidly reading every new Andeanist essay that came out, as well as producing more of her own, all handwritten as she refused to use a typewriter, let alone a computer. She felt that the later years of her life, since she was sixty, had been her most productive period. In addition to her prodigious academic output, she had recently created a comic book for children on the Incas and had written the text for a website. She had always been aware not just of the need for Andeanists to write accessibly (her own books in Spanish were admirably concise and clear) but to communicate with a readership outside their immediate peer group. She had just published a beautifully illustrated pamphlet for tourists on Pachacamac, the pre-Columbian pilgrimage site near Lima.

I came away seduced by her intellectual charm, and also determined to see the pre-Incaic cultures with Andean eyes, not imposing easy Western preconceptions on a world that tilted at such a different axis to our own.

*

María's office was not far from the historic centre of Lima, an area I rarely went to as it was some miles inland. Indeed the old 'City of the Kings' that Francisco Pizarro had founded in 1535 after defeating the Incas was now a soulless place. Lima's tide had ebbed out to more coastal areas like Miraflores, where I usually stayed, leaving wide traffic-filled streets, department stores and government offices with just the odd colonial building as a small island among the concrete. Visitors to the city inevitably wanted to go to the centre and were surprised when I suggested that they should walk along the modern seafront instead.

But this time I was curious to see what had happened to the statue of Francisco Pizarro that had stood in the main square, the Plaza Mayor. The statue had always impressed me, as full equestrian sculptures often did – Pizarro in body armour astride an equally armoured horse, moving forwards purposefully – even though in actual fact the illiterate Marquis was as bad at riding as he was at writing. He had been assassinated only a few yards away by political rivals one Sunday morning in 1541, at the time for mass, when they stormed his Governor's Residence which overlooked the square. Pizarro had been in Peru for less than ten years since the Spanish Conquest of 1532, but during that time he and his *conquistadores* had completely overturned the Andean world-order.

With great political fanfare, the new mayor of Lima, Luis Castañeda, had now decreed that his statue should be removed, as a symbolic gesture of liberation from the Spanish colonial past. Castañeda proposed that the flags of Peru and of the Quechua Nation should fly there instead. The rainbow-coloured Quechua Nation flag was popularly known as 'the Inca flag', although it was a later invention by the intellectual *indigenistas* of the 1920s and had nothing to do with the Incas.

Likewise, the mayor's motives for this particular political gesture were more complicated than might at first appear. For a start this was not a statue of Pizarro that had been erected by the Spanish themselves. It had only been put up in 1935, over a hundred years after Peru had already achieved independence; a group of conservatives, alarmed at the growth of the left-wing *indigenista* movement celebrating the country's Indian past, wanted a reminder of the 'civilising' influence of Spain.

Throughout the 1920s and 1930s, *indigenismo* had grown apace, as María Rostworowski had found when she had arrived from Europe; interest in pre-Columbian Peru was intense, and the more that was learnt of the wonders of ancient Peru by such archaeologists as Julio Tello, the more there was a sense of revulsion at the Conquest and Pizarro's knights who had swept it all away.

This process had culminated with Peru's current and first Indian president, Alejandro Toledo, who had not only been inaugurated at Machu Picchu rather than Lima, but had invested heavily in museums celebrating the pre-Columbian legacy. As his political problems had grown, so he had fallen back on beating the Inca drum; the statue's time was up. It had already been removed, which made the huge bleak square look even emptier. As Lima had originally been the viceregal capital not only of Spanish Peru but of all the Spanish dominions in South America, the square, together with the accompanying cathedral and palaces, had been built to a suitably imposing scale.

I got talking to an old man on a bench near by, who had been watching the workmen as they tried to tidy up the base of the plinth now that the statue had gone. He was interested in the climate in England – what could one plant there, when the sowing season came – and was incredulous when I told him that there was quite enough rain to do without irrigation canals.

In turn I asked him whether he knew what had happened to the statue. I imagined it being melted down in some ceremony of retribution: the metal running down into the earth as an emblematic reversal of the way the conquistadors' brute iron swords had cut through the tunics and flesh of a people helpless without the same metallurgical skills. Not long before, the statues of Saddam Hussein had come crashing down in Iraq.

The old man told me that this was far from being the case. Pizarro's statue had not been destroyed; indeed there were plans to erect it quietly in another part of the city, once the fuss had died down. '*Así es*, that's the way it is. When the play ends,' and he made a gesture with his hand as if of a curtain coming down, 'and the audience have gone home, the performance just moves elsewhere.'

Peru was playing a curious contrapuntal duet with its own history, like the celebrated *marinera* they danced on the coast, now advancing towards the European interlopers who had so dramatically changed it, now backing away, with what one commentator described as a 'schizophrenic historical consciousness'. Pizarro was a useful whipping boy for politicians; like Cromwell in Ireland, he had left a taste in the country like mustard in the mouth. But as Mario Vargas Llosa, the country's best-known writer, had just pointed out in a magazine interview: 'The *conquistadores* of five hundred years ago are not the ones responsible for the fact that in today's Peru there is so much poverty, such harrowing inequality, such discrimination, ignorance and exploitation. [Those responsible] are Peruvians of all races and colours who are very much alive.'

*

Three crumpled children sleepwalked into my arms at Lima airport after the twenty-hour flight from Europe. Sally was barely more awake. It took a weekend of breakfasts at the hotel's fabulous buffet bar to restore their balance. Unfortunately it also left the children with the impression that Peru had all the unaccustomed amenities of a five-star hotel.

I took them to the zoo, as a 'thing to do with kids in a big city'. We saw a guanaco.

'That's a llama,' said Leo, aged three, excitedly.

'They spit at you,' said Owen, seven: 'I read it in *Tintin*. One spat all over Captain Haddock.'

'Uugh,' said Daisy, nine. 'How disgusting. Let's not stand so close.'

'Don't worry,' I said trying to sound authoritative and calming: 'First, it's not a llama, but a guanaco, which is a bit like it but a gentler animal. And anyway, I've never had a llama spit at me in all the times I've come to Peru.'

The guanaco rolled a beady eye, snorted and expelled a quart of phlegm over us.

And then we were flying into Cuzco and down to the Sacred Valley where I had rented a house. Although I had not told Sally this, I had only seen the house briefly at night, so was unsure as to whether it was going to be suitable. Nor was I in good shape at the time. It had been after the inaugural launch of Nick Asheshov's train. As the inebriated passengers had made their way back from Machu Picchu, I had confided in Nick my wish to rent a house in Urubamba for a while.

'Aha, I have just the man,' said Nick, and took me over to a saturnine figure in a cape and wide-brimmed hat who was hunched up over the railway table: 'This is Carlos Rey, the architect. He's built some wonderful houses and you are going to rent one.'

Nick had a way of driving through a plan. Carlos looked up, surprised. He was about fifty, bearded, a successful architect in Lima who had got bored with chasing commissions in the city and wanted to pursue his interest in using pre-Columbian building materials, so had come to the Sacred Valley. I liked him immediately. He had the optimistic approach that architects need in the face of difficult clients and obtuse building regulations.

Carlos had built a complex of other houses around his own house on the outskirts of Urubamba, at a place called K'uychi Rumi, which means 'the rainbow stone' in Quechua; the houses shared a communal garden. By the time we reached Urubamba night had fallen. Carlos led me through wide gates into this garden, where his family and guests were sitting around a bonfire and in a stone circle that Carlo had designed to view the stars from.

Realising that I'd just spent twelve hours celebrating the launch of his railway with Nick and some of the biggest boozers in the whole of Peru, I concentrated on speaking slowly and not falling over. Carlos showed me around one of the houses with his dogs, giving the architect's tour: 'We've used adobe throughout, dyed with natural colours. The fireplaces use reclaimed stone.' They were handsome, spacious houses. Remember to check that there's a bathroom, I remember thinking to myself. All that was visible of the gardens were looming shadows against the sky. 'So do you want it?' Carlos asked.

I was leaving town first thing the next day. This would be my only chance to see the place. I committed.

And now I was going to have to live with that commitment. Sally had never been to Peru before. For her, as for the children, it was just the place I disappeared to for stretches at a time. I was determined that it should make a good impression. At least with an extremely active and curious three-year-old on the loose, I knew it had a garden that was walled and safe.

So to see that garden in full sun was as much a relief for me as an agreeable surprise for the others: a riot of hibiscus, abutilon, poinsettias and roses, with arum lilies growing alongside the small irrigation ditches that ran through the property. Carlos and his wife, Claudia, had also introduced some pre-Columbian plants – *polylepis* trees and quinoa. Yellow broom edged paths winding towards a large stand of eucalyptus at the far end of the property where the children would spend many happy hours swinging over the stream; immediately beyond rose the ravine up to Pumahuanca, one of the passes leading to the Amazon.

I remembered E. G. Squier's comments in the nineteenth century, the same American who had found bats in the Moche pyramids:

> A joy to behold, with its groups of trees and green, walled gardens
> … Although only 2500 feet lower than the Cuzco Basin, the Yucay
> [Urubamba] Valley, protected on all sides, enjoys a much more
> benign climate, similar to that of Nîmes and other parts of the
> south of France.
>
> Both healthy and fertile, easily accessible from the capital, and
> with a vegetation unrivalled in the Sierra, this sweet and tranquil
> valley, surrounded by some of the highest mountains of the Con-
> tinent, quickly became the favourite place of recreation for the
> Incas. The soil is rich and the climate, in spite of the fact that the
> Valley is enclosed by high snow-capped mountains, is soft and
> agreeable. A more beautiful place than this does not exist in all of
> the Andes.

The garden was largely the work of Carlos's wife, Claudia, who had helped arrange school places for the children, and this was my next nervous moment: it was quite something to go to a school where no one speaks your language, and naturally enough Daisy and Owen baulked at the prospect. Leo was anyway too young.

The school was called Llamk'achinapaq, which means 'work hard' in Quechua. This did not reassure the children. 'You realise', said Carlos, 'that it is a private school.' I blanched, knowing what this would mean in England. 'The fees are $10 a month.' We could afford it.

Llamk'achinapaq was in a graceful street of tall pisonay trees near the market. The class sizes were small – only ten or so – ideal for Daisy and Owen, and despite their age difference we had arranged for them to be together. Sally and I took turns to sit in class with them for the first couple of days, to help them settle and show solidarity.

The other children were amused to see me squashed into a child's chair at the back of the class, behind a small wooden desk. I translated for Daisy and Owen as the teacher, who spoke no English, explained that we would each draw a mountain landscape. He took the results, including mine, and divided them into those that were broadly realistic (the view, say, from Urubamba of the towering giants around it like Mount Pitusiray and the Chicón glacier) and those that were more *creativos* and fantastical, often involving giants and princesses. The 'Prof.' was hard on those who he thought were not up to the mark, addressing each pupil very formally as he went through their work:

'I congratulate you, Brenda, for the effort you have put into this painting.'

'Edwin, did you try to do this work as well as you could, or did you just try to get it over and done with?'

With admirable if inadvisable candour, Edwin responded: 'Just to get it over and done with.' This prompted a small homily on the dangers of such an approach in school and in life. It felt like a Victorian country classroom.

As a child of the same age I had briefly gone to a college in Germany and now I remembered the same advantages and disadvantages of being a pupil who didn't speak the language: on the one hand, no one expected you to do all the work, which was terrific, and you were outside all the usual strategic alliances being formed between class factions; on the other, you could become permanently disengaged as life continued in a foreign language, a sense made more acute for me now by being a full thirty years older than anybody else in the class.

But just as Daisy and Owen were soon accepted in their school, we all quickly found that Urubamba was an easy place to adapt to. The rhythm of such small market towns had always appealed to me: the Post Office that never seemed to open; the old men moving around the benches in the plaza to keep getting the sun – I overheard one telling another: 'Get it written down on paper because you know that words can be blown away by the wind'; a shoeshine boy playing his Gameboy while he waited for customers; the café on the corner of the square called, with the utmost simplicity, 'The Corner Café'.

Urubamba was a mountain as well as a market town; like a settlement in the Old West where the main drag is only a temporary slowing of a longer route through the wilderness, the high street past the gas station turned into a country lane, which led directly up to the Chicón glacier.

We rode up there sometimes from the town, using Nick Asheshov's horses, picking our way through the cobbled streets nervously as the odd *mototaxi* could shoot without warning from an alley and scare the horses, the drivers treating them as if they were errant pedestrians. By riding, we could get glimpses over the high patio walls of hidden courtyards, orchards and market gardens. The surrounding fields were a reminder too that Urubamba was organised not around its streets but around its water supply; there was a complicated series of irrigation canals, which could be diverted at different points during the day under a tightly regulated system. Woe betide the *campesino* who 'forgot' to divert a canal back to his neighbour at the appointed hour – or for that matter the three-year-old boy like ours, Leo, who enjoyed damming or diverting them at 'inappropriate' moments.

A local radio journalist called Amelia was waging a campaign to stop local politicians from privatising the water, a contentious issue throughout Peru. I had met her in the Corner Café, and she had invited me to appear on the local radio station to describe the discoveries at Llactapata. 'Sure, whenever you like,' I had replied, trying to be helpful.

'Let's do it now then. My show is on in five minutes. In fact I'm late for it.'

I found myself running through the streets with her and sitting at a microphone, broadcasting to the 'Urubamba nation' before quite knowing what I was going to say.

As we had decided not to release the news to the international press until we had written a full report on Llactapata, this was the first time I had talked publicly about it. Luckily Amelia was not interested in any archaeological subtleties, brushing them aside to get to the heart of the question: 'So how will this discovery benefit the local community?'

I mumbled about sustainable tourism and extending the Machu Picchu Sanctuary to include such sites. I wasn't quite sure whether my Spanish was good enough, but Amelia told me afterwards I had at least been '*entendible*, intelligible'. As it happened, the whole issue of Llactapata was about to raise its head in a far more alarming way.

*

Dear Sir

We have in our power a *denuncia* [accusation], in which it is said that in April of this year your group went to the sector of Llactapata in the District of Santa Teresa and made clandestine excavations, according to our informants.

If this is verified, we will action the appropriate legal sanctions.

May I also take this occasion to offer you my most cordial compliments.

Yours faithfully

The letter could not have been more explicit. It was signed by the regional Director of the Peruvian Instituto Nacional de Cultura, the INC, telling us that they had received a formal *denuncia*, a legal accusation, about our activities in the Vilcabamba.

Gary and Kim were by now long back in Colorado; it fell to Nicholas Asheshov and me to go into Cuzco and face the music with the authorities. My heart sank at the prospect. We were of course completely 'innocent of the offences as charged'. But explaining that to the relevant Peruvian authorities could take some doing – and the long and sometimes justified suspicion harboured against foreign archaeologists ever since the time of Hiram Bingham might play against us. If any of the mud stuck, it could prevent us working in Peru again.

Nick and I travelled together into Cuzco from Urubamba, leaving at dawn. I had already had a dreadful twenty-four hours: Sally's purse had been lost, stolen or otherwise mislaid the day before, and there had been all the usual problems of cancelling credit cards from the other side of the world; Leo had been bitten by a small dog and we were unsure whether it had been vaccinated against rabies (we later discovered it had been, as, naturally, had Leo and all the children, but the worry was considerable, given endemic rabies in the Andes). So I was not at my best, huddled into a cab in the bitterly cold early morning of the mountains.

At least if anyone was going to hold my hand, Nick Asheshov was by far the best qualified; in one of his many previous incarnations he had been editor of the *Lima Times* and was adept at dealing with Peruvian bureaucracy, as he showed when we arrived at the INC offices shortly after they opened. A large sign up on the door said: '*La hora cuzquena es la hora exacta*, Cuzco time is punctual time,' usually an indication that it wasn't. The lethargic secretary said that the Director might be able to see us. 'We have an appointment,' said Nick. She shrugged.

Nick adopted the tactic he told me later was infallible both in Peru and elsewhere: he stood in front of her desk and waved his blind man's cane around as if searching for something. When she asked whether he would like to sit down while waiting, he declined, saying he would stand until the Director saw them. Even in Peru, where embarrassment is a less potent weapon than in Europe or the United States, having a seemingly blind man standing in the middle of your office looking helpless was impossible to ignore, and we were duly ushered in to see the Director.

He had the quiet good manners of the professional INC operative: 'You're Hugh Thomson, the co-leader of this expedition, with Gary Ziegler?' he established. 'The *denuncia* does not name either of you, or you, Señor Asheshov. It is issued from the Santa Teresa district and names Pío Espinosa and John Leivers [he pronounced it 'layovers'] for having been *huaqueros*, looters, and digging at the Llactapata site in an unauthorised way. I believe they were members of your group.'

Nick and I understood the INC's natural discomfort at having to deal with a *denuncia*. The *denuncia* is an example of both Peruvian democracy and inertia at work. Anyone can issue a *denuncia*, a charge, against anyone else. It costs nothing to do so and does not require a lawyer. Once lodged with the police, or relevant department (and for archaeological matters, that means the INC), they are duty-bound to investigate it, although not to press charges. Most Peruvians respond to a *denuncia* by a prompt counter-*denuncia*, which can keep the whole system deadlocked, but this is not a recourse readily available to foreigners.

Luckily the Director knew of our previous work in the area and we had mutual colleagues in the archaeological world. The INC accepted our assurances that we had not excavated at the site, just cleared and examined it. This was particularly gracious of the Director, as it emerged that our paperwork for the expedition had not been as well submitted as it could have been. Peruvian paperwork is designed in such a way that it can never be completely in order, so as to give authorities the chance to assert themselves if they need to. Even so, ours had been casual to say the least, perhaps because we had been lulled by our many years of such expeditions in the area, none of which had run into problems before.

My concern was not that the case would ever come to court – as there were absolutely no grounds or proof for the charge – but that some vague opprobrium would hang over our expedition as a result. It mattered not that far more substantial archaeological expeditions had been issued in the past with *denuncias* – indeed, one could say that the only archaeologists with supposedly 'clean records' were too shy of their academic reputations to admit they had been charged. I was aware too that our friends and backers in Cuzco, who had arranged logistics and support for the expedition, could be tarred with the same brush, and so feel that their own reputations had suffered as the result of helping us. I felt particularly protective towards John Leivers, given that he had quite unfairly and randomly received the full weight of the *denuncia*. John spent a great deal of time in Cuzco, so was vulnerable to the suggestion that he had in some way acted improperly.

Then I remembered our final day at Llactapata, when we had met the road crew from Santa Teresa, and John had innocently given them his name in case they came across anything of interest while cutting through the *selva*. Certain comments I'd overheard from the same road crew came back to me – and also explained why Pío Espinosa, our chief muleteer, had been named in the *denuncia*, along with John. I realised what was behind the accusation.

Santa Teresa, where the road crew came from, lay at the bottom of the valley near Llactapata. Pío and his crew were from a small hamlet considerably higher up that same valley. There was much rivalry between his community and that of Santa Teresa. In retrospect it was understandable that the people of Santa Teresa, as the closest village to the site, should have taken umbrage not so much at us as foreigners but at a rival and more distant community getting all the work – and mule-hire – from an expedition to what might be considered 'their' site. We had worked with Pío and his crew because we always worked with Pío, and usually further away from his home base. It had never occurred to us that this might cause problems. Subsequent discreet enquiries in Santa Teresa established that this was indeed the root of the problem.

It was a reminder that one can never be too careful with the local politics of an archaeological investigation – and that any future plans for Llactapata would need to integrate the concerns of the local community rather better than we had managed so far.

*

The storm-clouds passed. The *denuncia* was effectively shelved by the INC. Sally became very friendly with Claudia, Carlos's wife, and the children settled into Llamk'achinapaq. Leo played endlessly with the clearly not rabid dogs. Within a few weeks of arriving we were invited to a local wedding and realised that we already knew most of the congregation. The bride and groom emerged from the town hall registry office to a full band playing in the town square, a band in which the bridegroom usually played himself.

I had met Joyo several times at the Corner Café, eating *empanadas* with a saxophone slung over his shoulder. He was an architect who had travelled in France, been an active revolutionary during the 1968 Sorbonne uprising, and had since settled in Urubamba with Lola, his French girlfriend and now bride, to play music; they were getting married to regularise both their own nationalities and those of their adopted children.

Unfortunately, as Joyo had told me, the Peruvian authorities had made a mistake and thought initially they wanted to get divorced, not married. Peruvian bureaucracy, once started, will move in only one direction; Joyo's protests that they could not get divorced because they weren't married had fallen on deaf ears. It had taken six months of bureaucratic confusion before their 'divorce' had come through and they could get 'remarried'.

Joyo unslung his sax and was leading his own wedding procession around the town square and up to their house for a wedding party that would last all day and all of the night. One of his band had played with the Grateful Dead. There were fond memories of the time Keith Richards had passed through with the Stones on one of their Peruvian adventures and had busked in the Corner Café (it had been a country that had always appealed to Mick Jagger, not least because when he was in the Amazon to film *Fitzcarraldo*, no one had recognised him).

Indeed, there was a bohemian diaspora around Urubamba of ponytailed hippies and Peace Corps veterans of a certain age, who had fetched up here in the cheap land and low regulations of the seventies, when dope could be grown in your back garden. The valley had changed considerably since then. In recent years the beginnings of the tourist boom engulfing Peru had spilt over from Cuzco and hotels were being built at an alarming rate, usually with our landlord Carlos as architect. There were also many exiled Limeños, like Carlos, who had moved here for the good life. Some had put jacuzzis into their haciendas. Even the taxi drivers now had mobile phones.

Carlos's son Rodrigo, at the wedding in a white suit with box-fresh trainers, was a fast-talking Limeño who always had plans. To Sally's and my amusement, he was proposing to start a model agency in Cuzco; one of the prospective models, his girlfriend Yjarri, was hanging on his arm with a revealing décolletage – unexpectedly, as she usually dressed as an urban cyclist wrapped in fluffy anoraks and ironic pigtails. If that didn't work out Rodrigo was going to start a cybercafé. One of Joyo's friends made felt slippers and sold them to designers in the States and Europe.

It intrigued me that the picture I had always had of Urubamba from afar – the small market town in the heart of the Sacred Valley, the grain basket of the Incas – should have such a touch of Laurel Canyon about it. Of course there were still plenty of local villagers keeping horses, minding their small plots and threatening to shoot the neighbours if the irrigation canal wasn't turned over to them at the appointed hour. But just when you least expected it, with the woodsmoke drifting past the eucalyptus stands and the sun setting on the Chicón glacier, a four-wheel drive would flash past blaring out rap music.

*

Carlos had built a ring of stone seats in his garden, perfect to sit around in the evenings while putting the world to rights and nursing a shot of *pisco*. Once the children were in bed, Sally and I would often watch the night sky with Carlos and Andrés, the nightwatchman, learning the names of the southern constellations and how differently stars were viewed in Peru.

Our Western tradition, largely derived from Sumerian, Egyptian and Arab astronomy, is to partition the sky into arbitrary constellations, joining up stars 'dot-to-dot' that may be as far apart as we are from them, but happen to look close to us, just because they make a neat pattern that we can interpret as a group or, better yet, shape. Our historical focus for both mythology and study has often been the planets of our own solar system, as some of the brightest and most prominent objects in the sky, and the narrow band of constellations we see behind them around the ecliptic (the line followed by the sun as the earth spins around), which make up the Zodiac.

By contrast the Incas and many of their modern Quechua descendants were more interested in the Milky Way, which they saw as a celestial river running overhead. They could use the Milky Way to divide the night sky and delineate areas, for during the year it shifts until it runs almost at right angles to its original position, thus neatly dividing the sky into quarters – the principle of quadru-partition being a natural way for the Andean mind to divide space, in the same way as the Incas divided their empire into four quarters.

In purely astronomical terms it could be argued that the ancient Peruvians took a wider view of the stars than we traditionally have, given that if our orientation has always been around our own, local solar system and the twelve major constellations of the Zodiac circling the ecliptic, their orientation around the Milky Way shows a much wider affinity to the whole of the galaxy of which we are a part.

In particular they paid attention to the so-called 'dark-cloud' patches, which form over the Milky Way and are caused by clouds of interstellar dust. One such dark-cloud patch was in the centre of the Southern Cross, the Southern Hemisphere's most celebrated celestial landmark.

Just below the Southern Cross was another striking example of this: the two bright stars that we know as Alpha Centauri and Beta Centauri, but which the Incas referred to as Llamacñawin, or 'the eyes of the llama'. Ever since I had been told this, I had noticed them far more and looked for the dark patches near by, a striking reminder that in the night skies, as in exploration, 'you only ever find what you are looking for'. At this time of year and of night, they were low on the horizon, but when they rose higher they were at the head of a much larger 'dark-cloud' formation, spreading across the Milky Way in the shape of a llama suckling her young, although it was not easy to make this out. The Inca chronicler Garcilaso de la Vega complained plaintively:

> They fancied they saw the figure of a llama suckling its young in some dark patches over what astronomers call the Milky Way. They tried to point it out to me saying 'Don't you see the head of the ewe? There's the lamb's head suckling, there are the body and the legs.' But I could see nothing but the spots, which must have been for want of imagination on my part.

Every culture projects onto the night sky its own concerns and myths, like a Rorschach Test for a civilisation, whether it be to see fish on the ends of long lines, Pisces for the West, or a llama suckling its young for the Incas. Other groupings that the Incas found in the sky were those of a snake, a toad, a tinamou (a pheasant-like bird) and an Andean fox.

One reason for their intense interest in the 'dark-cloud animal constellations' of the Milky Way was that they could be of immense practical use. They had learnt that if the visibility of any of these constellations was impaired, it was a harbinger of rain – for good reason, as the obscuring of the constellations would have been due to changes in the Earth's upper atmosphere, a point later noted in 1802 by Alexander von Humboldt, the pioneering naturalist and traveller, when he came to Peru:

> I have endeavoured to describe the approach of the rainy season, and the sign by which it is announced ... The dark spot in the constellation of the Southern Cross becomes indistinct in proportion as the transparency of the atmosphere decreases and this change announces itself the approach of rain.

Given the pan-Andean obsession with water supply that I had seen throughout my travels, I did not find it surprising that the Milky Way should have been thought of as a river that in some ways was an extension of the planet's own hydraulic system.

If I learnt one thing during our stay in Urubamba, it was that water and its supply was a constant preoccupation for the Andean mind, and at the heart of every dispute, from the local mayor and his plans to privatise the water services, to neighbours and their endless arguments about water allocation. One hotel owner had even publicly denounced another for having too many bathrooms.

No wonder that the Incas and their ancestors should have celebrated it so obsessively, or associated their *huacas*, their stone shrines, so closely with water.

*

Many months after our arrival in Urubamba and the day has begun as all our days in Urubamba seem to begin: the light coming up suddenly over the mountains, like a blind; dogs barking on the road; the hoot of Nick Asheshov's train passing at some ungodly early hour, moving slowly to make sure that there are no cattle or small children on the track; a hummingbird brushing so close to the window that its wings set the glass vibrating.

Then the firecrackers start, tight bursts of sound on the road. For this is the Principal Day of the festival of El Señor de Torrechayoc, a festival that the town has already enjoyably stretched out for weeks. It is the day when the cross with the figure of Christ will be removed from its dedicated chapel and carried through the town on a litter, decorated with oranges and pomegranates and roses, as if it was an Inca emperor. Behind and in front process a myriad of other crucifixes, some with corn, lilies and gypsophila, each with their attendant dance-groups.

By midday the procession has built to its height. It is a wild and fabulous scene; music is everywhere, from a couple of musicians on drum and flute to the full-fledged brass bands of Puno. The dancing girls gyrate their short skirts and strut in time to the simple but pulsating rhythm that seems to fill the whole town. The *ukukus*, the 'bear men', sweltering in their costumes, have unzipped them to the navel. As the cross progresses, pink and white confetti thrown on it scatters in the wind, some landing on the policeman who is trying to look authoritative with his padded shoulders and peaked cap, but now looks like a bride.

The whole of the main highway to Cuzco is blocked, stopping traffic up and down the valley. The cross sways incongruously in front of the truck-stop garage. A succession of dance-troupes pass: the male *chu'uncho* dancers with their high feathered headdresses from the jungle; señoras in bowler hats, pigtails protruding and falling to their waists; the Majeños in leather jackets and bulbous masks, enacting the surprisingly tender dance of the drunks in which they advance upon one another, beer belly to exaggerated beer belly, toasting the crowd. Other dancers dressed as mock professors in black tailcoats and *corbata* (ties) are using their canes to escort some improbably stockinged young female charges in mortarboards, who look like candidates for 'Miss Co-ed'. Some dancers whip each other in mock combat. Wide-boys from Puno sport space-cowboy suits with silver boots; a mock road crew in rough camouflage outfits are pulling a pole along and tossing it between them, like the Village People. The white-masked dancers of the mountains, the Colla; the costumes of the sun, *inti*, of bulls, of monkeys: all are proceeded by the Quechua rainbow flag, the symbol of a country trying to define itself anew by its pre-Columbian past.

The cross reaches an elaborate design that has been painstakingly laid out on the road with the most fragile and ephemeral of materials: green-grey eucalyptus leaves, flowers of yellow broom, and chalk-dust of white, olive, and above all, a red line weaving through the whole design. All the preceding dancers and crosses have made their way around this, but the principal cross of El Señor de Torrechayoc is carried straight through it, scattering the elaborate design to the wind, like the sand mandalas of the Buddhists which can take months to make and a nirvana moment to blow away.

The red, white and green of all the leaves and flowers swirl around the cross against the sun. One of the 'devil dancers', the maverick jokers of the feast, has climbed up onto the rooftop of a nearby house and shields his eyes from the sight in mock horror, as if Christ is vanquishing him.

And now a whisper goes through the crowd: 'The jungle girls are coming.' Men jostle to the front to be able to see better. Shimmering forwards in electric-green outfits, with feathers everywhere, in tight miniskirts and halter-neck tops, the jungle girls pass with all the confident assertiveness of those who know they are the stars of this particular show. They have been dancing for hours and the sweat glistens on their exposed flesh. More voluptuous and revealing than the other costumes of the traditional Serrano mountain dress, one noticeable difference is that while the 'mountain women' always dance in sensible shoes, the 'jungle girls' have thigh-length platform boots in lurid shades of purple and orange on which they can stomp through town. They use these to strut to the music with an enviable command and aplomb, knowing they are lighting the normally dry tinder of the puritanical mountain folk. This is a country where the jungle equates with sex, where a weekend in Iquitos means only one thing and even the best-selling condom is marketed as a 'Tropical'. Even in the time of the Incas, jungle concubines were the most valued. '*Ellas, ¡si que tienen pilas!*, They're really running on batteries!' murmurs a man beside me admiringly.

Elsewhere batteries are beginning to run out. I go down a small alley and find a troupe of musicians collapsed along the cobbles, their trumpets sprawled beside them, overcome by the heat and the alcohol. The consumption of drink has moved from conspicuous to prodigious – one store is now only selling beer by the crate, not the bottle. *Chicha* is being ladled into large plastic disposable glasses on the rock-festival principle that they'll never get returned and can't hurt anybody if thrown.

In the main square, the older men outside the church have the worst of it, as they are wearing full Sunday suits, unlike the young men in their football shirts and trainers. Many people are seeking shelter under the palm trees, or dipping their heads and hands into the fountain. Some of the devil dancers have thrown ropes up into the palms so that they can climb up and laugh at people. A startled bird crashes out of one tree as a devil's head pokes up beside it.

Small boys step right out of their *ukuku* bear costumes and reach for chilled bottles of Inka Kola; some of the musicians have their jackets pulled over their heads to protect themselves from the sun as they play; soap-bubbles float overhead from a machine operated by a street vendor.

The more prosperous townspeople watch from balconies around the square as the cross comes to a stop in front of the church and a long line of supplicants make their obeisance to it. Behind the church, the glacier of Chicón glistens in the heart of the mountain range from which the cross was originally brought; for this, unusually, is a 'Jesus of the Snows', a Christ-figure from the mountains.

*

The story of the festival and of El Señor de Torrechayoc begins, as so often in the Andes, with a geological catastrophe.

In 1650, a severe earthquake buried the main road from Urubamba to the nearby town of Lares. This was a substantial trade route along the valley, so the *caminantes*, the travelling salesmen, now had to use a much higher pass through the mountains, with harsh toll charges exacted by the owners of the hacienda through which the new route passed.

For two hundred years, nothing was done to rebuild the road – the Peruvian Government was not concerned about a local trade route used mainly by *indios*. Only in 1867 did a concerted effort by the townspeople themselves open the road, although they were persecuted, as if they were rebels, for doing so.

In celebration for the reopening of the valley route, a solemn mass was held on the high pass they had been using previously, and a cross placed there, with a figure of Christ carved in the Andean style. Soon afterwards, the inhabitants of nearby villages reported that they were having dreams of this Christ figure, who complained of intense cold, icy winds and that he felt himself abandoned. In 1882 the cross was therefore brought down to Urubamba and placed in a chapel, with a festival held every Pentecost to mark the occasion. By 1921 these annual festivities had been officially recognised by the Catholic Church, always good at syncretising local cults and beliefs with their own; for the worship of a mountain place, an *apu*, was a tradition that stretched back into deepest pre-Columbian times, and it was clear that this 'Christ of the Mountains' had carried a deep lode of meaning back with him from his pass.

Friends in the town told me that the festival had grown enormously. Twenty years ago it had been a small local affair; now marching bands from as far away as Lake Titicaca came to celebrate the event. Just recently, an annual pilgrimage had also begun to the spot where the cross originally stood on its mountain pass, starting with fifty pilgrims but growing to the extent that some two thousand of the townspeople had gone the week before, including Amelia, my friend from the radio station. To get there they had to make the ascent through the night, an arduous climb.

Today, after El Señor had been processed to the main church in the plaza, the cross was returned to its chapel, a large barnlike building in the poorer, higher end of the town above the market. We walked up there later. Over the altar, the Christ-figure's eyes were hooded and closed, a suffering rather than a serene Christ, in a rich red robe with gold armbands, the figure of the sun radiating out behind him giving a pre-Columbian effect. Swathes of gladioli, white lilies and carnations were laid at his feet.

Temporary stalls had been set up around the chapel, selling *chicha* in the usual way and offering simple gambling pleasures: throwing coins on a number, spinning a wheel and, to the great delight of my children, table football; they were less pleased to see racks of spitted and roasted guinea pigs, their heads still on to reassure customers they were not buying rat, along with beef-hearts and suckling pig. A stall sold *mate* made from *uña de gato* (the exotically named herb 'nail of the cat') as a protection against venereal disease.

We bumped into Andrés, the nightwatchman at K'uychi Rumi who had been helping me identify the unfamiliar constellations of the Southern Hemisphere. He told me that an *arranque de gallos* was taking place in a field above town. While I had no time for the occasional bullfights around town, the *arranque de gallos* was different, a spectacle of pure horse-riding skill that I had heard of but never seen.

By the time we got there, the horses had already thrown up a

circle of dust over the excited onlookers. In the traditional version
of the *arranque de gallos*, a fighting cock was dangled from a line in
the centre of a ring. Then horsemen would ride under it and try to
grab the cock with their hands, a task made more difficult by
attendants who used a rope to jerk the bird high up overhead as
the riders passed. In this modern version, a bottle was used instead
of a live bird (more it must be said because it was considered a
waste of a good fighting cock than for humane reasons), but it was
no less difficult for the horsemen, who in their excitement and
occasional intoxication would often fall as they leapt from their
saddles to try to grab the prize twitching high on its line.

Crammed up against the wooden seats of the makeshift ring that
had been set up, we got periodic glimpses of the mêlée of horses.
There were some younger men attempting it for the first time, as a
rite of passage, and finding it difficult to slow their horses down
enough for the jump. One, wearing a Brazilian football shirt, shook
up a Coke bottle and sprayed it over himself.

This was a sport for the villagers of the mountain uplands, the
communities where there were no roads and horsemanship was
both essential and prized. They were country folk in broad hats
and jeans. *Huayno* music was playing from a radio. A woman just
in front of me cradled two cocks she would probably use in a fight
later. She was looking at her partner, a man holding a glass of fruit
chicha in his hand, with complete adoration.

After riding under the prize, the horsemen would wheel round
and back under the rope to make another attempt. As the riders
dropped out through exhaustion, or fell off, the turning circle got
tighter and tighter as the remainder competed, until one horseman
finally leapt fully out of his saddle and was lucky enough to fall
back onto the horse, with the bottle in his hand. He wheeled round
victoriously, sending up a cloud of dust.

I knew that cockfighting would follow afterwards, so we left with
the children, passing the debris of the festivities in the town. And I
realised that after some months in Urubamba, I was ready to head
out again. I had explored the coast and Chavín in the millennia
before AD 1; now I wanted to investigate the next great phase of

Andean culture, in the years AD 1–700, as it developed at Nasca, one of the most celebrated of all the Peruvian cultures.

Sally and the children were well settled at K'uychi Rumi, where the gardens were in full bloom, and at the school. It was the middle of term-time, so it was not practical for them to accompany me; indeed, the children showed a positive disinclination to go and see 'some boring old lines in the desert'. They were far more interested in coming with me later on a visit to the Island of the Sun, which sounded tantalisingly exotic and warm.

And if I was being honest with them, I shared an initial doubt about how enjoyable a visit to the famous lines of Nasca might be. For I had been there before.

RECLAIMING THE DESERT:
THE NASCA

MY FIRST EXPERIENCE OF Nasca some years earlier had not been a success.

I had got into town very late, past midnight, after a punishing bus drive along the coast on a drug cocktail of antibiotics and Imodium to try to cure a rare bout of bad gastroenteritis: 'The drugs weren't working,' as the Verve used to sing, so I was in an altered state.

Bundled out of the Pan-American coach beside a petrol station somewhere on the outlying approaches to Nasca, near the budget hotels, I was reminded of being a stranger in a strange town way past its bedtime, a feeling I'd often had when I had first come to Peru. It was too late even for the hotel touts who hustle continuously in Nasca, but by now had moved on. A half-hearted girl was pushed out of a taxi at me to sell a flight over the lines near by the next morning (they obviously figured a girl made a better sell – with reason, as Nasca girls are exceptionally pretty).

I was not reassured by my own pre-booked hotel which had guests lying asleep all over the hall floor, waiting for a delayed long-distance coach. I had to pick my way over their bodies to get to reception. The hotel felt like a new build in the Middle East: stark white walls, too much space and not enough furnishings. I woke up to see a virtual bomb-site of fresh building work outside the window, part of Nasca's tourist boom.

So I flew over the lines at dawn with a scant five hours' sleep and in no fit state to take in one of the acknowledged marvels of ancient Peru (a book by the archaeo-astronomer Anthony Aveni was titled *Nasca: Eighth Wonder of the World?*). The plane was a small four-seater. The only other passengers were a Dutch couple who refused to talk to me. I sat next to the pilot, who insisted on speaking bad English and couldn't hear me through his headphones. He flew elegant figure-of-eight loops around each figure to make sure both sides of the plane saw it, a manoeuvre not recommended for passengers prone to motion sickness. His memorised running commentary sounded like a TV programme for schoolchildren: 'This ees the *monkey*. And this ees is the *whale*. And this ees the *hummingbird*.'

The iconography was so familiar from postcards, from films, from T-shirts, even now from tattoos (there was a 'body parlour' in Nasca selling the designs), that to see them in the desert was like actually seeing the *Mona Lisa* in the Louvre, where the first overwhelming reaction was the shock of familiarity.

Of course the actual lines were hallucinatory and extraordinary. But I did not feel the experience had been an engaged one. It was more like the archaeological equivalent of motel sex: a quick stopover and instant gratification. So I now wanted to return for a more sustained visit.

*

The Nasca lines, more perhaps than any other archaeological phenomenon in Peru, question our own perception and our aesthetic judgement.

The manner of their discovery – or at least, to borrow a phrase used of Hiram Bingham and Machu Picchu, their 'scientific discovery' – is largely responsible for this. For they were first seen, to their full, fabulous extent, from the air, when commercial flights were made by Faucett Airlines over the plateau in the 1930s. What must it have been like for those early pilots (and I was reminded once more of Cary Grant in *Only Angels Have Wings*) who suddenly realised that the whole of this isolated *pampa* between two river valleys, the Nasca and the Ingenio, was criss-crossed with geometrical lines and, most striking of all, with giant figures of birds and animals etched in the desert? Again, to quote Bingham at Machu Picchu, 'Would anyone believe what they were seeing,' even in a country like Peru where the miraculous was almost cotidian.

The sheer scale and quantity of the lines was overwhelming: more than a thousand designs spread over 1,000 square kilometres. And because they were seen so well from the air, and so easily, as I had done, the popular and natural impression was that this was the intention of their creators. The presumption that the lines were intended to be viewed from above, yet made by a people who could never view their own creation gave the modern visitor the supposed added satisfaction of seeing them in a way the Nasca would have liked to, but couldn't: a delayed gratification. The theory had all the mythical appeal of Bingham's 'lost city of the Virgins of the Sun' at Machu Picchu; it now seems to have been equally fallacious.

A series of coincidences gave rise to the initial way in which the lines were interpreted and publicised. In 1941, Paul Kosok was sitting in a Lima café when one of the Faucett pilots who had flown over the lines told him of what they had seen. The pilot had recognised Kosok because he had given a public lecture in Lima on his archaeological work elsewhere in Peru.

Paul Kosok was an interesting, maverick character; his day job was as a historian at Long Island University, but he also doubled as Director of New York's Symphony Orchestra – quite enough for most men, without becoming a self-taught expert on the more arcane realms of Peruvian archaeology as well. Pictures invariably show him wearing a bow tie. His interest in Peru had taken him to the north, where he had investigated the Moche irrigation systems. The research was to result in an influential book, *Life, Land and Water in Ancient Peru*, but the chapter of the book that attracted the world's attention was that on the Nasca.

For, intrigued by what the pilot had told him (and at this stage knowledge of the lines was largely confined to the pilots' mess-room), Kosok set off to see them for himself. He travelled to Palpa where the most well-informed man in the neighbourhood, the local doctor, took him to see a nearby line.

Kosok was beside himself with excitement when he realised that the line was man-made and yet clearly had nothing to do with irrigation. As luck would have it, the day he was there was 22 June, just one day after the June solstice. As he stood on the hill looking back at the line, he realised that the sun was setting directly down the line.

Few men could have resisted the interpretation he then made. According to Dr Tello, he exclaimed: '*¡El Calendario Astronómico más grande del mundo!*' and in his book he gave the Nasca chapter a similar title: 'The Largest Astronomy Book in the World'. The legend had been born.

*

The stage was set for the arrival of the most famous foreign figure in Peruvian archaeology, a woman who through her austerity and persistence has become the patron saint of autodidacts the world over: Maria Reiche.

Reiche had been sitting with Kosok at the Lima café when he first heard of the lines; she often worked there as a waitress when she was not helping Kosok translate archaeological texts. At nearly forty, she was about to be introduced to her life's vocation.

Born in Dresden in 1903, she had spent a restless and unhappy youth as a myopic loner. Out of tune with Weimar Germany and the coming Nazi regime, she escaped to Peru and a variety of peripatetic jobs as a penniless exile, from working as a governess in Cuzco (she was sacked after disagreeing with her charges' mother) to translating the works of the important German archaeologist Max Uhle. In Cuzco and in Lima, she had been part of the loose circle of academics, both Peruvian and foreign, who were trying with mounting excitement to explore the early pre-Columbian cultures which had first been highlighted by Uhle.

Kosok told her of his revelatory moment in the desert, when he had realised the astronomical import of the lines. He also described a bird-figure he had seen at Palpa (still known as 'Kosok's bird'). He himself had to return to the States, but he despatched Reiche as his emissary to Nasca to look at the lines and continue the work.

In December 1941, she arrived by bus in the small town, which then saw few foreigners, let alone the eccentric figure of a six-foot-tall blonde German governess who always dressed in the same clothes, and wore sandals and spectacles held together with sellotape. For over fifty years, until her death in 1998, she was to devote her life to studying the geoglyphs, spending long days walking in the desert sun.

At first she lived in a Spartan hut just by the Pan-American highway; then, as her fame grew, she moved to the main hotel in Nasca, giving nightly lectures where she explained her theory of the lines, a theory that, given the moral weight of her long investigation, became canonical.

Paul Kosok's initial interest in the geoglyphs was not sustained, partly because of his chaotic personal life – he drank heavily and was what one of my Peruvian sources described as a *mujeriego*, a heavy womaniser. But over her fifty years of studying the lines, Reiche extended Paul Kosok's initial insight. She saw the lines as being 'the most important astronomical monument of Peru and perhaps the world' – a vast, complicated series of alignments that charted the heavens with a sophistication and accuracy surpassing those of contemporary astronomers in the West. The figure of the spider she interpreted for instance as matching that of Orion, while she saw the monkey zooglyph as representing the Great Bear complex.

There were antecedents for this: the Maya were already known to have an elaborate system of calendrical time-keeping and were equally lauded as possessing a secret wisdom lost by the West, a theme that in the sixties and seventies fed the prevalent counter-culture's disenchantment with any easy assumption of our own cultural superiority.

Reiche attracted considerable publicity, which, despite her romantic image as an unworldly hermit, she cultivated assiduously. Bruce Chatwin visited her for the *Sunday Times* in 1975 and was taken by her intense blue eyes, blonde hair and boundless auto-didactic enthusiasm – all qualities, of course, that Chatwin shared. He was also impressed by her height; she towered over him. He accepted without question her assertions on the astronomical nature of the lines, about which he also commented: 'They look like the work of a very sensitive and very expensive abstract artist.'

While Reiche was impressive in the way she dedicated her life to the lines, those who followed in her wake were often not; chief among these was Erich von Däniken, the engaging Swiss waiter who sold the world the idea that the lines were landing strips for alien spacecraft. His *Chariots of the Gods: Was God an Astronaut?* was a best-seller that not only spawned many imitators but sold over two million copies, one reason why less successful archaeological writers dislike him so much.

A far more serious threat to Reiche's theories came from Gerald Hawkins, the archaeo-astronomer whose ground-breaking work on Stonehenge had revealed the extent to which that site was aligned on solstice and equinox sightings. Nasca was a natural sequel for him. Hawkins could be presumed to have come to the lines hoping to find similar alignments there, as Reiche and Kosok had suggested. The fact that he then didn't, having fed all the information into a computer, was damaging. Reiche contested Hawkins' findings, telling Chatwin: 'This Hawkins must have spent very little time here. He could not have taken proper azimuths of the horizon. What kind of astronomy is that?' But the way was now open for other interpretations.

*

When I returned to look at the lines, I went this time to Palpa, just north of Nasca and where Paul Kosok had first had his vision of 'the largest astronomy book in the world'. David Browne, a British Nasca expert, had kindly put me in touch with a team that was working on a section of the lines there.

Maria Reiche had not studied much around Palpa, partly because the local landowners had discouraged her and also because the lines on the actual Nasca *pampa* are more extensive. However, the Palpa geoglyphs are particularly interesting as they seem to have been made earlier than those at Nasca.

For the Nasca lines did not come out of nowhere, an impression sometimes given by Maria Reiche. There was a long prior history in the Andes of creating a 'sacred landscape', as I had seen at sites like Sechín, Las Aldas and Chavín on my earlier tour of the north of the country. More specifically, the Paracas culture on the coast, heavily influenced by Chavín, had begun to develop geoglyphs in the millennium before Nasca, from around 800 to 1 BC. One of the most remarkable of these was a giant flaming candelabrum etched into a slope that rose up from the sea. While it was difficult to date this accurately, other figurative images, like drops of water or images of whales, have been found in Paracas tombs as well as etched in the landscape, so the iconography matches.

As the influence of the Paracas culture slowly moved inland and south, it had been adopted first in Palpa, where the inhabitants began to experiment with more abstract geoglyphs of the sort Kosok had seen, some of them trapezoidal (the trapezoid being a shape that haunted the Andean imagination right up to the time of the Incas). In the next millennium, from AD 1 to 700, the Nasca people had developed this style yet further on the *pampa* above their river valley.

So at Palpa one could see the style as it first developed. The lines there were being investigated by a team of Peruvian and German archaeologists led by Johny Isla and Markus Reindel. It was a good partnership. Johny brought his knowledge of Peruvian cultural context, having worked on sites at Nasca, while the German team had some impressive technological tools, particularly photo-grammetry, a technique by which aerial photos could be fed into a computer and used to generate a 3D virtual-reality computer model of the landscape.

Johny used it to 'fly me over' the Palpa geoglyphs when I met him at his team's headquarters just outside Palpa, a plush set of whitewashed buildings (one advantage for the Peruvians in working with the Europeans was they brought not just technology but considerable funds). The virtual-reality model was powerful because it gave an opportunity to 'fly over' a particular geoglyph again and again, and it was in 3D, so gave a vivid idea of the terrain the lines were on: 'the topographical context', as their German colleague Karsten Lambers had put it in his PhD thesis, so far the only work that had been published on their research at Palpa. Simple aerial photos had a tendency to flatten out the geoglyphs and encouraged a simplistic reading of them, a point I had noticed when flying over the famous hummingbird at Nasca and realising for the first time how neatly it fitted into a small plateau at the edge of the *pampa*.

But while the virtual-reality model was impressive, and computer simulation was clearly the way forward for a whole range of archaeological interpretation in the coming years, I had come to Palpa to do precisely the opposite; I wanted actually to walk on the lines. For it was impossible to do so at Nasca itself. Quite rightly the *pampa* was protected from anyone randomly wandering (or worse, driving) over it. The pilots who flew the many tourists were quick to report anyone seen there without authorisation. This was one of Maria Reiche's best legacies, as she had ceaselessly campaigned for the lines' preservation as an archaeological monument, a concept that had at first been difficult, given the vast expanse of the *pampa*.

However, at Palpa I could join Johny and his colleagues as they walked and studied the geoglyphs on the ground; in particular, the so called Reloj Solar, the 'Solar Clock', the most famous of the Palpa lines. This was a beautiful maze set just below a hill; unlike many of the lines, it could therefore be viewed from land, from the hill's summit, so that I could see the elaborate design of spirals and lines doubling back on themselves before descending to them.

The first thing that struck me was how satisfying it was to walk, satisfying in the childish way of walking a line, something I had done recently with my own children in a small maze Nick Asheshov had constructed in the garden at his hotel in Urubamba. It was an immediate reminder too of one of the most significant and remarkable features of the geoglyphs – that they are all 'drawn' with a single continuous line, like a thread in a weaving; a far harder way of creating them and clearly for a purpose.

The lines also always finished where they began (no loose ends), which for anyone walking, or indeed more formally processing as a group, had a neat symmetry. And it was this intuition, that the Nasca people may indeed have designed the lines to be walked on, not seen from above, that had become predominant in recent years, as a reaction against the 'astronomy book' proposal put forward by Paul Kosok and Maria Reiche.

*

The Nasca lines are often loosely described as being 'in the desert'. However, this is not the long sand desert that stretches along the Pacific coast, but an inland and upland desert, on a plateau above the rich valleys of the Nasca and the Ingenio rivers, which cut through it on either side. It is a desert of stones, which have oxidised darker than the surface below; remove any and you create a distinctive pale mark, instantly visible both from the air and on the ground. It is a subtractive process, often compared to an etching.

While not perhaps quite as dramatic as the way Bruce Chatwin described it – 'If you so much tread on the Pampa you will leave a white footprint that will last for centuries' – it is considerably easier and faster than might be imagined. Local schoolchildren were able to create a 'line' in a matter of days when they tried it as an experiment (scrupulously erased afterwards). So the question is not how the Nasca people made the lines, but why?

In books, the geoglyphs are reproduced in isolation from one another and appear neatly diagrammatic. Seeing them when you fly over the *pampa* is more disconcerting – the lines are clearly visible, but in what is otherwise a wasteland. Floods have washed portions of the plateau away. Moreover lines overlap and in some cases almost obliterate other figures. It looks like urban graffiti, albeit on a gigantic scale; some of the figures enclose areas of 50,000 square metres, while if all the straight lines were added together they would stretch 1,500 kilometres.

In the late 1970s a new group of American visitors started to arrive at Nasca to study the geoglyphs. At different times, this group included Tom Zuidema, Anthony Aveni, Gary Urton and Johan Reinhard. Crucially their academic background was more anthropological than archaeological; they wanted to place the lines in their cultural context.

Tom Zuidema and Anthony Aveni arrived fresh from intriguing work on the *ceque* system of lines radiating out from Cuzco, on which Zuidema was the acknowledged expert. Gary Urton, a graduate student, was to become one of the leading Andeanists of his generation, studying both astronomy and the *quipu*, the knotted cords used in the Andes to keep records. And Johan Reinhard, then unknown, was to achieve fame as the man who discovered the 'ice mummies', the sacrificed bodies of young children on Peruvian mountain tops, as a result of his sustained interest in the 'sacred landscape' of the Incas.

They were all proponents of the new discipline of archaeo-astronomy that had grown out of Gerald Hawkins' work at Stone-henge and a new interest in how ancient cultures practised sky-watching. They were naturally drawn to Nasca. But perversely, given their background, the interpretation they came to about the lines was to take them away from astronomy in a different direction.

Aveni's first impression was that he was looking at an 'unerased blackboard at the end of a busy day of classroom activities'; he also thought of the surface of the moon. Like Hawkins, when he and his colleagues ran tests on the geoglyphs, they showed little direct correlation with astronomy, and certainly did not seem to have been a great 'sky-map'. However, the team did spend a considerable amount of time walking the lines, at a time when, if you had Maria Reiche's permission, you still could. Doing this made them realise why the 'astronomy book' theory of Nasca had always been so popular. Walking the lines was hard, hot work compared to viewing them from the air, as most visitors did. It made them respect Maria Reiche, who had been crossing the plain on foot for decades, even as they reached conclusions at variance to hers.

Within the cultural context of the Andes, something Reiche had paid scant attention to, the notion of pilgrimage and of walking a sacred landscape had a rich tradition, one that continues today at immense pilgrimage festivals like Qoyllurit'i, or even small local ones like the El Señor de Torrechayoc celebrations I had witnessed at Urubamba.

The growing hypothesis of the young anthropologists was that the lines were laid by succeeding generations of the Nasca to walk along in ritual procession. This hypothesis was also developed by the enterprising British film-maker and investigator Tony Morrison, who drew a comparison with Bolivian peasants, who still process ceremonially along certain lines at certain times of year. And as I walked around the spirals and doubled-back lines of the Reloj Solar at Palpa, it was easy to imagine a procession around it, with participants wearing full ceremonial costumes. I could see how the lines would have been enjoyable and ritualistic and strange to build together, as well as binding to walk together. It was a theory that intuitively made sense to me.

From the investigations of Aveni and Reinhard, it seemed that the longer, geometric lines often pointed towards water sources, or towards summits that symbolised water; they also concluded that those lines at Nasca that did seem to have some astronomical function marked the time of year (November) when water would first appear in the valleys.

For anyone who has been to the Nasca area, it is clear why water should be such an obsession. The hydrology is a peculiar one. It hardly ever rains in the towns of Nasca or Palpa themselves, but water from the rainy season in the mountains is borne down both by the rivers and also the natural aquifers that the Nasca people extended and manipulated with an elaborate system of underground aqueducts. As long as the water system is working, the valley is an extremely fertile one, but the supply can be erratic.

As it happened, I had arrived in the area after three years of drought and water was again an obsession for the local community. In the Palpa town hall, a crisis meeting was being held, which I only witnessed because I went there with Johny Isla to see his exhibition on the aerial work they had done on the local lines. While agitated farmers petitioned for the right to sink more personal wells ('*pozos particulares*') on their land, they were looked down on by giant photographs of their ancestors' geoglyphs, which may well have expressed similar concerns. We know from climate research on the ice-cores of glaciers that there were periods of extreme drought during the Nasca culture, as well as equally devastating floods.

I travelled on from Palpa to Nasca. The heat was intense and after my previous experience I decided this time to stay in an hotel with a pool; indeed, not just any hotel, but the Hotel Nasca Lines, a hotel with a peculiar fascination as it was where Maria Reiche lived for the last decades of her life. There was a 'Maria Reiche sandwich' on the menu, made from 'Tenderloin Roast Beef with Hot Mustard, Lettuce and Tomato'; I wondered whether the inclusion of the mustard was a quiet joke, as she cannot have been the easiest of guests. The hotel management had given her free board and lodging (and even laundry, although they told me this had never amounted to much as she always wore the same clothes). This was a magnanimous if not wholly altruistic gesture, for by the 1980s the town had come to recognise that Reiche, once seen as a marginal, eccentric character, was the key to its prosperity.

One reason for her virtual beatification in Nasca – and many of the inhabitants still referred to her simply as 'María', as if she had been a saint – was that she had single-handedly created a tourist boom bringing 80,000 tourists a year to the town; doubtless even more would come if the airport ever expanded to allow commercial flights from Lima and abroad.

I met Josué Lancho by the hotel pool. Now about sixty, he had been at the centre of investigations into the Nasca for decades, both as a teacher at the local school (it was he who had conducted the experiment with the schoolchildren in creating a 'line') and also as regional director of the INC, the National Institute of Culture. He was charming and forthcoming, with an ingrained schoolmaster's habit of doing little diagrams in a notebook of squared paper to illustrate what he was talking about.

Over a coffee and a 'Maria Reiche sandwich', he told me a bit about her: 'Nobody wanted to contradict Maria while she was alive. She could be very closed, very "German" sometimes, but she could also be open as a child. She found it difficult to make friendships – *un carácter muy fuerte*, a very strong character.' Josué imitated the birdlike voice with which Maria would deal with detractors and journalists. He also told me the story of the inevitable clash between Reiche and the young American newcomers, which he had witnessed.

At first she had welcomed them. They were after all fellow archaeo-astronomers, precisely the area that interested her. She even took Aveni and Zuidema out into the desert to show them how she measured the lines.

But there were problems. Like many autodidacts, she felt insecure with those who were more academically trained. And Josué told me that she always found it much easier dealing with women. The young Americans failed on both counts. Worse still, they disagreed with her, although they were too courteous to do so directly; they were beginning to favour an interpretation that stressed the walking of the lines rather than an astronomical connection. And they were inclined to point out that even Reiche's astronomical interpretations concentrated on constellations more prominent in her native Northern Hemisphere – like the Great Bear and Orion – than those central to the Southern Hemisphere cosmology, which Gary Urton and the others had studied around Cuzco. Given that Reiche's theories were astronomically complex and most lay people could not understand them, it needed astronomers to refute them.

Things came to a head one year when Aveni and Urton tried to take low-altitude pictures of the *pampa* from a balloon, as photos from aeroplanes often failed to give enough detail and the planes moved too fast (the same problem we had experienced at Llactapata with our infra-red footage). Unfortunately the balloon came loose from its moorings and started to drift at speed. The support team on the ground were forced to drive at an equal speed across the *pampa* to retrieve it; worse still, the incident was photographed by Renate, Maria's formidable sister, who had joined her in Peru and now flew over the Americans to witness them trespassing over the *pampa* in their jeep.

Josué laughed: 'All hell broke loose. Everyone was called to the hotel – the mayor, the chief of police and me, as the local director of the INC. A *denuncia* was issued against the young Americans for "*profanaciones en la pampa*, desecrating the *pampa*".' It didn't help that, in their cowboy boots and dishevelled seventies clothing, Aveni, Urton and the graduate students looked more like Lynyrd Skynyrd on tour than *estudiosos*, serious scholars. Their older colleague, Tom Zuidema, was not with them at the time.

Josué described the scene in a perhaps unfortunate phrase, given Renate's alleged prior association with the Nazi Party, as being 'like the Nuremberg Trial; the authorities were lined up in their ties and jackets on one side of the room, and on the other side were the *gringuitos*, looking worried and conferring with each other.' Aveni and Urton, with their graduate student charges, were naturally alarmed that they had incurred a possible legal investigation. Maria Reiche herself was not present, having retired to her hotel room, but Renate Reiche was there as 'her presence on earth', triumphantly brandishing the still-wet photos she had just developed, which showed the Americans driving across the *pampa*.

In Josué's words: 'On seeing the photos, the chief of police looked like a man who had just found the last cold Coke in the desert.' The Americans' papers were examined and in the usual way it was discovered that there was an inconsistency somewhere which could be prosecuted. Renate wanted blood. Just at the point when the finest Andeanists of their generation were about to be thrown into the Nasca county jail, Josué was able to show that they were not common *aventureros*, despite appearances, but men of science. This was largely because of the reputation of Tom Zuidema, their older and absent colleague, and a man of considerable standing.

Josué had a far more substantial involvement with the geoglyphs; he was one of a series of quieter but persistent Peruvian investigators into the lines who had been less publicised than the Western interpreters. Indeed, it is little known that the lines had actually been reported before Kosok and Reiche publicised 'the largest astronomy book in the world'. In 1927, Toribio Mejía Xesspe, a young follower of Julio Tello, had published a paper in an obscure archaeological journal, following his early sighting of some of the lines the previous year when he had ascended a nearby hill. Given his Peruvian background, his intuitive assumption was that they were like the *ceque* system of Cuzco, lines marking out the landscape, and that they were ceremonial walkways. It may have helped that he first saw them from land, not the air, and that he was an archaeologist investigating Cahuachi, the main Nasca site near the lines, so he was already trying to put them in context with what he knew of that civilisation. However, because he was young, Peruvian and modest, and the Nasca lines unknown, his findings were not remarked upon for many years, by which time Paul Kosok's more flamboyant 'astronomy book' thesis had gripped the public's imagination.

Josué had developed a new theory of his own about the lines, based on an intriguing feature of both the Nasca textiles and the Nasca lines, again with a more natural grounding in a Peruvian context. The textiles were all woven from a single thread of llama wool – and as I'd been reminded at Palpa, the designs created on the *pampa* were all done with a single line etched in the desert. Josué thought that it was the Nascas' proficiency as weavers that allowed them to execute such pictures on such a large scale in the desert, the preconceived designs emerging slowly and 'blind' just like a weaving – and that the Nascas created them as a way of preserving textile designs for future generations, almost as templates, just as they buried their mummies in those same textiles.

Whether directly linked to weavings or not, the fact that the Nasca designs were made up of a single line supplied a vital clue to their ritual use. It would have allowed the *pampa* markings to be used as continuous ceremonial walkways – both the circular self-contained designs, like the animal figures and the double spirals, but also the long straight ones that run across the *pampa* for miles.

Josué had himself recreated a procession along the line he had built with his schoolchildren; he also agreed with the suggestion that the Nasca not only processed on the lines but danced along them. One pointer to the Nasca love of the ceremony and of dance is the remarkable number of musical instruments that have been recovered, from small drums and tiny whistles to pan pipes, made unusually from clay rather than wood and often decorated with the same images as occur on the geoglyphs.

Indeed, one impressive result of recent work at Cahuachi, the main Nasca site, is that we now know far more about the culture that actually produced the lines. I drove there with Josué down a difficult dirt track, past ancient and rapidly disappearing stands of carob trees. Few of Nasca's 80,000 visitors a year went to Cahuachi, as there was little to see, for one simple reason: on exposure to the air, the friable adobe was exceptionally vulnerable and the rare but possible chance of rainfall made it even more imperative that, once excavated, the city should be buried again. So apart from a few test trenches on the Great Pyramid, all that was visible of the complex, twenty-four kilometres square, was a few large mounds which, if Josué had not told me otherwise, I would have mistaken for sand dunes.

When the American archaeologist William Strong first dug here in the 1950s, he naturally assumed that such a vast site must be the residential capital of the 'Nasca Empire'. Strong was an archaeologist who favoured the direct approach; he was remembered locally for having drunk half a barrel of beer a day when on site and for using a bulldozer to drive a test trench straight through one of the smaller pyramids.

More subtle investigation had taken place since. Both Helaine Silverman and Giuseppe Orefici, on separate digs, concurred that Cahuachi was not a residential capital at all; instead it was a place of pilgrimage, a ritual site, a meeting place, perhaps only occupied at certain times of year and somehow linked to the geoglyphs on the desert *pampa*.

From a viewpoint on the summit of the Great Pyramid, the imperative of the landscape was obvious. Cahuachi was on the upper desert slopes of the Nasca river; looking down from it one saw the green valley, and then beyond the high desert *pampa* where the lines were; beyond that again were the distant dim silhouettes of the mountains from which the water came. Below these mountains and across the desert *pampa* of the geoglyphs lay Ventilla, another Nasca site, but one that is thought to have really been a residential population centre.

So the supposition was clear. At certain times of year (for example November, when the water came down from the mountains), the population of Ventilla would cross the desert *pampa* to get to Cahuachi for what archaeologists loosely describe as 'ritual activities'. While crossing the *pampa*, they could construct and process along a line, perhaps forming into different kinship groups to do so (as it happens, there is a high concentration of lines ending at the side of the river valley directly opposite Cahuachi, although they could have fanned out all over the *pampa*).

What do we know of the Nasca from excavations at Cahuachi and elsewhere? They flourished from around AD 1 to 700. Like the Moche in the north of Peru, they were people of considerable artistry; their early ceramics, of peculiarly fine ware, are often playful. One frequent theme was the innocent pleasure of watching different hummingbirds sip from the same flower. Other pots show foxes, lobsters, toads and a myriad of seabirds, which seem to have had a particular call for this people close to an inland desert (some of the most striking geoglyphs are of a frigate bird and a plunging cormorant with a long neck, loosely referred to as the 'flamingo').

Many of the same themes survive on the textiles, which are far better preserved here than in the north, as the southern soil has a higher nitrate content. Despite the passing of time and the efforts of looters, as heroic here as in the Moche area, there are still plenty of mummified bodies to be found, wrapped not only in contemporary textiles but often in textiles that significantly pre-date the deceased, as if deliberately burying them with antiques.

It was the frivolity of some of the findings made at the buried site that moved me: the tiny flutes and *zampoñas* made from camelid bones; the small woven bags used to store personal supplies of coca leaves and the little cut stems of sugar cane used for keeping needles and thread; most of all, three woolly hats displayed together at the site museum, one red, one green like a tea-cosy, the last beige and floppy.

Headgear and hair seem to have obsessed the Nasca, as with other Andean cultures (at Chavín, I had noticed that the priests undergoing hallucinogenic rituals were often pictured with their hair in elaborate topknots). The Nasca fetished the braiding and the cutting of it, perhaps because the braiding of hair is so naturally allied to weaving. At different Nasca burial sites during my travels, I had been shown hair worn up, down, long, fringed or backcombed, together with a variety of turbans, hairnets and combs made from cactus spines. Some Nasca women grew their hair long so that it could be cut and worn by shamen as wigs. One shaman recovered from a Nasca grave had such hair hanging down to his waist, with an elaborate headband. I was also shown a tiny, woven doll that had been found at Cahuachi, about two inches high, with immaculate, miniature braided hair.

But not all of the Nasca themes were so playful and innocent. Careful dating of the ceramics shows a change in subject-matter as the centuries rolled by. From the straightforward representation of the animal world, other themes emerge, usually associated with human sacrifice and in particular trophy-heads − for which long hair was useful, to hold the heads by − often seen in association with whales (shades of Sechín and the carnivorous fish), or with a feline, winged deity.

And this emergence of a darker side to Nasca art coincided with climatic changes. For we know that, then as now, Nasca was an area particularly susceptible to climatic variables, even by Peruvian standards. There has been speculation that over the centuries the Nasca people found it increasingly difficult to obtain water − hence the great expanse of their aqueduct system. And this ties in with the lines. For the biomorphs, the drawings of life-forms, seem to be much earlier than the geometric lines and the trapezoids that sometimes almost blot them out. If many of the geometric lines point towards water sources, or mountains as the symbols of water, as Aveni and others have suggested, one can imagine a scenario in which the Nasca first celebrated the diversity of life with their biomorphs, much as they did on their pottery, but then turned to straight lines 'that lead to water' as the precious commodity started to dry up and become rarer, almost as if the lines were dowsing rods, which would take them there.

Finally it seems that around AD 350, when the culture was at its zenith, the temples at Cahuachi were struck by floods and earthquakes so violent that some of the temples were split in half. Dead bodies were found under the collapsed walls. Archaeologists like Giuseppe Orefici have argued that this was when the Nasca religion seemed to lose its power, or at least some gods or the ceremonial centre itself lost power, and the place was abandoned. Before leaving the site, the Nasca completely covered it over with a layer of clay, just as archaeologists do today, to seal the monuments. To all intents and purposes the Nasca culture disappeared. It was not until those first flights over the *pampa* that the lines they left were brought properly to the world's attention.

*

I flew over the geoglyphs again. My earlier disengaged experience, and the fact that they were probably never intended to be viewed from the air, any more than the builders of European cities cared what their streets looked like from above, did not prevent this from being a terrific kick, particularly as I liked flying. The view from the small Cessna dipping and weaving over the lines, now that I could put them in context, was as exciting as when I had flown over Machu Picchu and Llactapata.

One way of looking at the lines arose directly from the topography. The Andean peoples liked to create meaning out of landscape. The relationship between the key constituents of their world – the sea, the mountains and the jungle – seems continually to have fascinated them, in their ceramics and textiles, and they loved to play with the iconography that each produced.

But the desert *pampa* was wasteland. It did not fit into this world order. It was some of the most sterile land in the world, with a rainfall of less than an inch every four years.

The lines can be seen as a heroic effort to reclaim this desert, to give meaning to an otherwise blank part of the landscape. So they filled it with all the fecundity of their world – with images of whales, of condors, hummingbirds and monkeys, of fish-eating birds plunging down into the sea and of a frigate bird puffing out its chest as it flew – and then may have processed along these figures to bring them further to life.

If art creates meaning and order out of the inchoate and sterile, the lines can be seen as one of the greatest aesthetic achievements of the pre-Columbian world.

Whether the lines have an astronomical or hydrological interpretation is still open to debate, although it is perhaps simplistic to assume that they need to be 'read' in predominantly one way. After all, if the lines were the Nasca people's equivalent of writing, a 'text in the landscape', as Anthony Aveni described them, why should they exclusively have written about a single subject, whether it be astronomy or hydrology? To extend Aveni's useful comparison of them to an 'unerased blackboard at the end of a busy day of classroom activities', the lines could deal with a whole variety of subjects that caught the Nasca imagination, from the stars to water to biomorphs of particular animals that may have had special kinship associations for the group that made them. When people ask me why the Nasca made the lines, I am tempted to ask them in return why people fly kites; not all human activity is reducible to the primary colours of religion, death and warfare.

What also seems to have misled many interpreters of the geoglyphs, whether from the air or the ground, is the assumption that what mattered exclusively to the Nasca people was the finished result, rather than the pleasure and importance of making them. I question this.

It is useful to take an analogy with the Neolithic and Bronze Age peoples of Britain, who, according to the archaeologist Francis Pryor, were often more interested in the collaborative effort needed to build their ceremonial centres than the actual final structure. Indeed, in some instances he cites evidence that they tore down part of a finished structure so that they could continue building it.

And this connects with another question, so simple that it is rarely asked. Why did the Nasca keep making so many lines? It seems clear that for them too there was no notion of completion, or of particular interest in lines that had already been created, which were often 'drawn over', or partially erased. This is similar to many other Andean cultures, where pyramids were continually being rebuilt, with one layer ritually buried so that the next could be added. This was not out of any sense of dissatisfaction with the previous layer – like, say, a country house being continually remodelled in a newer contemporary style – as often the layers that followed were remarkably similar to what had gone before. No, what mattered was the process of working together in a ritual, communal activity. We know that for the Incas the process of *mit'a*, of shared collective labour, was one of the binding principles that held the Inca realm together and enabled their substantial projects to be built. Emperors such as Huayna Capac had to invent quite spurious building projects for their subjects, and it is a principle with deep roots in the Andean world.

Here was a place where the Nasca people could come together in their kinship groups to make the geoglyphs as communal projects, given that they had no other interest in the *pampa* as a piece of waste ground between two fertile valleys.

The notion is a radical one, for the Nasca may have been completely uninterested in the lasting results of their labours. It is only we, with our Western tradition of passive aesthetic consumption, who assume that the lines were designed to be 'seen' at all.

THE HUARI: THE PEOPLE OF THE
WHITE BUILDINGS

THE E-MAIL BUREAU IN Nasca doubled as the local tattooing parlour; it was open-plan, making it occasionally distracting when I was trying to write while some good-looking girl near by was having a copy of the hummingbird geoglyph tattooed on her buttock. But I found out that an old friend, Adrian Gallop, was in the country and we arranged to meet up at Toro Muerto, in the Majes valley some 200 miles down the coast from Nasca.

Toro Muerto was a site I had heard about from Roz Savage, a member of the Llactapata expedition who had later travelled there, but from virtually no one else. There seemed to be no academic literature on it either, and certainly no tourist infrastructure. Yet as I discovered when I arrived, it was one of the largest petroglyphic sites in the world.

Adrian and his girlfriend Marilú met me at the only place to stay in the vicinity of Toro Muerto, the Majes River Lodge, which belonged to the deeply eccentric Don Julio Zuñiga. Don Julio was in his late fifties and a local landowner of varying fortunes. In a quixotic way, he had tried out every possible form of enterprise, from commercial river-rafting in the local Colca canyon to making *pisco* and staging bullfights; he had built a small bullring at the back of his yard, now disused. Nothing had quite worked out and with considerable enthusiasm he had designated himself instead the unofficial protector and promoter of the Toro Muerto site.

Large and voluble, he reminded me of the 'Majes dancers' I had seen at the El Señor de Torrechayoc festival, with their leather jackets and bulbous masks enacting the dance of the drunks, advancing upon one another, beer belly to exaggerated beer belly, toasting the crowd. Majes was a famous wine- and *pisco*-producing area and its merchants had travelled the country selling (and sampling) their beverages. Now Adrian, Marilú and I were invited by Don Julio to an extensive tasting of his own *pisco* production.

Then we drove off in his pick-up truck to see the site. Julio kept up a running commentary: 'So you've just been to Nasca, have you? You know of course why the lines were built?' I murmured politely that no one seemed quite sure. 'Rubbish! It's obvious. They were designed for punishment. If you were a *delincuente*, a criminal, in Nasca society you were forced to "run the lines".' Adrian and I coughed politely.

It was good to be back with Adrian again. He was half Peruvian, and a man of great gentleness and knowledge of Peru's backwaters. I had travelled down to Espíritu Pampa with him to see Vilcabamba, the last city of the Incas, some years before. He divided his year between London and Peru and was learning to play the *cajón*, the Peruvian box-drum. I had not met his girlfriend Marilú before, who lived near Arequipa, as they had not been together that long.

We were driving close to the Colca river, a valley that even in Peru was remarkable for its spectacular scenery. The river had cut a deep gorge through the valley – so deep that it was difficult to descend from the upper to the lower reaches, as the intervening canyon was too savage. An intrepid Polish team had managed to set up a whitewater-rafting route down the canyon, but most rafters stuck to the lower, more placid reaches, where we were. The upper reaches of the valley, accessible from Arequipa, were a perfect spot for condor-watching, as the birds caught the thermal currents rising up from the gorge.

Don Julio gestured at a village high above the river on the other side. 'And that's where all the local witches come from,' he said forcefully. I was puzzled until Marilú whispered to me that he was talking about his first wife.

Before we got to Toro Muerto, we stopped at one of the many ancient cemeteries on the higher sides of the valley. Turkey vultures were flying overhead in graceful movements – the 'guardians of the tombs' according to Don Julio. After 2,000 years they had not left much meat on the skeletons, which were scattered over the surface together with tomb detritus. I had come across such open cemeteries before in Peru, where erosion had uncovered shallow tombs and looters had done the rest – Huaca Prieta on the northern coast was just one such place – but there was a peculiar desolation to this particular cemetery. It was hard to walk anywhere without treading on skulls. As I unfurled a bit of fabric wrapped around a bone, the vivid flash of cochineal red could still be seen inside the bleached outer layer of cloth. Near by was a spool of wound cotton ready for weaving, together with a fragment of pot showing butterflies on a red background.

More elaborate rock tombs could be found up against the cliffs. Much as in the Nasca valley, there was a striking contrast between the green and productive lower slopes beside the river, with their sugar-cane plantations and vineyards, and the barren wasteland of the higher slopes. It was on these higher slopes that Toro Muerto itself could be found.

The Toro Muerto site was covered with large boulders, 5,000 of which had been covered with petroglyphs, rock drawings. We know that there are 5,000 because they have been counted by Antonio Núñez Jiménez, a Cuban diplomat and former fighter with Fidel Castro and Che Guevara. After the revolution, he was posted to Peru and decided to catalogue every single example of 'rock art' in the country. Luckily Cuban diplomatic postings are infinitely extendable, as it took him many years to complete this Herculean task and Peru has one of the most extensive, dispersed and least-known collections of ancient petroglyphs in the world.

The resulting four volumes of his catalogue were published in a limited edition in Cuba. I had managed to obtain a copy when I had visited Havana some years before. One entire volume of *Petroglifos del Perú* was dedicated almost exclusively to Toro Muerto, which Jiménez hailed as 'the most notable site for petroglyphs in the whole country'.

If it had been difficult to assess the Nasca lines, on which millions of words had been written, how much more difficult was it to view the drawings on the Toro Muerto boulders, in many ways equally extraordinary artistically, but on which virtually nothing had been written at all.

Five thousand individual drawings made up one of the largest fields of rock art in the world – indeed, displays of any sort of art. To give some comparison, at any one time the Tate Modern has 500 works on display, the Guggenheim a similar number. It was difficult to date the stones and there was no large settlement near by, as at Nasca, from which to draw inferences, but the style of the designs would suggest a late Nasca or Huari influence, and the graveyard not far away, with its Huari tombs, would confirm this. The only laboratory dating, conducted by German researchers, had suggested AD 800–900, which again points to the Huari who were flourishing at that time.

The Huari were a highland culture that emerged towards the end of the Nasca period and were based further inland near Ayacucho; they drew many of their influences and style from the Nasca and in many ways were the missing link between that culture and the Incas themselves. Comparatively little was known about them, aside from some fine abstract ceramics and weavings. It was they who had produced the exquisite miniature turquoise figurines I had seen in the Cuzco Museum with the Young Presidents all those months before.

The petroglyphs of Toro Muerto were not labelled or signposted in any way. Since the first report of the lines, which was made only in 1951, little had been done to catalogue them aside from Jiménez's magnificent and eccentric solo attempt. As far as the eye can see, these boulders stretched across the slope, each with its drawings; as I wandered through them, surprise came after surprise, in the knowledge that one was inevitably only seeing a fraction of what was there.

Just as at Nasca, some drawings were figurative, some abstract, while some blended the two. What they all shared was a kinetic energy and vibrancy of design. Many showed dancing figures, often masked and some with strange protruding headdresses. Often they were shown with llamas, condors and other animals, although others were scenes of pure natural history. In one, a fox hid behind a cactus, but ineffectively, with too much of himself showing, so that the bird he was stalking could clearly see him; in another, a landscape was clearly illustrated, with on one side of the boulder a river flowing down to a mountain valley, and on the other, as if crossing a watershed, a different river descending to the jungle, with monkeys and jaguars. Some reminded me of tapestries, with their zigzag lines, abstract swirls and dotted edges. Don Julio compared the abrupt zigzags, which decorated many of the petroglyphs and were a recurring element, to pulse-rate monitors. A more useful comparison might be to musical notation, as the zigzags (and accompanying dots and swirls) were often seen around dancing figures.

There were men with trophy-heads, with elongated fingers, with heads that looked like the sun, or with geometric weavings wrapped around them; some were jumping over animals or touching an eagle's beak with their hands. In all, it was a very populated artistic universe, more so perhaps than the Nasca lines, where the abstract images dominated the figurative ones.

Toro Muerto was aesthetically overwhelming in that on just one rock one could see over 150 individual drawings, using every face of the boulder. At no other point on my journey through ancient Peru had I felt so much like a nineteenth-century traveller confronted by an as yet unassimilated cultural phenomenon. Alongside my wonder at the profusion of drawings was the inevitable question: how was it that such an extraordinary body of work had yet to be properly studied?

Viewing the rock art was hard work. The sun was intense and reflected harshly off the white boulder field and the cliffs above. It was disorientating picking one's way through the petroglyphs and we were exhausted and hungry by the time we had finished.

Don Julio dropped Adrian, Marilú and me off at a small shack down by the river where they served freshwater prawns. People came from far and wide to eat these prawns, far more than came to Toro Muerto. The prawns were kept fresh in underwater cages in the river; stepping out from her kitchen, the woman who owned the place would scoop a handful up straight from the water and into the pan, adding garlic and tomatoes, and serving them with beers kept equally fresh by the cold waters of the river.

The shack had a small television that was showing live images from Celia Cruz's funeral in Miami, together with her music. The death of the old salsa singer, who had spent half a century in exile from her Cuban homeland, had prompted a wave of emotion across the Hispanic world:

> *No ha que llorar, que la vida es un carnaval,*
> *es mas bello vivir cantando.*
> *No hay que llorar,*
> *que la vida es un carnaval*
> *y las penas se van cantando.*

> There's no need to cry, because life is a carnival,
> it's more beautiful to live singing.
> There's no need to cry,
> for life is a carnival
> and singing makes the pain go away.

We were the sole customers in the place – the Majeños came only at weekends. There was a mellow melancholia to the moment: Adrian and Marilú, clearly in love; the TV playing 'La Vida es un Carnaval' as a salsa elegy for Celia Cruz; the priest intoning a funeral oration; and the forgotten gallery of pre-Columbian art we had just seen at Toro Muerto. But this was banished when the cold beers and prawns arrived. Any fresher and they would have been jumping into our mouths.

*

In the little village museum at Aplao near by, no more than a single room, pride of place was given, rightly, to the most extraordinary Huari headdress, which was still wrapped around the skull it had been found on.

The headdress projected forward a full six inches from the forehead, like a second proboscis growing from the skull. Knotted cords, feathers and copper implements were stuck into it. At the very end of the headdress, cactus spines had been threaded through the 'nostril', perhaps in reference to the San Pedro cactus and its shamanic powers. There had been figures with similar unusual headdresses depicted on the Toro Muerto drawings.

The headdress had been dyed red with cochineal. Nearby was a *porra*, a six-pointed sling-stone; there was no indication of whether they shared provenance, but the Huari were known to have been more militaristic than most preceding Andean cultures.

It is with the Huari that one feels most frustration with the lack of written information. Their culture, which flourished from around AD 600 to 1000, left behind unusual cities and heavily influenced the Incas, who learnt much from them, and may indeed lay claim to having been the first to create an 'empire' or sphere of influence right across the Andes – and yet we know less about them than the Chavín or Nasca peoples who preceded them.

Almost to point up this frustration, in the same little museum was a *quipu*, a cord from which other knotted cords hung down. While of all the ancient civilisations, it is true that we know least about Peru because, as an illiterate society, they had no writing, they did leave these *quipus*, the elaborate knotted cords mentioned by the Spanish chroniclers, which have still not been fully deciphered. They remain one of the most tantalising challenges in archaeology, comparable to the Maya hieroglyphics which have only been translated in the last few decades, and potentially as revealing.

There are around 600 known *quipus* around the world, either in museums or private collections. *Quipus* are made up of a central cord from which subsidiary cords are hung. There are numerous variations in colour, weave and even in the knots with which the subsidiary cords are attached to the main one (the word *quipu* simply means 'knot' in Quechua). Along the subsidiary cords, more knots are placed at strategic intervals.

We know from the chronicles that the role of the *quipucamayocs*, the *quipu* interpreters, was an important one in Inca society, from the royal court downwards. Garcilaso de la Vega tells us that even the smallest settlement was supposed to have a minimum of four *quipucamayocs*, often engaged in recording the same statistics so that their tallies could be compared.

These records were used to itemise everything in the Incas' possession, from llamas to weavings. This purely numerical aspect of the *quipus* has been largely deciphered. Using a decimal system, and ascending knots from units of 1, 10, 100, 1,000 and 10,000, the Incas could manage complex accounts. Moreover the amounts recorded in each individual *quipu* could be 'carried forward' to a top-string above it, or a quite separate master *quipu*. Sometimes groups of *quipus* would be tied together, as if a finished set of accounts. From duplicate copies sometimes found with the originals, it seems there was some cross-checking to make sure that what Gary Urton has euphemistically called 'data manipulation' (and we would call 'double accounting') had not taken place.

But only some of the *quipus* follow this relatively straightforward numerical pattern. Others are more random and difficult to interpret. And even with the numerical *quipu*, we have no way of knowing what the numbers refer to, as for the vast majority there is no provenance – the *quipus* have arrived in collections from dealers, from the booty of conquistadors, from looted tombs, or by accident. They could be counting anything from llamas to spondylus shells. The only obvious exceptions are the handful of unusual *quipus* with figurative ornamentation, some of which, for instance, have a figure drinking *chicha* above the main cord, suggesting a tally of drinking supplies. However, this is unusual; as elsewhere, the Incas resisted figurative illustration.

A few *quipus* have known 'provenance'. In 1956, twenty-two *quipus* were found in a earthen jar at Puruchuco, a site near Lima. And there was great excitement in 1996 when a further thirty-two were found at a previously undisturbed burial site in Chachapoyas, at the Laguna de los Condóres. Not only did many of the *quipus* graphically illustrate the principle of numerical hierarchy, where totals from one were carried through to the next, but some were clearly calendrical and broke down a two-year period into twenty-four months and individual days of the year.

A team led by the same Gary Urton who when young had been nearly thrown into jail at Nasca, and was now an eminent professor at Harvard, had recently been trying to analyse these *quipus* and others. The 'language' of the *quipus* and their subsequent decipherment was complicated by the range of different variants within each subsidiary cord. The way in which it was knotted to the main one was a signifier; so was the choice of left-spun or right-spun line with which it was woven. In particular the colour is important, for while most are now faded, it is apparent that the cords come in endless and presumably carefully chosen shades of dye, of a far greater number than the letters in our own Western alphabet.

Gary Urton was the most recent of a long line of distinguished Andeanists to attempt the decipherment of the *quipus*. Determined to unravel their mystery, Urton had started to program the variants of all the known *quipu* into a computer to see exactly how blocks of 'data' repeated themselves, as it was clear they did, often with slight variants, as if a story were being retold. What story that was, we still do not know.

Yet there is a danger that our overwhelming desire for the *quipu* to be proved a form of language could force us into unnatural contortions to demonstrate that what may still just be an accounting device is actually much more. We long for the pre-Columbian civilisations to be able to speak to us direct from beyond the grave; is there some Homeric tale, some Peruvian *Gilgamesh*, of which we know nothing? At the very least, the hope is that the non-numerical *quipus* may have been some mnemonic prompt to a storyteller or historian. The Incas and doubtless their predecessors were interested in the expression and manipulation of their own history, and would presumably have recorded details like reigns and the genealogy of the complicated kinship system.

Almost every major anthropological museum in the world has a *quipu*, usually displayed so that the subsidiary cords spread out in a fan. At one of Urton's first lectures on his attempted decipherment, he showed multiple examples of *quipus* laid side by side, with the cords together, for ease of interpretation. En masse, they looked curiously like a set of the bar codes used by shops to price goods, and the hope for the future is surely that one day they will eventually be 'swiped' and read with as much ease.

What has also become apparent only very recently is the antiquity of the *quipu* system in the Andes. The mass of known examples are naturally Inca. However, some earlier Huari ones also exist, from around AD 900 – one of which I had seen in the rooms of a private collector in Lima. And just prior to the writing of this book, Ruth Shady's team discovered an example at Caral that is over four thousand years old.

The great dream of the Andeanists is that a 'Rosetta *quipu*' will be found, a *quipu* alongside its translation into Spanish. This is not as fanciful as it might sound. The Spanish were interested in the *quipus* and had several translated, more it must be said because they wanted to find out about land yields and legal titles than from a spirit of cultural enquiry. We have some sixteen of these translations. Unfortunately, no one has yet been able to match a translation to an existing *quipu* from which it might have come.

This is partly a matter of materials. The Rosetta stone inscribed demotic and hieroglyphic forms of Egyptian next to the Greek translation on the same tablet. But even if the Spanish had felt the least interest in preserving the skills of the *quipucamayocs*, which they didn't, attaching a *quipu* to a corresponding sheet of parchment is neither practical nor permanent. They are incompatible elements, like the game children play of 'paper, scissors and stone'.

It is perhaps this very incompatibility that drew me back to the *quipus* with fascination whenever I came across them. For it was not just the precise meaning and stories that may be buried in the coloured knotted cords, but a more basic and undisputed truth that they revealed: when the Andean peoples chose to record information, whatever that information was, the medium they chose was not writing, as with every other ancient civilisation, but cloth – for what is a *quipu* but a form of weaving?

*

The display in the little Aplao Museum reminded me of the very first time I had seen such weavings.

The Museum of Archaeology and Anthropology at Cambridge is stuck away in a courtyard and little visited, which is a shame, for like its better-known equivalent at Oxford, the Pitt-Rivers Museum, there are wonderful treasures concealed in its old-fashioned cabinets.

As a student I had always been fascinated by the fragments of Peruvian textiles on view – not just the *quipus*, but the weavings. There was one fragment from Paracas that especially intrigued me: a strip of dark black cloth across which red and yellow hummingbirds chased each other and, in a stylised way, sucked from flowers. Smaller green hummingbirds darted after them. Elsewhere, in a closed cabinet, was a magnificent and rare surviving shirt made from the tiny feathers of the hummingbird, of the sort the Inca emperor and his nobility wore.

I knew that Peru had the longest continuous textile record in world history, but this bald fact sometimes obscured the sheer opulence and artistic vitality of the work to a Western world as blind to weaving as the pre-Columbian world was to writing. We are still predisposed to think of weaving as fundamentally utilitarian and that a woven cloak is a garment; yet Andeanists have come to recognise that this was not necessarily so for the pre-Columbian mind.

William J. Conklin, an archaeologist based at the Textile Museum in Washington, has said, 'The role of textiles in Andean societies as carriers of meaning and power is different from anything else that I know.' Citing the example of Huaca Prieta, a north-coast site dated to about 1500 BC, and some early textiles there that were not apparently intended to be worn, Conklin notes 'the incredible fact that weaving [in Peru] was invented for what we might call "conceptual art" – to communicate meaning – and only afterward was it used for clothing'.

While at Urubamba I had been able to visit some of the local weaving communities, particularly those near Chinchero, a village some thousands of feet higher than Urubamba, where a local family, the Callañaupa, had revived traditional weaving methods that had fallen into disuse, not least because of the lure of cheap synthetic yarns which today's weavers often preferred to the old, naturally dyed fabrics.

The grandmother of the clan, Justina Callañaupa, insisted on giving me a freshly killed guinea pig to eat while we talked; this was disconcerting as I disliked the taste, yet it would have been rude to refuse. I knew also that my children were so sensitive on the subject of 'eating pets' that they would give me considerable grief when I returned home.

Sitting outside her hut above the village, Justina had brought out old pieces of weaving that she had been left by her grandmother. Many were dyed with cochineal red. Cochineal comes from an insect that lives on prickly pear cacti as a parasite; it is both dye-fast and produces a red of extraordinary intensity. The Spanish conquistadors were amazed, as they had seen nothing like it before – indeed, along with the potato, if less heralded, cochineal was one of the great exports from the New World to the Old. The Spanish commanded a monopoly of the trade back to Europe, and so were able to exclude England; 'the fiery Latin red' attributed to the Mediterranean countries by the colder Protestant North may well come from this. Certainly cardinals were able to obtain a much richer scarlet cloak after the conquests of Peru and Mexico, where cochineal was also found.

On a previous journey Adrian and I had stopped at an old hacienda in Limatambo and seen fields of these cacti. I had rubbed the parasitical mould between my fingers to stain them red. Cochineal was a valuable crop, selling at $12 a kilo in Peru and between $50 and $80 a kilo on the world market. The Andean peoples had always used a variety of ingenious methods to sustain it, planting new cacti from stock already infected by the beetle and then fertilising each cactus with wood-ash. They also kept animals away by enclosing the plants and even lit fires and put up cloches on cold nights to prevent the insects from freezing. Some 200 tonnes of cochineal are still produced in Peru each year, a fabulous amount when you consider that each insect weighs less than an ounce. Peru is the only country in the world to produce it in such quantity; it is the country that has dyed the world red.

For Andean weavers, cochineal has always been infinitely versatile. When mixed with urine, lime or old *chicha*, it can produce many shades of red. Other colours can be extracted from plants – beige from cactus stalks, soft green from a plant called *chilca*. But the cochineal insect was the most important source of dye; it gave a red of such vibrancy that it is still used for Campari and certain shades of lipstick.

'Red is the colour of strength for weavers,' said Justina. 'My grandmother needed it. Once it rained for forty days and forty nights. There was no food. Many died. Another time the village was afflicted by the "blood-coming-out-of-mouth" disease. Our shaman got rid of it by putting all the victims' goods onto a llama and sending them down the mountain to the next village.'

Although in the weavings Justina showed me, no two hand-woven pieces were ever the same, there were motifs that recurred: the diamond pattern of *inti*, the sun; figures of eight formed by the scythe, the *cuti*, turning back on itself; and Incaic flowers, like the *loraypo* and the *cantuta*, the bright red flowers that the Incas held in particular regard. The emperors were showered with them when they passed, and their attendants followed behind to sweep up the flowers after the litter.

The use of cochineal seems to have extended back to the very earliest weavings. On my travels I had seen it on five-thousand-year-old scraps of cotton, stained into the floor of Moche pyramid-tombs, and wrapped around the head of a Huari shaman. It had bled through the prehistory of the country.

When the Italian geographer Raimondi visited the Nasca area in the nineteenth century, he managed to miss the lines completely (perhaps because they were so unusual, he wasn't looking for them), but he did note that the inhabitants still maintained the ancient tradition of obtaining and using cochineal.

The tradition had survived the Conquest. After leaving Justina (with some uneaten guinea pig surreptitiously hidden in my handkerchief), I had visited the church in the same village of

Chinchero, which the conquistadors had erected over an old Inca palace, an ostentatious symbol of cultural domination. At first sight it had seemed a classically beautiful seventeenth-century church, with altars and frescoes in the Spanish baroque style, and an image of the virgin of Montserrat. But looking closer, one could see that the roof had been dyed a deep cochineal red, unusual for a church. The Indian artisans had also smuggled their own iconography into the Christian decorations – there were images of the sun, moon and *cantuta* flowers, just as in the weavings, with puma heads among the angels.

In a similar altarpiece in Cuzco cathedral, Christ and his disciples could be seen eating guinea pigs at the Last Supper. The Spanish may have conquered Peru, but the pre-Columbian inheritance runs deep within it.

*

Back in Urubamba I could spend more time with weavers in the high local villages above the Sacred Valley, where not a mobile phone or jacuzzi could be seen. I hired mules and horses, and travelled with Sally and the children on a journey of some days over the high passes to Lares, an area which produced some of the best weavings. Outside the adobe huts, or just inside where the light could still reach, women sat on the hard baked clay and wove on their looms, with corn drying around them and a few children and pigs rooting around.

Any suggestion that this was a case of 'from time immemorial, Quechua Indians have woven their textiles and kept their pigs', like some dull anthropology book, was dispersed by a bit of direct conversation. A millenarian evangelical cult had been sweeping the hills, converting many, who now formed isolated and different communities from the rest; they were known as *Israelitas*, and abstained from alcohol. There was friction between the evangelical cult and other villagers. One reason that the Maoism of the Sendero Luminoso had taken such root in the mountains was the native taste for such millenarian cults.

At one small isolated homestead, I talked to the daughter of the house who was using a loom outside the door. A Peruvian friend with me, who knew the family, told me that the father had refused to let the attractive girl marry, or go to the local *tinquys*, the highland fairs that were also marriage markets, because she wove so well and he wanted her to look after him in his dotage.

It was winter now in the Andes and the fields were lying fallow, the red clay showing through the stubble. Mules were set to work to trample the beans in teams of four, while the women trod down the potatoes themselves, to extract the moisture so that they would dry into *chuño*, a nutritious but dull store-cupboard ingredient for soups that could last for two or three years (and tasted as if it had lasted for twenty). As we passed by the high valleys, we saw the women in their full layered skirts clomping up and down on the potatoes with the exaggerated high steps of pantomime horses.

Riding proved a great success with the children. Leo was at an age when he was too small to walk far and too large to be carried. But on small sure-footed Andean ponies, he and the other children could get up some substantial passes and see the highlands of the Andes at their best; one night we camped at 14,000 feet by a beautiful spot near a lake, with the jagged twin peaks of Pitusiray in the distance. Even though we had to end the trek abruptly when the weather closed in and one of the children became ill, overall the experience of parachuting into a foreign culture and school had worked well; neither Daisy nor Owen would necessarily remember much Spanish but Sally and I felt that in later life they would always be able to jump out of the plane.

One day an unusual visitor arrived at our house in Urubamba. Vera Tuleneva was a young Russian woman who had studied fine art in St Petersburg and had been a guide at the Hermitage. After a strange series of coincidences, she had ended up in Peru as a protégée of Nicholas Asheshov, through his Russian connections. Nick had told me: 'When Vera arrived at the hotel, after a hard time travelling, she had virtually nothing, not even a pair of boots. She spent the first few days eating more than I have ever seen anyone eat.' Following marriage to a Peruvian, quickly annulled, she had settled in Cuzco and made it her base for a series of peripatetic expeditions.

For Vera was an explorer. She had already travelled through areas of the Vilcabamba that I knew nothing of, and had ranged further afield to Bolivia, in search of traces of Paititi, a supposed lost city of the Incas, which enterprising adventurers still occasionally tried to find as a good excuse for an expedition. Vera's interest, however, was more rigorously academic – she had traced the story of Paititi through the libraries of Cuzco, before setting off on her own to find it, and she could be dismissive of those whose standards of scholarship were not up to hers.

Vera had striking good looks – Russian pale skin with dark hair and brown eyes – and her arrival at the house for discussions with me on Paititi, however rigorously academic, caused a certain amount of domestic tension. Sally was already quite tired enough of hearing visiting male explorers discuss their exploits. Rather than begin any other long journeys away from the family and our Urubamba base, I was reminded when talking to Vera that the Huari had left cities near Cuzco that I could visit within a day; what was more, one of these, at Choquepukio, was being excavated.

*

A good deal of the ethno-historic information about Andean religion seems to have been concerned with appropriating the ancestors of conquered peoples so that their spiritual powers could be harnessed for the good of their conquerors.

(William Isbell, *Mummies and Mortuary Monuments: A Postprocessual Prehistory of Central Andean Social Organisation*, 1997)

I had passed by Choquepukio many times on buses from Cuzco without noticing it, or even hearing of it. Like many of the key archaeological sites in Peru, it was not listed in a single guidebook. Yet in recent years it had produced some of the most remarkable finds about the Huari, the culture that had emerged from the ashes of the Nasca and swept across the Andean highlands in the first millennium.

Choquepukio lay on top of a small tableland just off the main highway and railway line between Cuzco and Bolivia, a little before the far more famous and extensive Huari site of Pikillacta, the so-called 'place of the flea'. Looking up from the road below, you could see a few of the ruined buildings, if you knew where to look, although their red and ochre colouring blended in with the landscape far more naturally than the austere grey granite of a classic Inca site. It was only on top of the tableland that Choquepukio's true extent was revealed, with its imposing walls twenty-five feet high and its dominating position over the valley and Lake Muina.

I had come here at the archaeologist Gordon McEwan's invitation. Although he had yet to publish much on his findings (a book was in the offing), he had been excavating Choquepukio for the previous ten years and Pikillacta for twelve years before that.

It was a long time since I had been on an archaeological dig in the area or, indeed, that I had been able to; since Ann Kendall's pioneering work at Cusichaca in the early 1980s, there had been precious few other excavations to visit. The Peruvian Government had concentrated resources on restoring ruins for tourists, not digging them up (even Machu Picchu had yet to be properly excavated), while foreign archaeologists seemed more interested in the sites closer to the coast that I myself had been visiting.

Of all the great ancient Peruvian cultures, the Huari had perhaps been least investigated. It was bizarre. Here was a civilisation that lasted some four hundred years, dominating the highlands of Peru and imposing an order and structure that the Incas had inherited – and yet not a single book took them as its main subject. Many Huari settlements remained unexcavated. Indeed, one of their principal sites, at a nearby town called Huaro, had been discovered only in 1995.

This was partly because no one had even been aware of their existence as a separate cultural entity until the 1950s, thinking they were just an offshoot of the neighbouring Tiahuanaco culture in Bolivia. Moreover their eponymous capital, Huari, lay near

Ayacucho, the centre of Sendero Luminoso guerrilla activities and so off-limits to investigators in recent decades. From there they had spread out north and south across the Andes and as far east as here, their border with the Bolivian altiplano and the Tiahuanaco culture that had grown up around Lake Titicaca. The Huari had thrived between AD 600 and 1000, when, like their Tiahuanaco neighbours, the culture seems to have collapsed as an 'empire', around the same time as some abrupt regional changes in climate and rainfall. The most lasting testimony to their memory was that the coach service that covered the same area had named themselves 'Expresso Huari'.

If anyone was finally going to put them more on the archaeological map, it was Gordon McEwan. I sensed that after twenty-five years of study, he had imbibed deeply from the Huari spring. A Texan with a quiet manner, like many archaeologists he had the slightly rumpled, down-to-earth air of an off-duty plumber.

He showed me around the site, conjuring up a vision of how Choquepukio would once have been stuccoed dazzling white. Gordon thought that it was 'primarily administrative, not residential' and a gathering place for the Huari and their subjects. As he put it, 'With no writing, the business of running their large dominions had to be done face to face, and so there had to be substantial and impressive meeting places to get it all done.'

The Huari had a huge area to administer and to do so they had created an impressive infrastructure of roads and cities like Choquepukio right across southern Peru, which the Incas were to follow. Gordon saw the Huari as imperialistic, a tough culture that had imposed these architectural and trading patterns on client nations.

I wondered, diffidently, whether perhaps the Huari culture had been more like the Chavín influence a millennium before, something that had percolated across the Andes by cultural example rather than by force. Choosing my words carefully, as I had already heard Gordon's brisk views on a fellow archaeologist whose field methodology he thought 'insufficiently rigorous', I asked: 'What would you say to anyone who claimed that Huari was an influence, or trade-style, like Chavín, rather than an empire?'

'That they were complete idiots!'

Gordon continued, more temperately: 'No, it is a fair question, but there are clear differences – the Huari imposed a town-settlement plan on sites right across the Andes. If you took the Viracochapampa site near Ayacucho and placed it over Pikillacta, the two would match almost perfectly, as if created from the same template. These were sites designed for administration, places of power, where the local population could be impressed by the imposing architecture on their occasional and restricted access to it.

'The Huari relocated whole peoples from one area of their empire to another, just as the Incas were to do later. They were dictatorial.'

Just a little further along the valley from Choquepukio was the vast and far better-known site of Pikillacta, which likewise seems to have been not residential but instead a centre for trade and for the all-important reciprocity ceremonies in which *chicha* was drunk (and hallucinogenic drugs consumed). Gordon told me, 'You certainly didn't get into Pikillacta – or here at Choquepukio – without privileged access. You went there as a guest, perhaps of the local government. Indeed, once inside you wouldn't have been able to get around without a guide. Imagine narrow passageways, forty-foot-high walls, all painted a blinding white and designed with labyrinthine complexity. Even the floors would have been covered with white gypsum plaster. It would have been deliberately dis-orientating for any visitor.'

I remembered that when I'd visited Pikillacta in the past, I had found it peculiarly difficult to assimilate. While Machu Picchu had an intuitive architecture accessible to anyone, and thus has become the world's favourite archaeological centrefold, Pikillacta was, to say the least, counter-intuitive; there were hardly any windows, doorways or even streets, yet over 700 buildings, many with those high intimidating walls.

However, it shared one feature with Machu Picchu: both were cities built in an unlikely, difficult location. Pikillacta was situated on the slopes of the extinct volcano of the same name. As Hiram Bingham had pointed out on his first visit in 1911, it was a curious place to choose, for the local soil was poor and the volcano had no natural source of water. As at Machu Picchu, water supplies needed to be brought from afar by canals that had since decayed, so the site was never reoccupied after the Huari by the Incas or the Spanish.

There was a puzzle over what these buildings could have been used for; they certainly didn't seem suitable to live in. One suggestion was that they were vast storehouses for goods which the Huari extracted as tribute from the local population. The high windowless walls might have been good for storage, but very few artifacts had ever been found to indicate such use, as one would expect, despite extensive excavation. I couldn't help wondering whether some of the storage sheds had deliberately been kept empty, like the dummy warhead-silos of the Cold War, suggesting a huge concentration of stored wealth to the client peoples who, Gordon suggested, would have come here in supplication to the Huari.

We looked across the valley. As with the Incas, the Huari were not afraid to landscape on a massive scale. Gordon pointed to evidence of their extensive canalising around Lake Muina, which glittered in the morning sun: 'Yes, they liked "terraforming" their dominions.'

He rolled the word 'terraforming' around his mouth as if it were a fine Merlot. Every so often Gordon would slip into such archaeology-speak, but then plain Texan English would break back through again:

'Now this really is something else – it may have been a "mummy storage depot".'

I did a double take. We had reached the most substantial building of the Choquepukio site, with niches set high up in the walls, a building Gordon referred to loosely as 'the temple'. The recessed niche was an architectural motif I was familiar with from Inca architecture. Yet, as Gordon reminded me, the Huari had already developed it as part of their corporate branding of sites across the southern Andes almost a thousand years before the Classic Inca period.

He theorised that the high niches might have held the mummified remains of both the Huari's own ancestors and those of client nations, to keep them under control. Then state business would have been conducted in front of these mummies for added weight and legitimacy, what Gordon described as 'administration carried out in front of lineage ancestors'. I remembered the old Addams Family cartoon joke when a character turns to a skull and says: 'Well, at least Grandfather agrees with me.'

The idea of holding the mummies of client nations effectively hostage was one the Incas were later to use, as we know from the Spanish chroniclers, although there is less confirmation of the use of niches to do so. The stored bones of ancestors were not just for veneration. Traditionally in the Andes they had a practical advantage: they proved you had inherited from your ancestors the land and water rights to the area.

As Gordon put it: 'I think the Huari used this belief to create their empire. They captured other peoples' mummies or ordered them to bring their ancestral bundles to places like Pikillacta or Choquepukio for storage. The only access you then had to your ancestors – and so to your land and water – was through the state. If you didn't comply, the Huari destroyed your ancestors, which left you destitute. The Incas did the same thing, but it was probably the Huari's idea.'

Gordon pictured a scene in which the impressed and disorientated visitor would have been confronted in this dazzling-white plaza by costumed priests, before reciprocal drinking ceremonies and the possible consumption of psychotropic drugs (much as at Chavín), all in front of the mummified remains of local ancestors. As a way of psychically instilling obedience and fear in a client tribe, it was a form of highly developed mind control.

The Incas never acknowledged their considerable debt to the Huari. They liked to cling to the belief, as Cieza de León reports, that before them there were only naked savages and that 'these natives were stupid and brutish beyond belief. They say they were like animals, and that many ate human flesh, and others took their daughters and mothers to wife and committed other even graver sins.'

Like any state-sanctioned view of history, this was a self-serving one; the idea that the Incas had created themselves *ex nihilo* was a powerful myth, which the Spanish accepted without question. In an oral culture, remembering back more than a hundred years inevitably led to a foreshortening of events. But recent subtle studies of Inca historiography have shown that the Incas extended this further, by ignoring not only their predecessors but their own early successes and making it sometimes appear as if the spread of their enormous empire had been the achievement of just one Inca emperor, the great Pachacuti, and his dynastic succession in the century just before the Spanish arrival. Pachacuti had been a usurper, and the achievements of the previous line of emperors may consequently have received short shrift. I remembered the old English tag: 'Treason shall never prosper, for if it prosper it is no longer treason.'

At one end of the main temple-building, Arminda Gibaja, Gordon's Peruvian colleague, had made an important discovery some years previously: a stone *huaca* or shrine, with offerings around it including fine ceramics, spondylus shells and the small beaten-gold figure of a llama. This *huaca* had at some stage – perhaps quite close to the Inca period – been ritually buried, one reason for its preservation from looters. On uncovering it Arminda's team had found the bones of llamas, which seem to have been sacrificed at the interment.

Excavation had also revealed a complicated set of five channels across the floor of the temple, directing water through rather than around the building, so that the combination of water and stone, so potent later for the Incas, could be present for ritual occasions. The name Choquepukio, while the traditional local name for the site and not necessarily the historical one, means 'Golden Spring'.

It was in this same building that Gordon and Arminda had concentrated much of their digging; a test trench crossed it. And it was a reminder of one question that I had: why bother to excavate here at Choquepukio as well as at the much larger Huari site of Pikillacta just down the road, which Gordon had already looked at? His answer was that, unlike at Pikillacta, there was a much longer occupation at Choquepukio that both preceded and followed the principal Huari occupation, probably because of the natural water source. This led to a rarity in such sites: what archaeologists call a 'stratigraphic column' starting at about 375 BC and stretching right up to Inca times, a record of continuous occupation. One reason that so few similar sites existed was that the Incas tended to 'terraform' away all traces of previous occupation before they occupied a site. At Choquepukio, a relatively small settlement, they couldn't be bothered.

So Gordon and his colleagues could study the direct development between the Huari and Inca cultures in a way that had never been possible before. The work at Choquepukio was a confirmation of what other scholars had long suspected: that as one influential commentator, Michael Moseley, summarised it, there had been a far more 'incremental expansion' by the Incas that had begun long before Pachacuti and probably drew on deep Huari roots and their notions of statecraft and state control.

It was impossible to understand the Incas without understanding the Huari. My sense was that this process, which I had seen develop since 1982 and my first visit to Peru, was going to roll on remorselessly as scholars demythologised the Incas' accounts of their own origins and revealed the Huari layers underneath. Even Cuzco, for long thought of as the capital the Incas built for themselves on a green-field site, may actually have been a Huari city beforehand.

Gordon and I settled down to a cup of coffee at the tent that served as his headquarters. Looking out over the site and the fieldworkers below, I reflected that while the results might be intriguing, the process of archaeology had to be one of the dullest spectator sports ever invented. Watching tortoises race would be more fun (at least you could take bets). And the excavations here seemed initially to be no more exciting than those I had witnessed in the past. I recognised the slow ennui, the paperbacks read on little camp stools, the whistle blowing at regular intervals, the local workers waiting for their pay because it was Friday. Moreover the exposed position on the plateau, with an enervating and constant wind whipping dust into our faces, meant that I was still wearing a down jacket long after I would have taken it off back in Urubamba.

I prepared myself for a lengthy cold day before we headed back in the team van to Cuzco.

But while I was still talking to Gordon, at just after 11 in the morning, a workman rushed up to hand him something. There was a sudden and huge commotion coming from one of the digging areas below. The graduate fieldworkers were shouting in the background. I had never seen so much excitement in the usually somnambulant world of archaeology. It was as if a pike had entered a millpond.

Gordon was looking at an object in his hand. He could hardly contain his excitement. I came closer to see what he had cradled on his palm.

He held up the miniature turquoise figure of a man, exactly like those I had seen in the Cuzco Museum. It was so intensely green that for a moment it looked like a child's toy from a cereal packet, a plastic Ninja Turtle. But this was made of turquoise. In over twenty-five years of excavating, Gordon had never found anything like it. Of course there had been many ceramics and fragments of bone, useful for dating the site and charting cultural influences. But this was the real thing, even for the most sober-minded archaeologist, and everybody on the site knew it. The workmen and graduate students all crowded around. Arminda Gibaja came up from her tent below.

The only such figurines ever found before on a Huari site were way back in 1927, at nearby Pikillacta. These were the set displayed at the Cuzco Museum, which I had seen with the Young Presidents delegation at that strange cocktail party so many months before. A few had percolated through to the international art market from looters, but were of much lesser archaeological value as no one knew where they had come from, so they were 'without provenance'. An archaeologist will say that an artifact comes 'with provenance' with the same tone of reverence as others use for saying that a mother is 'with child'; it is their holy grail.

The detailing on this one was exquisite – and as I held it in my own hand, I realised with a shock that it had precisely the same protruding headdress that I had seen on the mummified figure at the small museum in Aplao and on some of the Toro Muerto petroglyphs near by. Gordon pointed out to me the fine detailing on the feet of the figure, which helped establish authenticity, not that in this case, having been found on site, it was needed.

Later, as we relaxed over lunch (for the rest of the day was effectively declared a holiday) Gordon told the story of the previous find in 1927. Then a *hacendado*, a local landowner, and his men had come across the set of forty figurines when they were 'prospecting' a corner of Pikillacta. In the general excitement, one of the figurines had 'accidentally dropped' into a labourer's boot; he had later sold it for a bottle of beer. Another landowner, jealous of the find, had immediately embarked on extensive digging near by and found a further set, again of forty pieces.

Each set was of the same number and included figurines with markedly different regional characteristics. It was hard to escape the inference that they might somehow represent all the client states of the Huari – that just as they may have held the physical remains of their subjects' ancestors as hostages, so too this was symbolic of their possession of other tribes. There were figures with jungle dress as well as more naturally Huari mountain costumes, as if each one was a member of the Huari confederation. And there is still in the highlands a fetishisation for the miniature, the token of the real thing, like the little gold llama found here at Choquepukio beside the stone *huaca* in the temple. One of the Spanish chroniclers most sympathetic to Inca traditions, Juan de Betanzos, who married an Inca princess, recounted how a set of miniature gold figures representing the Inca dynasty was buried in the main plaza of Cuzco at a dedication ceremony held by Pachacuti.

Gordon blessed the earth with a whoosh of beer, '*pagando la tierra,* paying the earth' in his own dedication ceremony, using the local formula of propitiation for good fortune. One of the graduate students told me that she had 'never seen Dr McEwan looking so happy'. The usual dyspepsia of any archaeological supervisor had been momentarily relieved. Certainly I couldn't believe my own luck in being there on the one day when such a find had been made.

I wandered further up the hill to a few *chulpas*, small tombs, dotted above the ruins. These looked more characteristically Inca, with a trapezoidal entrance, and may have been built later. The area seems to have maintained its spiritual potency after the Huari's demise, as Huascar Inca, one of the last Inca emperors before the Spanish Conquest, had a *moya*, a 'country estate', near the lake (the Spanish were convinced that his treasure had been deposited in its waters and made fruitless attempts to find it).

Looking down I tried to picture Choquepukio below when it was inhabited by the Huari: the lords in their feathers at the centre of an enclosed maze with shiny white walls; their supplicants drugged or drunk with ritual intoxication: the water flowing though elaborate channels to a *huaca* and then leaving again; the mummies or deities of local client peoples perhaps stationed in the high niches of the walls so as to be visible to all.

Not for the first time, I was reminded of something Gordon had said earlier: that the pre-Columbian civilisations are so removed from Western conceptions of civilisation, empire and literacy that they are the nearest we can get to encountering an absolutely alien mindset.

THE ISLAND OF THE SUN

I COULD NOT BE in a more different place. While at Choquepukio the hills, valleys and even the Huari remains were unremittingly brown, now everything around me is suffused with an intense blue.

I am on the shores of the Island of the Sun, on Lake Titicaca, at 12,500 feet. The Island of the Sun is so called because the Incas believed it to be the sun's birthplace.

Nothing can compare to the quality of light over Titicaca; the clear air at high altitude combines with the fast-moving clouds and weather system to create a constantly shifting theatrical display of such a deep blue that the resulting photos often look as if artificial filters have been used. From my island viewpoint, I can see small twisters forming on the lake and spinning like tops across its surface; the locals fear the twisters not for any physical destruction they cause but because they are thought to suck the moisture out of the soil.

The lake looks as if it has been brushed with one of the cactus-spine combs the pre-Columbians used, so fine are the lines radiating out from the small islands. To the east, the sun is slowly coming up over the low ridge of the Island of the Moon and burnishing the soft honey-coloured walls of Pilko Kayma, the Inca ruins right on the shoreline of the Island of the Sun. I let the sun warm me, as it is a bitterly cold dawn, even with the flask of coffee brought from our small lodgings along the headland.

Such a picturesque spot naturally drew the attention of nineteenth-century travellers in the Andes, like the pioneering American again, E. G. Squier, who tried to capture it in watercolours, drawings and early photographs, copies of which I have with me. I can see from these that much has decayed in just the last hundred years, but Pilko Kayma is still a building of character and force.

It has an impressive eastern frontage to the sea, although the upper storey has slipped away considerably over time. On both this and the southern side, the doorways into the complex are flanked by two blind niches of an equal size, well over the height of a man. The central doorways lead into an intimate warren of connecting rooms, some with fine corbelled roofs, a rarity in pre-Columbian Peru. However, my eye is drawn more to the blind niches on either side of the doorways, a good example of a recurring theme in Inca architecture, the juxtaposition of the revealed and the hidden: through this door you can enter, if privileged to do so; through these other two you cannot.

There is a peculiarity to the Inca architecture that I immediately notice: interspersed with the usual grammar of niches and trapezoidal doors are the step and diamond motifs of an older Andean style, that of Tiahuanaco, the contemporaries of the Huari who built the great site that bears their name at the southern end of Lake Titicaca. It is as if the Incas deliberately wanted to refer to an older Andean tradition but assimilate it very clearly into their own, rather like Napoleon's fascination with Egyptology, or Mussolini's with ancient Rome.

For what might now seem a romantic setting was part of a much more calculated design when it was constructed. This was the first building of substance that the thousands of pilgrims who came to the island from all over the Inca realms would have encountered. The Incas exerted an obsessive control over the ritual experience that these pilgrims were to undergo; from the moment they began the pilgrimage, they were to be reminded of the authority that the Incas wielded over the birthplace of the sun.

The best description of this pilgrimage that survives comes to us from Father Bernabé Cobo, a Jesuit priest who visited the island in the early seventeenth century. Cobo was a sympathetic and scrupulous observer of Inca customs and religion who did not let his own beliefs bias his account. This may have been because he was principally a naturalist – most of the books in his vast *Historia del*

Nuevo Mundo concern the wildlife of the New World – but just as Newton wrote more on alchemy than on physics, so Cobo is remembered for the small part of his output that deals with Inca customs, which he recounts with the detachment of a biologist.

He was particularly interested in *huacas*, the Inca shrines, listing them carefully and visiting many, like the Island of the Sun. He reported that 'Titicaca', as he called the island, had previously been a sanctuary but that the Incas had enlarged it considerably and had instituted a pilgrimage with various prescribed rituals for the participants, which began before they even landed.

The pilgrims would first approach along the peninsula that extends into the lake from the south and helps divide modern-day Peru from Bolivia. There is a point where the peninsula narrows and forms a natural point of control, and here they were taken aside by 'confessors', Cobo's Jesuitical choice of word, who, if the offences merited it, would drop a heavy stone on the penitents' backs. After this they had to refrain from salt, meat and *ají* peppers, much to Cobo's disgust as he thought this fasting feeble by Catholic standards. Although he does not say so, they would also probably have foregone sexual relations, the custom elsewhere. The pilgrims would then advance further along the peninsula for more confessions and purification, before setting sail to the Island of the Sun in small reed boats.

Looking out over the lake, I remembered Cobo's strange and poetic description of how 'the water of this island, and on clear days the rays of the sun, shimmer in such a way that from the beach the waves seem like painted snakes of various different colours'. A flock of small black birds with a yellow stripe across their bellies was circling the ruins. Apart from the birds, I had the place to myself and could wander through it in a happily haphazard way. The heat of the dawn sun outside contrasted with the cold, dark interior of the building. From inside the rooms that led off the eastern side, each window and doorway framed a view of Koati, the neighbouring Island of the Moon across the water.

I tried to imagine the intoxication of grace that pilgrims must have felt on arriving. Pan-Andean belief held that this was where both the sun and moon had first emerged from the earth. To be able to look from one birthplace to another, as they gazed over the waters from the Island of the Sun to the Island of the Moon, fulfilled all the conditions of reciprocity that satisfied the Andean mind. Hidden on the other side of the Island of the Moon was a substantial temple for the mysterious rites of female celebrants, mysterious because the distaff side of Inca religion was relatively unrecorded; even the Inca emperor was said by Cobo to be unsure what they did.

It is likely that to be selected or allowed to embark on the pilgrimage was a privilege in the empire, and that those chosen to undertake this once-in-a-lifetime journey from their homeland enjoyed much the same kudos as Muslims who had been to Mecca. Ahead of them lay a five-mile pilgrimage route to the far north of the island and the Sacred Rock, the exact spot from which the sun was believed to have emerged.

They would first have made their way around the coast to the natural harbour of Yumani, either on foot or possibly by boat. At Yumani, the pilgrims climbed up an imposing stairway with high treads, which still delays many visitors unused to such effort at 12,500 feet (local boys make a roaring trade carrying their bags). There was a formal bath called 'The Fountain of the Inca', another indicator of ritual purification as the Incas, like their Christian conquerors, believed in the efficacy of water to wash away sin.

To either side of the stairway were terraces, probably for growing the famous sacred maize of the island. One chronicler suggests that special topsoil was imported to achieve this. Maize does not grow easily on the high altiplano around Lake Titicaca but it can flourish on the microclimate of the islands and we know that the Incas valued maize from the Island of the Sun above all others. The maize was grown not as a simple foodstuff but as the principal ingredient of *chicha*, the corn drink essential to all ritual celebrations. Early Spanish visitors estimated that there were as many as a thousand women employed on the island just to make *chicha*.

As I followed in the pilgrims' footsteps I passed a few modern huts that had sprung up around Yumani offering simple lodging to visitors. The Islands of the Sun and of the Moon were on the Bolivian side of the lake and had never had the same number of tourists as the more organised islands on the Peruvian side − indeed not that long ago the Island of the Moon had been an island penal colony, therefore unvisitable − but a smattering were starting to arrive, drawn to the name, it must be said, more for the idea of heat than culture. I passed two French girls on a hotel terrace just below the ridge-summit who were telling a third that the best thing about the island was the sunbathing.

Certainly Sally and the children were enjoying it. After a memorable ride over from Cuzco on a train kitted out with all the luxury that Orient Express could manage (panelled woodwork, observation car, armchairs that moved around within the carriage), we had settled into a hostel with views over to the small Island of the Moon; Daisy, Leo and I had taken a boat trip over there and found ourselves the only visitors. The hostel was simple and extremely cold at nights − we had huddled together on a pile of mattresses and blankets − so the chance for them to soak up the sun while I went off walking today had been a popular one.

Most visitors to the Island of the Sun had little sense that the island had once been a pilgrimage route − information about it was not readily accessible − and so they were content to enjoy the spectacular sunsets over the lake or to take a small boat around the coast to the main ruins near the Sacred Rock. But I wanted to walk to those ruins, and to follow the traditional high path the Incas would have taken, switchbacking along the long ridge that ran up the island's length.

It was a fabulous path that, by keeping to the highest point of the island's spine, opened up different views of the lake and its archipelago of islands. I felt on a high myself, with just a light pack, an apple in my pocket and the whole day ahead. The sun was shining. To the west, the yawning blue waters of the Bahía Kono made deep inlets in the shore.

The pilgrims taking this route would have been accompanied by musicians and dancers, with the sound of *ocarinas* shrilling in the air. The occasional eucalyptus tree that I passed was a reminder of the much more extensive *polylepis* forests that the Incas would almost certainly have planted (we know that the area nearer the Sacred Rock was forested, for instance), so they could have walked in and out of groves of trees. Scholars are not always good at thinking of the route as being as important as the destination; in this case the experience and process of travelling to the Sacred Rock was at least as important as the ceremony upon arrival.

As they walked down the island the pilgrims would have passed small colonies or control points that the Incas established, the remains of which were still visible. I wandered around one of these called Apachinacapata, the doorways of which had been filled in by locals to use as cattle corrals. Architecturally functional rather than remarkable, it was a reminder that the Incas had brought in colonists to help them run the islands, and moved many of the original inhabitants out, in the brutal policy of *mitamayo*, which the Incas enforced throughout their realm.

Bernabé Cobo records with some amazement that the Incas tried to grow the coca plant on the island, as it usually only grows at lower and more humid altitudes:

> Since it seemed to the Inca [Topa Inca, the emperor] that the only thing lacking which could enhance the grandeur of this temple and shrine was the plant called coca, which was among the most highly esteemed offerings that they had, he decided to plant it on the island itself. In order to compensate for the plant's aversion to this highland location, he made up his mind to have such a deep place dug on the island that it would be warmer there. But carrying out such a difficult undertaking was impossible. Since the island is small and completely surrounded by water, moisture soon seeped in and stopped the work before a very deep hole could be dug. In spite of all that, they made such a large hollow that the coca was planted and it started to grow, though this was accomplished with great difficulty.

Coca was a prerogative of the nobility forbidden to the common man, so this would have been another symbol of status and imperial power to visiting pilgrims, if somewhat mitigated because, as Cobo reports, eventually 'the high part of the gully caved in, burying the coca and along with it many of the Indians who were in charge of cultivating it. Therefore the Inca rescinded his order because it was too difficult to carry out.'

As with so much in the Andes, serious investigation of the Island of the Sun had got going very late. Bernabé Cobo's compendious *Historia del Nuevo Mundo*, including his account of Titicaca, was finished in 1653, forty years after he had visited the Island of the Sun, but lay in manuscript form in a Spanish library for 250 years, only finally to be published in 1890, when interest in Andeanist studies was awakening. Adolph Bandelier, a Swiss archaeologist, made the first examination of the island a few years later, in 1895, and shipped many findings, including some beautiful silver llamas and tunics, back to the American Museum of Natural History in New York. He left a jaundiced account of the contemporary inhabitants of islands, which Hiram Bingham tried humanely to counterbalance when he visited in 1915 after his successes at Machu Picchu:

> The present day Indians known as Aymaras, seem to be hard-working and fairly cheerful. The impression which Bandelier gives in his *Islands of Titicaca and Koati* of the degradation and surly character of these Indians was not apparent. ... It is quite possible however that if I had to live among the Indians, as he did for several months, digging up their ancient places of worship, disturbing their superstitious prejudices and possibly upsetting, in their minds, the proper balance between wet weather and dry, I might have brought upon myself uncivil looks and rough, churlish treatment such as he experienced.

Tactfully put. Bingham went on to point out sympathetically that the Indians did have to deal with 'the most trying conditions of climate and environment', in that after a few months of intense heat they then suffered torrential rains, which could wash away topsoil. His remarks were published in *Inca Land*, a book that is little read nowadays as the Machu Picchu section was superseded in his own later *Lost City of the Incas,* but includes some wide-ranging investigations right across the Andes.

Although Bingham and many subsequent visitors were intrigued by the Islands of both the Sun and the Moon, it took another century before any really substantial work was done, by Brian Bauer and Charles 'Chip' Stanish in 1994–6.

Bauer and Stanish were in some ways the dream ticket of Andean archaeology, in that both came to Titicaca after impressive achievements elsewhere. In his fieldwork around Cuzco, Brian Bauer had rolled back the carpet of Inca history to reveal that their origins were far earlier than their state propaganda and some later archaeologists would have us believe. His colleague Charles Stanish had studied some of the earlier cultures of the Bolivian altiplano, with a hard-headed emphasis on political economy. Their subsequent joint investigation of the Island of the Sun was a model of lucidity and the results, published in 2001 (*Ritual and Pilgrimage in the Ancient Andes*) were refreshingly free of the usual jargon of such archaeological reports.

Bandelier and other early investigators had not realised that the island was a pilgrimage destination before the time of the Incas. By immensely careful work (they reckoned to have walked over every square foot of the island), Bauer and Stanish revealed that the Incas had inherited a tradition of pilgrimage from the earlier Tiahuanaco culture.

And this was one reason I had come here after Choquepukio; for while a seemingly very different site, it was one of the few other places in the Andes where one could see how the Incas had built on the legacy of a previous culture, in this case on that of the Tiahuanaco, the Huari's neighbours in Bolivia. Choquepukio marked the edge of the Huari sphere of influence, and there was a very natural watershed and pass to the east as a transition to the Tiahuanaco culture began – not that in some ways they were that different. Rather like the countries of Peru and Bolivia today, the Huari and Tiahuanaco could be seen as having shared cultural values under different administrations, and in some places they seem to have coexisted without conflict.

It was the Tiahuanaco who had built the first pilgrimage shrine for outsiders to the island, near the Sacred Rock at a place called Chucaripupata. Excavations show that from around AD 700, when the Tiahuanaco state was expanding, the site seems to have been important, with great numbers of *qeros*, drinking vessels, being found, as well as elaborate objects in turquoise and metal brought in from afar. Bauer and Stanish argue that Chucaripupata was already 'a pilgrimage centre of regional significance' for the Tiahuanaco. They also threw offerings out at sea to the north of the island and built a temple on the Island of the Moon, from which at least six golden Tiahuanaco pumas have been recovered and numerous other signs of their presence.

So when the Incas 'terraformed' the island into a place of pilgrimage, which legitimised their own rule and place in history, they were building on the work of a previous civilisation, or at least reviving it. There had been a lapse of some four hundred years between the demise of the Tiahuanaco culture in around AD 1000 and the growth of the imperial Inca state from AD 1400, during which time the mass pilgrimage tradition had lain dormant, or was celebrated just in the locality. Cobo is explicit about this in his telling of the story – that an old guardian of the site, a Colla Indian, had journeyed to Cuzco to tell the then emperor, Topa Inca, about the shrine and how revered it was locally; that Topa Inca had travelled to the island himself and immediately seen how appropriate it would be to adopt it, 'taking into consideration how much the Incas boasted of being descendants of the sun'. He had set about building the various temples and lodgings necessary 'to extol it with all sincerity'.

In the process the Incas had simply razed Chucaripupata to the ground. A site that mirrored Tiahuanaco was not appropriate. Bauer and Stanish put it brutally and succinctly: 'In a word, the Inca destroyed any vestige of the remaining Tiahuanaco occupation.'

Even the path I was following was a legacy of the Tiahuanaco and earlier cultures, adapted by the Incas for their own ends, just as many of their famous roads in Peru were built over Huari ones. But the Incas were not simply harnessing the cultural power of an earlier mighty civilisation – they were making a claim for a mystical origin themselves. They had always been concerned to exalt their origins and the whole cult of mummified dead emperors was designed to build up an unstoppable genealogical weight behind their power – exemplified by the sun-shield, the Punchao, which was meant to contain the dried hearts of previous rulers. Now they linked the Island of the Sun to one of their creation myths: that the original Adam and Eve of the Inca line, Manco Capac and his sister Mama Occlo, had emerged from this same island.

In a complicated way, on which much ink has been spilt by academics, this story ran in parallel with a quite separate origin myth: that Manco Capac and Mama Occlo had emerged from a cave much nearer to Cuzco, a legend probably far closer to the actual emergence of the tribe as a dominating force in the Andes. But the idea that the Incas could simultaneously enjoy two quite separate accounts of their beginnings was not so unusual. It was similar to Britain in the Middle Ages, which on the one hand could trace its political and civic traditions back to Rome, but still enjoy an appeal to Arthurian legend, with the idea of a patriotic legitimacy being forged on the Isle of Avalon along with Arthur's sword.

After walking the pilgrims' path for a while, I felt I had its measure: striding across agriculturally arid land in a proprietorial way, it was broad and purposeful. I could see how it could have formed part of the cleansing ritual of purification for the pilgrims. Although it lay less than a thousand feet above the lake, the perspective down to the water's edge gave the illusion that one was walking off the end of the world. The sun had risen to the point where the lake's surface was glowing an incandescent white.

I was getting close to the Sacred Rock and the northern end of the island, and I could see the last snaking headlands descending to the lake ahead of me. The rich maize-growing areas of the island were lower, down by the shore, so I had met no local farmers on the path but only a few children scampering past to the island's only school. When the enterprising Joseph Barclay Pentland visited the island for the British Government in 1827, while undertaking the first real geographical survey of Bolivia, he found a mere 120 inhabitants; it is still sparsely populated today, with just three villages of any size.

To see how the Incas had staged the climax of the pilgrimage, I followed the route of the traditional path as it slipped down towards a place called Kasapata beside the lake, almost certainly the site Bernabé Cobo referred to when he talked of 'an impressive *tambo* or inn for the pilgrims to stay in, one quarter of a league before one reaches the temple'. Today the overgrown remains of a large five-doored building well over a hundred feet long blend so well into the surrounding fields that they are easily missed. The remains of large *chicha* jars found here confirm that this was a place of feasting before the pilgrims entered the sacred area itself. The five-doored building faces onto an area whose most remarkable feature is a large carved stone of the sort the Incas liked to celebrate so much; the stone complements the monumental peaks of the Bolivian cordillera in the distance.

Each feature of the landscape now started to be dramatised with great intensity for the pilgrims. Approaching the Sacred Rock, they passed through three ritual gateways: the first was called Pumapunku, meaning 'the door of the puma' because a stone puma guarded it; the second, Kentipunku, 'the door of the humming-bird', was covered with the minute feathers of that bird; the final gateway, Pillcopunku, 'the door of hope', was covered with the larger green feathers of the pillco bird. At each of these passages, the pilgrims would have been interrogated by the confessors and guardians of the shrine to see whether they could proceed further. At the very last gate, Pillcopunku, in the words of one Spanish chronicler, 'Its custodian priest effectively persuaded the pilgrim to examine his conscience thoroughly, because there was absolutely no passing this last door with a guilty one.'

There is reason to think that not all pilgrims were necessarily able to proceed through even the first gate, regardless of the extent of their sins – that due to lower rank or status, they may have been siphoned off to a viewing platform just outside the sanctuary walls; from here they could see the Sacred Rock from a distance and the ceremonies in front of it involving the more elite participants.

However, even an Inca emperor, and all Topa's successors visited the Sacred Rock, would have followed his example and removed their shoes respectfully before approaching the ceremonial area.

The Sacred Rock today is not immediately impressive. A large sandstone outcrop, the pilgrims' path first approaches its longer side where it slopes down towards the sea. Then, having passed the sites of the original three gateways, the path crosses around the rock to its inner, more concave side, which faces onto a ceremonial plaza.

There is a simple reason why the rock does not immediately command attention. In the Incas' time, the longer side sloping down to the water, which the pilgrims first saw, would have been covered, in Cobo's words, by 'a curtain of *cumbi*, which was the finest and most delicate piece of cloth ever seen'. Given the primacy of cloth in the Andean world, no greater statement of its importance could have been made. The cochineal red and the black of the enormous weaving would have stood out in relief against the deep blue of the lake.

When those elite pilgrims who were allowed to go through all three gateways came around to the other side of the stone, they would have seen the concave side covered in gold and silver, with some hollows for offerings. In front, on the walled plaza, was a receptacle for *chicha*, 'admirably wrought, about as large as a medium-sized millstone', according to Cobo. Moreover when Bauer and Stanish excavated the plaza they discovered an elaborate floor of crushed greenstone, now covered in rubble. There were also finely cut blocks of andesite scattered over the plaza, suggesting a high-status structure possibly torn down by the Spanish as being idolatrous. As andesite does not occur on the island, these blocks must have been laboriously transported here by the Incas, another indication of the site's importance.

Not much remains today. A few of the andesite blocks have had a slab placed over them as a spurious recreation of what 'an Andean table' might have looked like. A plaque on the wall, inaugurated by a recent Bolivian president, states that this was the birthplace of the original Inca couple of mythology, Manco Capac and Mama Occlo, and of the Inca empire, so that the myth instigated by the Incas still lives on – if marred by the fact that the plaque gives the Incas' dates as 1400–1532 BC, not AD.

Brian Bauer and Charles Stanish made a remarkable discovery here and one that interested me because it reflected on our findings at Llactapata. From the plaza the remains of two towers were visible on the peninsula beyond. No one had ever quite known what to make of them, as they were not hollow like the cylindrical tombs or *chulpas* of the altiplano, but filled with rubble. However, the recent interest in the archaeo-astronomy of the Incas led Bauer and Stanish to an inspired observation, made with another colleague, David Dearborn. For those standing on the Sacred Plaza, the sun would have risen precisely between these two markers at the time of the June solstice. Although it had long been known that the Incas used such calendrical markers, none had ever been found before, as the Spanish destroyed all those around Cuzco.

Bauer and Stanish had gone further, building a virtual-reality model of the Island of the Sun at the University of California in Los Angeles, where Stanish was a professor, so that they could plot the sun's course. They had fed into their model the variables required to recreate the precise solstice position 500 years ago, which is marginally different from today. I had seen Charles Stanish demonstrate this model; such expensive but powerful tools were set to revolutionise archaeo-astronomy when applied to similar sites.

The significance of the twin towers had led them to some intriguing deductions about the layout of the area around the Sacred Rock. Given that not all pilgrims were allowed through the entrance gates and that those of lower status (or excessive sin) were directed to the small viewing platform just outside the low walls of the Sanctuary, Bauer and Stanish realised that this platform also lay directly in line with the centre of the Sacred Plaza and the calendrical markers beyond. In this way the lower-caste attendants could also witness the June solstice, if from a greater, more respectful distance; indeed, they would have seen the sun at the solstice rise over the heads of the Inca nobility on the Sacred Plaza. Charles Stanish told me that he compared it to those Christian celebrants who were allowed to sit further away or closer to the medieval altar, depending on their status.

Beyond the plaza and off to one side lay the Chincana, a complex described 'as labyrinthine as Crete' by Bernabé Cobo in the seventeenth century. The name means 'the place where one gets lost' and it was indeed a confusing maze of buildings, configured around closed plazas, with a magnificent setting, looking out over the sweep of a turquoise-fringed bay.

In a slightly magisterial tone, Bauer and Stanish complained of the 'general carelessness of construction here', in that architectural proportions varied considerably across the site, although this may well have to do with a mixed workforce of *mitamaes* drawn from across the Inca realm, all bringing their own building styles.

I was reminded of the *mitamaes* by a local gang of workers from the little village near by, a pretty place I had passed earlier with boats pulled up on its beach. The workers were ostensibly repairing part of the path, with heavy jumpers stripped off in the sun and left draped over the ruined walls of the Chincana, but much of their conversation was about the inebriation of the previous day's Pachamama ceremony, from which many were still recovering. There was a thriving local industry pandering to New Age tourists who came to the islands looking for cultural authenticity, something the locals were more than happy to stage for them, both for the money and because like most Andean Indians, they enjoyed nothing more than putting on a show.

Charles Stanish had told me a story that perfectly illustrated this. When his team had first realised the towers were calendrical markers for the solstice, they had shown the locals, who were deeply impressed, as they had known nothing about it. On coming back for the next season's dig, the archaeologists found that the same locals had now adopted this as a long-held piece of traditional wisdom and were holding profitable solstice ceremonies for French tourists, dressing up as shamen to welcome the sun's arrival between the calendrical stones.

In a way, this showed that the deepest tradition in the Andes was not that of celebrating the solstice but of creative myth-making.

Stripped of its mythological meaning, the actual landscape around the Sacred Rock was relatively unimpressive. The Incas had taken this unprepossessing scrag end of the island, completely useless for crops (they were never ones to waste good agricultural land), and managed to invest it with a historical swirl of pageantry that had elevated it in pilgrims' minds to the centre of the Andean world, or at the very least its birthplace.

E. G. Squier had marvelled in the nineteenth century how

> at almost the very northern end of the island, at its most repulsive and unpromising part, where there is neither inhabitant nor trace of culture, where the soil is rocky and bare, and the cliffs ragged and broken high up, where the fret of the waves of the lake is scarcely heard, and where the eye ranges over the broad blue waters from one mountain barrier to the other, from the glittering crests of the Andes to those of the Cordillera, is the spot most celebrated and most sacred of Peru.

The power of myth and of spectacle was one the Incas knew how to wield as well as any latter-day totalitarian state. To control a large territory you needed more than just armies – you needed a cohesive ideology. By participating in a pilgrimage to a place that was held to be both the birthplace of the sun and of the Incas, the pilgrims bought into this powerful myth and took it back to their homelands across the Andes.

It was a lesson they had learnt from earlier civilisations and, indeed, one that ran deep in the fabric of ancient Peru. From the very early days of Chavín through the making of the lines of Nasca and the earlier pilgrimages here of the Tiahuanaco culture, it was clear that the Andean capacity to generate powerful myths from landscape was one of the most distinctive features of the pre-Columbian mindset. And it continued to this day, as I was to find out by travelling to the most extraordinary of all Andean festivals, Qoyllurit'i.

A PARLIAMENT OF BEARS:
QOYLLURIT'I

The said cross remains up there on the glaciers until the Monday night after the Sunday of Holy Trinity (*de Santísima Trinidad*), a sad night, a melancholy night, of unimaginable cold, when the *ukukus* both of Paucartambo and Quispicanchis climb up to the cross.

From the unedited papers of Juan Ramirez,
The History of our Land of Koyllur-Ritti (1968)

MY FIRST VIEW OF Mahuayani was dreamlike: awakening in the bus at four in the morning, through the windows smeared with condensation I could just make out the low-voltage lights of a shanty town, with shadowy figures moving between blue tarpaulins. There were shouts and cries from outside, indistinct, many in Quechua.

The bus had slowed to a continuous crawl, never quite coming to a complete rest, as it searched for a place to stop and the pilgrims tensed themselves to get off. The couple from the jungle huddled together beside me – the man had been joking for much of the journey with his *negrita*, his gold teeth flashing, but now he fell quiet.

The pilgrims were already battered after the six hours we had driven through the night from Cuzco. Many had held handkerchiefs over their faces to keep out the thick dust thrown up by the other pilgrim trucks and buses on the dirt roads. I had managed to sleep fitfully on the back seats that John Leivers had commandeered for us, perhaps on the old intuition that this was where the bad boys sat at school – if so, it had been a mistake, as the higher seats kept slipping us forward during the night. I had awoken at regular intervals to find myself perched precariously on my buttocks, half on the seat, half on the floor.

And then we were out and standing in the centre of an open sky-bowl of mountains. I suddenly felt wide awake, and very cold. A truckload of *ukukus* came by, sitting high up on the side wall of their pick-up and careering in the potholes. With one particularly savage jolt, a woman *ukuku* on the corner fell off, from a height of some twenty feet, and hit her head hard. She was semi-concussed and a concerned crowd gathered round her, asking whether her teeth were all right. The other *ukukus* on the bus fell silent, but did little to help her. There is a tradition within Qoyllurit'i that the *ukukus* should live a bit on the edge, that some should die on the ice (as indeed some do this year).

The *ukukus* are the officiating guardians of the Qoyllurit'i festival. They have a fearsome reputation, dressing in bear costumes with full balaclavas and criss-crossed as if with war-stripes. The *ukukus* speak in high-pitched screams and carry whips, which they use on each other and on pilgrims who do not follow the unwritten laws of the Qoyllurit'i pilgrimage. But there is also a playful, anarchic edge to them.

More *ukukus* pulled up on another crowded pick-up truck shouting, '¡Que calor, que calor! How hot it is!' in the blue mist of the dawn. Some begin to practise their high-pitched camelid squealing, a frightening noise that cut through the dawn like cheese wire. It is meant to be the voice of the llama speaking through them, or rather through the small mannequins of themselves that they carry strapped to their waists, a curious form of ventriloquism, that allows them to be both other-worldly and frivolous.

From the remote road-head village of Mahuayani, a path led up to the Sinakara valley, where Qoyllurit'i, the greatest and most extreme of all the Andean festivals, is held. It culminates in a night-time ceremony on glaciers 17,000 feet high and has a reputation for intense cold. The pilgrims huddled around me on the bus had discussed it nervously as '*un matador*, a killer'.

John Leivers and I had come with Ramiro, the cook who had accompanied us on the Cota Coca expedition, and two friends from

Urubamba, Javier and Henri, who were themselves *ukukus*, and had been to the festival before. I had persuaded my landlord and now friend Carlos to join us as well, although he was worried about the cold, and Claudia was concerned for his health. The reason that most Peruvians gave for never having been here, despite its fame, was its reputation for punishing exposure.

This reputation was probably precisely what had attracted John Leivers. After a bit of regrouping after the *denuncia* against him, which he had naturally taken as a personal affront, he had gone off traipsing on his own through the Vilcabamba to work the injustice out of his system. He had stayed with us briefly in Urubamba. And now we were teaming up again for our most ambitious journey.

The little *pampa* on the outskirts of Mahuayani had become a gigantic car-lot; trucks and vehicles were scattered in all directions. In the black-blue of night, the metalwork on the trucks gleamed fluorescent, and the dreamlike abandonment of the place was compounded by the silhouettes of mule teams wandering through it, looking for business.

We took on a muleteer at the going rate, half what they would have charged closer to Cuzco, for this was an area of bone-dry poverty compared to the lush pastures of the Sacred Valley. It reminded me more of Bolivia, with its high *puna* above the treeline and the moorland grazing. As we had driven here, crowds of children had gathered along the dirt roads, begging the pilgrims to throw food to them as they passed.

Many locals had set up temporary stalls around Mahuayani to sell goods for the festival. Through the cloud-mist that was rising up from below, and the stalls lit with candles and low-voltage electricity, shapes blurred together as the pilgrims bought provisions for the journey: pork *chicharrones*, candles, soap and gloves. It was already bitterly cold even before we began the ascent higher, as Mahuayani lay at 13,000 feet, well above Cuzco. There were cries of '*plásticos, plásticos*, plastic bags', and I remember a *huayno* song playing on a market radio, 'Los Hombres son como Picaflores': 'men are like hummingbirds / they just pick at women / but their consciences come back to haunt them.'

Chavín: the Lanzón in its cruciform gallery;
'like a vertebrae that had been forced back and out of
someone's skull'.

Petroglyphs at Toro Muerto: *'one of the largest fields of rock art in the world'*.

The Huari head at Aplao Museum: '*The headdress projected forward a full six inches from the forehead, like a second proboscis from the skull.*'

Gordon McEwan moments after the Huari turquoise figure has been found.

A quipu: *'still not fully deciphered, they remain one of the most tantalising challenges in archaeology. We long for the pre-Columbian civilisations to be able to speak to us direct from beyond the grave.'*

The festival of Qoyllurit'i:

Left Chu'uncho dancers with their feathered head-dresses.

Left below The *ukukus* with their whips and furred costumes: '*the officiating guardians of the festival, with a playful, anarchic edge*'.

Right An ukuku with one of the crosses high on a glacier.

Below Massed *ukukus* beside a glacier at dawn.

A Sacred Landscape:

Above The Island of the Sun: the pilgrimage route down the island.

Below Pilko Kayma at first light, *'the doorway into the complex flanked by two blind niches of an equal size . . . The Incas exerted an obsessive control over the ritual experience that pilgrims were to undergo.'*

Machu Picchu seen from Llactapata and [right] through the doorway of the Overlook Temple.

Below The reverse view: looking from the Sacristy at Machu Picchu towards Llactapata (the sunlit ridge on the right).

Sunlight down the long sunken corridor at dawn.

Hugh Thomson in the field-tent at Llactapata.

We set off in the dark, stumbling through the maze of blue tents, and almost immediately lost John, who had been walking slowly and abstractedly as he was recovering from flu (most people would not have embarked on the toughest of all Andean pilgrimages when ill, but then John was tougher than most people). Ramiro went off with a head torch to find him. I finally made out the distinctive silhouette of John's Australian hat in the distance. He had hunkered down at a stall selling chicken soup, where we joined him. Ignoring the carcass of bird floating in the bowl, I gulped down the hot liquid and the *chuño*, reconstituted dried potatoes, floating in it, together with some *mate de coca* to try to keep out the cold.

Leaning back on the thin poles of the hut, Javier played a beautiful flute song for us, and my first memory of the festival proper was this, Javier's music, the faces of my companions through the steam from the chicken soup and the *mate*; it was a moment of stillness among the streams of pilgrims who were passing us, a moment out of time.

'You'll need that for the walk up the hill,' observed Javier darkly as he watched me drink the chicken soup. After finishing his song, he had hunched down in his poncho. I remembered his answer during one of our many pre-Qoyllurit'i discussions over coffee in the village square, when Carlos had nervously asked what he needed to bring with him to the festival: 'Just faith, Carlos, just faith.'

Javier liked to cherish the times he had been to Qoyllurit'i, and to play up its hardships when talking to novices like Carlos and myself. Yet despite his patina of experience, I could tell that he was nervous. Although he had been to Qoyllurit'i several times before, this was the first time he had come as an *ukuku* rather than as a musician. Indeed I thought of him as more naturally musician material than an *ukuku*. He was a gentle soul, bespectacled and quietly voiced, who lived with his pretty German wife Grit in a fairytale cottage above us in the hills at Urubamba, with two children and various dogs and livestock.

As might be expected, the initiation necessary to become an *ukuku* was both intense and secretive. Javier had never witnessed it, but had been told that he would be whipped naked on the glacier at midnight, enough to make anyone go quiet in the anticipation.

But Javier had another preoccupation – he was a Limeño, one of the seemingly many who had moved to Urubamba in search of their roots, like the emigration to Wales and to Woodstock of the 1970s. He worked in Urubamba as an architect with Carlos. He was therefore, by definition, Peruvian middle class.

By contrast, most of the *ukukus* were tough men of the mountains, who put the costume on as if it was a second skin. Javier was like an accountant wanting to become a Hell's Angel. Now he had dressed in a poncho and distressed his accent to the same sort of slurred mumble that Mick Jagger used for interviews. Much of the time I could no longer hear nor understand him.

Javier's friend and mentor Henri had been an *ukuku* for longer, having first come five years ago. He had at once realised, he told me, that this is where his heart lay. An artisan by trade and inclination, he made pottery in Urubamba, and was ponytailed and tough.

It was Javier and Henri who had originally invited me to join them for both the pilgrimage and the further extreme heart of the ceremony, the midnight vigil on the glacier, which is usually the exclusive preserve of the *ukukus* and to which outsiders are forbidden. If I survived that, then I could join them on the so-called twenty-four-hour pilgrimage, when the *ukukus* leave Qoyllurit'i by a special route and walk through the night to bring El Señor de Tayankani, the crucifix at the heart of the ceremonies, back to his resting home across the mountains, while the other pilgrims left Qoyllurit'i by the much shorter descent.

As such, Javier and Henri had seemed to be my protectors. But now I found myself being protective towards Javier, lending him a good sleeping bag that a film company had given me to go up Kilimanjaro, rather than the flimsy one he owned, and bringing extra food and drink, as I knew that part of the hard-core *ukuku* stance was that they travelled light, so wouldn't have enough.

When we had first discussed the festival, Henri had said: 'There are two ways of going to Qoyllurit'i – either during the day, on Monday, which is the easy way – there are even some tourists who take photos! Or travel by bus right through Sunday night, arrive at dawn and walk up through the dawn,' his voice rose exultantly, 'past the stations of the cross, to see sunrise at the Sanctuary.'

There was no doubt that this was a choice with only one possible answer: 'I'll take the night trip with you.'

So now, groggy with sleep deprivation, we started up the hill. The low-voltage lights of the market stalls were still just stronger than the thin light of pre-dawn. I could make out streams of pilgrims on the path up ahead of me, and there were other paths high up on the hillside threading their way to the Sanctuary from all over the region. Many of the groups were being piped along by musicians and one man was bent over with the weight of a heavy harp. There were continual cries of '¡Jahu, jahu! Make way, make way!' Boys came racing down the track on horseback, whooping with laughter as they steered mules back to Mahuayani to pick up more pilgrims and another cargo. The mules jostled through the constant flow of walkers and just beside me one man suddenly lost his drum, which bounded down to the stream below. The crowd yelled instructions as he ran down the steep slope to retrieve it, and then laughed good-naturedly when they saw the drum had jammed safely in a rock.

I settled into a stride to keep up with Javier and Henri, who were attacking the ascent as if they'd been held back on a leash. Henri had refused my offer of some spare space on the mules for his tent and gear – 'Carrying it all is my annual penance,' he said – and Javier had followed suit, although he occasionally gave the mules a wistful glance. They made much of the fact that the previous year they had completed the long forty-kilometre exit walk over to Tayankani, a walk that entailed a forced march with other *ukukus* right through the night. '*Hombre, fue buen duro*, it was serious, man,' said Javier, 'we just had to keep going on coca and stamina.' He stared moodily into the distance.

Something kicked in for me as well and helped more than the *mate de coca* to keep me going: the sense of being part of a *riachuelo*, a stream of humanity, drawn by faith up a hill. It reminded me of the Indian pilgrims I had seen walking to the source of the Ganges in the Himalaya – the same simplicity, the same innocence and often the same ignorance about what conditions would be like that high: a few blue plastic sheets for shelter, some provisions wrapped in a cloth, surprisingly young children being carried as they cried from the cold and the altitude.

High up on one hill I saw a long line of pilgrims being piped along, like some vision from the Scottish highlands. The tiny black figures were silhouetted against the thin ridge light. Many of the surrounding communities had already walked for days to reach here, and their paths slipped down off the hills to meet ours.

In the changing swirls of walkers up the path, I would sometimes fall behind groups of musicians and whenever they started up with a song I felt re-energised. It was not long before I was high enough to look back with the first gleam of dawn and see the extended encampment of Mahuayani below, with mountains beyond.

Carlos was panting beside me and I was worried for him, given that he was in his fifties and had a heart condition. But he wore his humour swept around him like his poncho, an incorrigible cheerfulness that seemed to ward off any problems.

We came to the first station of the cross, of the twelve that mark the route up to the Sanctuary. It was a simple shrine made of stones, almost like a glorified cairn, with the cross at its centre. There was smoke coming up through the stones from the many candles that pilgrims had placed around and under the shrine. The great massif of Mount Ausangate was in the distance, and gave a fragility and smallness to the cross. Mount Ausangate was often seen as the partner to Mount Salcantay in the west. Between them they were the 'fathers of the mountains' for the Incas, and just as Machu Picchu lay on the slopes of the Salcantay massif, so the Qoyllurit'i festival was played out around the Ausangate massif.

A few solitary figures had isolated themselves away from the path and were praying quietly. A chapter of musicians arrived while I was standing there, removed their hats and piped their respect to the crucifix.

A group of women passed the shrine, all carrying heavy wood-framed pictures of the Lord of Qoyllurit'i. Others were carrying *taytachas,* banners with a replica of the same picture embroidered on them. A little behind were three young girls of between twelve and nine, in wide hats and red cloaks, their bells making them tinkle as they walked. A man was carrying up a whole mattress for his family.

John had fallen some way behind us, taking it slowly with his illness, and I got many curious looks as the only European face among the thousands (the few others who go up travel by the day), and a fair amount of good-humoured ribaldry. Along the way were stalls selling provisions and offering diversions. Some sold fake money in bills of $1,000; the idea was that if you bought the fake money now, you would earn the same amount for real later on. They came in bundles of $30,000, far more than a lifetime's income for most here, but when I bought mine the young *cholo* joshed me for getting so little: 'Surely that's what you spend for breakfast,' he said.

'What can I use this for?' I asked.

'It's for the *juego de las casitas,* the game of the little houses,' he answered. I didn't know what he meant.

The climb was one of the most peaceful and entertaining I have ever made, as the sun slowly rose with me: a pilgrim's progress past the stations of the cross, with all the accoutrements of a medieval fair. I passed a decapitated mule's head beside the path, advertising a medicinal paste made from the mule that was supposed to cure stomach and altitude sickness. Another popular stall had two parrots on a stick; the birds first touched the supplicant with their beak, then selected a 'fortune' from a tray of prepared paper slips. Mine told me that I should avoid eating greasy foods and any prospective partners with blue eyes.

We were reaching the high llama pastures and flocks of them were grazing on either side of the stream whose course we were following upwards. As we got closer to the Sanctuary, the pilgrims around me became visibly animated, and picked up pace. Most were hill people, some in bare feet, but there were many from Cuzco and some affluent enough – or unfit enough – to have hired horses as well as mules. They certainly rode like townspeople, as if sitting in an armchair, with no pretence at moving to the rhythm of the horse.

None of the approach had quite prepared me for the scale and noise of the Sanctuary when I came round a corner, over the lip of a ridge, and saw it, lying at the head of the stream. Down from a great bowl of mountains came the long tongues of four glaciers, each with its prescribed place in the rites that would take place later that night. At the bottom of this natural amphitheatre was the Sanctuary, a long low building erected around the main shrine to El Señor de Qoyllurit'i, 'the Lord of Qoyllurit'i'. Around the Sanctuary spilt an endless array of temporary stalls and simple tarpaulin tents, crossing the stream towards the other landmark of the bowl, the Q'eros rock, so called because the Q'eros people, some of the most indigenous of the tribes who came, made it their own.

John and I later independently reckoned that some 30,000 people had come here for the festival and were sprawled across the high valley bottom, from the Sanctuary on one side to the Q'eros rock on the other. There was a cheerful spread of home-made tents, many made from just a blue plastic sheet, and stone corrals marking off the separate 'nations' from one another in a haphazard way. Even more chaotic was the noise. On the way up, there had been the occasional single line of musicians leading us. Now there was a swirl of competing music from the dozens of dance troupes parading around the site, with the amplified voice of an MC booming across his own feedback.

In many ways, it was like a rock festival without the bands. There were tents for lost children, rudimentary toilets with queues and enough food stalls to feed an army. The emergency medical services were working overtime, as the effects of altitude kicked in on pilgrims from the city unaccustomed to it. One of the doctors later told me that a peculiar problem was the kudos that resulted from being born at the festival. Heavily pregnant mothers would come especially because they knew that any resulting child would be showered with both presents and respect.

One striking difference between this and the Peruvian fiestas I had been to (let alone rock festivals), was that there was no alcohol. Qoyllurit'i was an unusually teetotal celebration, a rule enforced by the *ukukus* who whipped anyone seen to drink, in public at least. More privately many, including the *ukukus*, had small 'medicinal' hip flasks to keep out the cold – but there was none of the communal drunkenness I had seen at the Urubamba town fiesta of Torrechayoc, with bodies lying in the street and institutionalised, sanctioned inebriation. (It is said that Quechua has more terms for the different stages of drunkenness than any other language.)

Which is not to say that the atmosphere was sober or solemn. The *ukuku* bear men were everywhere, laughing, carousing, dancing. Their dance took a strange form: first an *ukuku* danced on his own; another then approached and lashed at his feet with a whip; the two embraced and danced up to the standard of El Señor de Qoyllurit'i, arm in arm, bowing to it. Then they danced away backwards, at which point other *ukukus* would hurl themselves on the ground to trip them up, much to the boisterous amusement of the crowd.

There were dancers from every one of the seven *naciones* or 'nations' that made up this gathering of the Peruvian tribes. Besides Quispicanchis, the mountainous areas near Qoyllurit'i itself, there were jungle dancers from Paucartambo, groups from Canchis, towards Puno, and from the plains of Anta, from Paruro, from Chinchero and the Sacred Valley, and from Cuzco itself, each with its own regional variation of costume and musical style. This was one reason for the congenial anarchy of the place, in that while nominally a single *hermandad*, 'brotherhood', served the Lord of Qoyllurit'i, in reality each *nación* was following its own way, and there were often disputes over prime camping spots.

In the midst of this confusion, it took a while for our small group to find each other and a clear space to make camp. Once we had gathered near the Q'eros rock, Carlos said it for us all: 'I'm just lost for words – I never imagined it would be anything like this.' After a sleepless night and the climb up, the sensory overload was intense and after putting up a tent, I lay down with an altitude headache. John had already been feeling ill – not even coca tea helped him. As I lay in the tent, I could hear the screeching voice of the MC exhorting the pilgrims to pay obeisance to the Lord of Qoyllurit'i and occasionally to leave the Sanctuary building so that it could be cleaned.

There are various Catholic accounts of the origins of the festival of El Señor de Qoyllurit'i, which vary in detail. However, most agree that it celebrates a miracle that is said to have occurred in 1783. A young shepherd boy named Mariano Maita was sent to the high Sinakara valley, where the festival is now held, to look after some llamas who needed the high pasture. He was around twelve to fourteen years old. Some accounts say that he was badly bullied by an older brother; all agree that he was unhappy and lonely in the valley until befriended by a young boy of about his own age, a *mestizo* stranger, who helped him to such an extent that the herd prospered and his father asked how he could reward the helper.

Mariano wanted to buy his friend some new garments, as little cloth was to be had in those parts, and his father consented. Mariano took a scrap of his friend's poncho to Cuzco to see whether he could buy anything similar, but the cloth was so fine he was told that only Archbishop Moscoso had anything of that quality. When he went to the archbishop's palace, Moscoso became inquisitive and sent a delegation back with Mariano to meet his companion.

The delegation travelled to the remote valley of Sinakara, but on approaching Mariano's companion, they were blinded by a dazzling light. As the leading priest put out his hand to try to touch the young boy he found he was holding a tree; on looking up at the tree's branches he saw a vision of Christ in agony on the cross. Mariano cried out that they had betrayed his friend and fell down dead beside them.

From that moment the spot was considered sacred. The first chapel was supposedly built on the site by a miner who had tried to drown himself when his gleanings from a nearby river were low. At the last moment he changed his mind and prayed to El Señor de Qoyllurit'i. He immediately sieved enough gold from the river to pay off his debts to the company store. By way of thanks, he founded the chapel around the stone that was venerated by local

Indians as the site of the miraculous vision. Over the years this chapel had grown in size, as had the annual festival. By 1953 it had become big enough to need an organising committee and by 1965 a new church was built to accommodate the flood of pilgrims. This had already been outgrown, so there was now a long queue snaking right around the Sanctuary, patiently waiting to see the image of Christ engraved on the rock at its centre.

Over the PA system, I heard the MC summon one man to the church because he had left his costume on a mule going back down and the mule-handler was concerned that he wouldn't be able to dance without it. Crawling out of the tent, I found Carlos and we wandered up the hill behind the church, both still feeling groggy. We passed some dancers from the jungle near Paucartambo, the *chu'uncho*, with their tall headdresses made from the feathers of jungle birds. Just as at Urubamba, the 'jungle girl' dancers were wearing less than anybody else, and it was only by continuously dancing that they could hope to keep warm. Some of the girls were at least wearing tights, but not all.

The sun was setting early over the high mountains, at four in the afternoon, and the feather headdresses of the *chu'uncho* were dramatically backlit. The headdresses had a broad red headband, matching the deep cochineal red of their tunics, and the headbands were festooned with feathers of pink, yellow and turquoise. More feathers cascaded down their backs.

Streams of other dancers were also coming down from the glaciers and passing us on either side. Accompanying musicians were playing pan pipes, flutes, harps and marching drums. Red was again the dominating colour, in their flags, *taytacha* banners, masks and elaborately embroidered backplates. Then came the crosses that had been left up on the glaciers and were coming down to be blessed. Each cross was borne by four *ukukus*, struggling with the weight of the heavy wood. Now that the *ukukus* were carrying the crucifixes, the red crosses dyed into their black costumes stood out in relief. Other *ukukus* were dancing behind them with whips.

By nightfall the noise level had, if anything, increased. I had brought earplugs and, by jamming both headphones and a woolly cap over them, just about got some sleep, despite the rockets that were being let off continuously around the bowl. Some of these misfired and crashed back down onto the crowd; one tent near us received an almost direct hit.

I had asked Javier to wake me in the middle of the night to go up for the *ukukus'* meeting on the glaciers above, as we had arranged, one reason for trying to get some rest during the day beforehand. But when it came to it, Javier was obviously overwhelmed by a novitiate's sense of the proprieties, and by the constant dancing and music beforehand, and didn't wake me. Ramiro did so instead, to tell me that the *ukukus* had gone up already. Did I still want to go?

*

It is a decisive moment: I have finally reached that state of perfect equilibrium in the sleeping bag where I am warm and have achieved deep sleep. I can hear Carlos snoring in a nearby tent. Do I want to get up in the middle of the night and climb a glacier when we have been abandoned by the *ukukus* who were going to take us? On the other hand I haven't come this far just to lie in a tent. With a supreme effort of will, unusual in that I find it hard enough to get up at 8 a.m., let alone 1 a.m., I struggle up.

I can see my breath freezing in the air against the clear night sky. Ramiro cooks some porridge and I have a hit of good old-fashioned English breakfast tea, strong enough to stand the spoon up in. This is a time to test the old climbers' motto that you can do anything with a clean pair of underpants and a brew.

Ramiro and I set off, trying to climb our way up to the glaciers by moonlight. We can already see a stream of torches heading to each of the four icefields above. Different chapters traditionally go to different glaciers for their climactic moonlit vigil. Neither Ramiro nor I know which way Javier and Henri have gone, so we fall in with the first group of *ukukus* we come across and tag along behind them. In the dark, they are too cold and weary to take much notice of us, as we walk up in single file. The *ukuku* in front of me has hunched his head down so deep into his bear costume that I could probably have been a real Andean spectacled bear for all he cared.

As it turns out, these *ukukus* belong to the Nación Canchis, who come from around Puno, and are characterised by the bigger, brass sound of their music, compared to the more traditional Andean instruments favoured by the *naciones* closer to Qoyllurit'i. I am grateful, as there is nothing like a marching band to get you up a mountain in the small hours. The sound of trumpets around me is echoed across the mountain bowl, as snatches of music go off like fireworks for all the other *naciones*. It is a cloudless night, and thin trails of torches are threading their way onto the other glaciers far away from us.

The musicians stop and start up again at stuttering intervals, sometimes paying obeisance to a passing shrine, sometimes with a dance. Only when we get close to the top do they leave us, remaining at a discreet distance below.

Our party of *ukukus* arrives at the bottom of the glacier just as the *convenio* or parliament begins. It is an extraordinary sight. By the pale gleam given off by the moon and its reflection on the ice behind, I can see the standards of the various chapters spread out in a line, along with the Peruvian national flag and the rainbow flag of the Quechua. In front are the *ukuku* leaders, addressing their troops, and listening are the assembled bear men, in their suits of fur and striped balaclavas, some hundreds strong. The *ukukus* around us press down on the ground and against each other to keep warm as their leaders address them. I can smell the coca on the breath of the *ukuku* closest to me.

As the first speaker points out, this is a rare conference of *los hermanos*, 'the brothers', an annual opportunity for the spirit of the mountain people to be invoked and celebrated. There is much whistling and applauding. The name of each chapter is called out – of Sicuani, of Maranqani, of Putamarca, of Chihuaco – and the *caporal* or 'foreman' of each chapter shouts a response. Occasionally a chapter has yet to arrive and the speaker of this parliament of bears repeats their name several times to shame them.

Then the session begins in earnest. It is at this point that I wish they were speaking in Quechua or Aymara – yet unfortunately, because the chapter spans both dialects, they speak Spanish as a lingua franca and I can understand every tedious word. For what follows is a bureaucratic discussion about the proprieties of their organisation which would make the meeting of a water board seem dynamic. It is not just that the placemen have to be elected to central committees, but that every nomination and objection has to be accompanied by a preamble in flowery and rhetorical Spanish, expressing gratitude to the parliament's speaker for being given the floor and wishing his companions well.

Only once does the debate spark into life and that is when the thorny question of admitting women to the *ukuku* ranks is raised. While women have always come to the festival, and have been some of its most devout pilgrims, it is only recently that they have participated in the dance rites reserved for the *ukukus*. The same arguments for and against their inclusion are trotted out as must occur in every remaining male-only institution: that on the one hand women are equal – indeed, that both genders are equal in the eyes of Christ – but on the other the vigil on the snow has always been an all-male affair, and 'tradition must be respected'. One magnificent old *caporal* of a chapter, in a padded bear costume, points out to my delight, 'Señores, gentlemen, we should never forget that woman was after all created from a man's rib.'

But however long-winded the parliament is, the pre-dawn faces of all those around me grip me. It is the first time I have seen the *ukukus* in repose. Most are young, in their twenties, if that, with short, cropped black hair and wide Quechua faces. Their bear costumes make them look even broader and stronger than normal. It is a tough discipline. Those who transgress the *ukukus'* rules (particularly against drunkenness) receive a serious whipping; four of the *hermanos* tie a victim's feet and hands together, suspend him in the air, mask upwards, and then lash him until blood is drawn.

Time is no longer running to its normal rhythm. I look at my watch and find that five minutes may have gone by, or an hour. The stars above are as clear as I have ever seen – it feels as if there are 30,000 visible, one for every pilgrim, with the milkiness of the galaxies like the bloom on the ice behind the *ukukus*.

The tongue of the glacier slopes up and away from the gathering. Lining the ice are clusters of candles lit to El Señor de Qoyllurit'i. Many *ukukus* have spent the whole night beside the glacier, and have settled into a trance of faith and sleep deprivation, jolting themselves awake into an occasional epiphany of joyous celebration. Although wrapped in blankets and ponchos, they are now almost blue with cold. Ramiro and I share some of our *mate de coca* with them.

The parliament slowly breaks with the beginning of dawn. The musicians come up from below to welcome the sun, and small groups of *ukukus* begin to ascend the glaciers. They cut blocks out of the ice in honour of El Señor de Qoyllurit'i and will then carry these down to Cuzco for the ceremonies that follow on Corpus Christi, a few days later. The ice that comes from the very highest section of the glaciers is the most prized.

We go with them. The casual way in which the crevasses, ice-bridges and glissades are treated by the *ukukus* would give a Swiss guide palpitations. Some wear football boots with studs so as to be able to grip the ice better, but that is their only concession to the treacherous nature of the glacier slopes. Each year they take a certain amount of pride in reporting that some unlucky *ukuku* has fallen into a crevasse; these stories are part of their self-mythologisation.

At one point I see some *ukukus* tie their whips together to pull each other up an overhanging lip of ice. They are laughing as they do so. There is an atmosphere of release after the long night's vigil, helped by the dancers and pilgrims who have come from below to join them. A few intrepid bowler-hatted señoras have struggled up the glacier on their hands and knees to get to the wooden crucifixes erected right in the centre of the ice field, as a display of determined faith.

The scene around the crucifixes is a curious one. Each cross stands on the snow, with a few devotees around it paying homage. There are others walking in the distance. It feels allegorical, like a tableau. I remember stories of how the Victorians liked to promenade over Alpine glaciers as a diversion.

Off to one side, I see a venerable long-haired man, dressed in white, conducting some ceremony to the mountain spirits. 'He must be a shaman,' says one of the *ukukus* respectfully.

'No, he's not,' says Ramiro. 'I know him. He's just an old hippy yoga teacher from Urubamba.'

We are now at over 17,000 feet, and the effects of altitude and cold are taking their toll on some of the *ukukus* and pilgrims, who sink down into the snow. Others seem re-energised by the ceremony; some go higher up the ice slope and sledge themselves down, whooping in high-pitched camelid voices to one another, their mannequins at their sides bouncing on the ice. In their bear costumes, the surreal effect is of St Bernard dogs taking to their owners' sledges after one too many brandy flasks.

I reflect ruefully how I have lectured people on not ascending Kilimanjaro too rapidly because of the resultant altitude problems, having been up the mountain a few months before coming to Peru – and yet I have climbed far faster here than even the most ambitious tour agent on Kilimanjaro would suggest. The coca tea and the headiness of sleep deprivation drive me on. With Ramiro and four *ukukus* I go up to the very head of the glacier, where there is a steep ice field over the top of the pass.

I have always loved passes – the ability to see through to another, parallel landscape – and despite the lack of crampons (or football boots), and the fact that the sun is beginning to soften the ice, Ramiro and I push on with the small group until we get up to the col. We can see a nameless glacier descending to a broken ice field, and a 20,000-foot peak in the distance. None of the *ukukus* with me knows its name. One looks around him. 'This is a place of *apus*,' he says; the *apus* are the spirits of the mountains.

I let the moment fill me. On the side we have come from, the Qoyllurit'i glaciers peel away back towards the Sanctuary campsite below, with thousands of small figures crossing the mountain bowl, every inch of the valley a sacred landscape; on the other side there is an unpopulated, empty vista, barren of meaning but with its own, unholy beauty.

*

The whole Qoyllurit'i festival can be seen as a transference of the power of a sacred landscape. The festival begins with a cross brought from its chapel at Ocongate and placed here on the glacier, as are banners from all over the region. Then these crosses and the banners are returned to their homes, recharged with the spiritual energy of the *apus* of the highlands, of a place that has always had tremendous spiritual power.

The scenes on the glacier were a reminder that while Qoyllurit'i might ostensibly be a Christian festival, its roots went much deeper to a pre-Columbian past. I remembered talking about this with Robert Randall twenty years before at Ollantaytambo, when I had first heard about Qoyllurit'i. Randall had come to Ollantaytambo with his wife Wendy Weeks and had spent years studying Andean customs before dying tragically from rabies. He had written a short and influential paper on Qoyllurit'i.

Randall had pointed out that it was not for nothing that the miraculous apparition of the Catholic tale was supposed to have occurred in 1783, for this was a momentous time in Peruvian history, shortly after Tupac Amaru II's great uprising against the Spanish.

Tupac Amaru II was a charismatic descendant of the Inca emperors who led one of the first concerted rebellions against Spanish rule, a revolt that although it failed initially (and led to Tupac's execution in 1781) set off the first waves of liberation on the continent, culminating with Bolivar's wars of independence in the next century. Tupac was still widely admired as an indigenous hero, and one of the guerrilla groups of the 1990s, the MRTA (Movimento Revolucionario Tupac Amaru), had taken their name from him.

One of the persecutors of Tupac Amaru II at the time of his revolt was Archbishop Moscoso, the self-same archbishop who had instigated the cult of El Señor de Qoyllurit'i. The story attached to the miracle (the lonely shepherd boy, the apparition in a high valley) resembled other stories that the Catholic Church was attaching to native sites of veneration, as it tried to extirpate the last vestiges of indigenous belief, which had suddenly become as suspect politically as it was religiously.

Tupac Amaru II had been inspired by the writings of Garcilaso de la Vega, one of the few indigenous accounts of the Inca past, and Garcilaso's work was promptly banned. A concerted attempt was made to root out any last remaining strongholds of pre-Columbian belief and clearly Qoyllurit'i was such a place.

For one can see, even from some of the Catholics' own writing on Qoyllurit'i, that there had always been a considerable importance attached to the site of Sinakara in pre-Columbian times. The stone on which the image of Christ was now carved, and which was contained by the Sanctuary church, had previously been worshipped as a *huaca*, a stone of worship. In his paper, Randall quoted the First Lima Council convened by the Church in 1551, which had declared that such '*huacas* should be destroyed and a church built in the same spot, if appropriate, or at the very least a cross erected there'.

Qoyllurit'i lies on a line directly east from Cuzco, and much work has been done to show that important *huacas* were placed on such lines, called *ceques*, radiating out from the old Inca capital. Qoyllurit'i would have held a particularly important place in such a system, as it also marked the division between the north-eastern section of the Inca empire, Antisuyo – the quarter of the jungle – and the south-eastern section, Collasuyo – the quarter that extended away towards Bolivia and Lake Titicaca from where the Incas claimed their mythical origins. As such it was perfectly placed between jungle and mountains, the two guiding principles in pan-Andean beliefs. No wonder that the *apu* or spirit of the place should have held such importance and been worshipped, and that modern-day pilgrims should wish to bring back some essence of it to inform their daily lives.

The chapter of *ukukus* with whom I had come up to this glacier were from the highlands towards Puno and Lake Titicaca, so precisely the area of Collasuyo; historical records showed them to have been one of the first chapters associated with the festival, and they were still one of the foremost. And the *chu'uncho* dancers who were so ubiquitous were primarily from the Puacartambo *nacion* in Antisuyo, and were thought of as the 'jungle dancers'. This was a meeting place, a *tinquy*, for both the spirits and peoples of the mountains and the jungle, and it was this that gave Qoyllurit'i its unique feeling and connection to the deepest roots of Peruvian identity.

The *ukukus* themselves were the anarchic guardians of this assembly and many of their traditions stemmed from ancient pan-Andean customs that had not been sanitised within the ostensibly Catholic setting of the festival.

Why had we spent a vigil by moonlight on the glacier? One Catholic priest suggested that this might have something to do with the charming Peruvian habit of celebrating a birthday on its eve as well as on the actual day itself, and that the *ukukus* were in some way simply extending the celebrations of El Señor de Qoyllurit'i. However, a more likely explanation lay in what could be seen in the night sky above. For the Pleiades, the Seven Sisters, were due in the heavens, having been absent for over two months.

I had spent the nights of the previous week trying to spot them with Carlos in the garden at Kuchi Rumi, in sessions that had usually happily degenerated into drinking sessions and speculation as to how we would survive Qoyllurit'i, with little success at stargazing. But what better place to try to see them than above the clouds, here at 16,000 feet on a glacier?

In the Southern Hemisphere, the Pleiades have always played a useful astronomical role, in that they disappear from sight around the end of April, and reappear in early June. This temporary disappearance of the Pleiades was used as a seasonal indicator by the Andean peoples, neatly marking both the autumn harvest period and the planting time for potatoes. As it happens – and very conveniently for the Catholic Church – this also coincides broadly with the Easter period, so that pre-Columbian ceremonies that were traditionally held to mark the Pleiades' absence and return could be adapted into Easter ones.

The Catholic Church had skilfully fused ancient pan-Andean beliefs into a more recognisable miracle legend that it could use for its own purposes – I particularly liked the way the Andean obsession with cloth had been incorporated into the story, with the search for a textile to match the Christ-boy's leading to the bishop – but equally intriguing was the way the Indians had allowed the Church to do this, while continuing with their own beliefs. Indeed, it was too easy to say that the Catholic Church had 'appropriated' the festival, as if stealing it. Qoyllurit'i seemed a more interesting mixture of both Christian and pre-Columbian festivities, united by the deep faith of the participants.

The pre-Columbian origins of Qoyllurit'i also seem to have been deeply bound up with a necessary propitiation of the spirits to look after the people's livestock. This was herding country; I had seen llamas grazing on the approaches to the Sanctuary, and camelids had been domesticated since the very earliest signs of Peruvian civilisation; worked camelid bones had been found at Caral. In the vicious weather of the Andes, it would have been natural to look to the *apus*, the spirits, for protection of their most valuable commodity, never more so than in late autumn, when Qoyllurit'i was held, just before the onset of winter in the Southern Hemisphere.

The Catholic Church had certainly incorporated the Andean concern for their livestock into the story of the martyr Mariano, who had been a herdsboy – and emphasised Christ's nature as a shepherd of souls, the stranger who helps Mariano increase his flock.

The Q'eros people, one of the oldest and least-changed of the Andean communities near to Qoyllurit'i, came to the festival explicitly to ask protection for their flocks. It was said that they congregated around the Q'eros rock and waited until the other pilgrims departed, before entering the empty church and making obeisance to '*el Señor del Ganado*, our Lord of the Cattle'.

But if the festival had originally been a primarily rural one, with rural concerns, over recent years it had changed greatly in character. What once had been the exclusive preserve of the local mountain people – a celebration of the autochthonous Indian, and photographed as such by the celebrated Peruvian photographer Martín Chambi in some iconic portraits – had cast its net far wider. Now people came to it from right across the southern Andes, and from many of the major cities like Cuzco. In just a decade, it had grown from 20,000 to 30,000 participants. Communities like Urubamba had only recently started sending large groups there. There was even a ceremony held in its honour in distant New York by the immigrant Peruvian community.

This increased urbanisation and attendance was deplored by some, in much the same way that people have always complained that England's Glastonbury Festival 'is not the same as it used to be', but seemed a potent sign of what had happened in Peru as the country had become so much more aware of its spiritual home in the mountains.

Qoyllurit'i was a myth of Andean origin that the modern nation needed just as much as the Incas needed their own creation myth.

*

As we descended and the effort of the night began to catch up with us, Ramiro and I came across a peculiar ceremony beside the bottom of the ice field: men and women were kneeling in front of the glacier, where the standards of each *nación* had been placed. Then an *ukuku* would whip them, hard, three times on the buttocks.

This was the 'initiation ceremony' that Javier was presumably experiencing elsewhere, both for entrants to the *ukukus'* order and for those who wanted to progress higher in each chapter – or simply as a penitential act. There were three *p'ulkas*, three strokes of the whip to represent the Trinity.

Nor was the whipping simply symbolic. Much pride was taken both by the flagellator and the recipient in the fierceness of the lash, and women were whipped with the same force as the men. The older señoras being initiated sensibly wore thick layers of petticoats as a precaution, but one young woman in fashion-conscious tight jeans suffered considerably.

Afterwards, both men and women would kiss the whip that had been used on them and embrace the *hermano*, the brother, who had done the whipping. As we were watching, a señora turned to Ramiro and asked him to be her *padrino*, her godfather and initiator, as the intended one was not present. Ramiro accepted with embarrassment, and an awkward glance at me, but still whipped her with gusto.

Just above the Sanctuary, and near a small shrine to the Virgin, we came across perhaps the strangest part of the whole Qoyllurit'i festival: an area of the site completely covered with miniature buildings a few inches high, using small loose stones from the hillside immediately above. Some of the houses were simple little rectangles laid out in the bare earth, a few inches high; others were more elaborate complexes, with two-storeyed central buildings and out-houses. They looked as if built by children, but near by were their adult owners, grave-looking men and women crouching over their model homes, adding string as electricity supplies to some, or putting in model cars and goods that they had bought at stalls supplying them.

For this is a serious business, the *juego de las casitas*, 'game of the little houses', in which people build their dreams. The participants believe that you will actually acquire whatever you build in mini-ature, with the aid of the Lord of Qoyllurit'i, so that you must meticulously consider what you ask for. In the words of the old saying: 'Be careful what you set your heart on, for you will surely get it.' So these men and women move slowly, as if in a sort of waking dream, as they deliberate whether to add even more white pebbles (llamas) to a field, or buy more goods from one another. They use the paper money I had seen when I first arrived, the large bundles of fake 'thousand-dollar' notes. Sometimes a man will just buy the whole of another's model, realising that someone else has created his dream for him.

They can use the money to acquire academic certificates, com-puter qualifications, tickets to travel abroad, driving licences and everything else being sold by the salesmen who rove around the plots of the houses. Some men and women are just sitting in a contemplative attitude, making their houses as if 'dreaming awake'.

The level of detail is phenomenal: small sticks represent eucalyptus groves (eucalyptus being the equivalent of poplars in France, a cash forestry crop), and there are tiny fridges, food-blenders, pick-up trucks and even Volvos. On the slopes above, those who want to be *transportistas*, 'truck drivers', carve long descending routes in the stone and dust for their model lorries. A priest who has studied the phenomenon over the years, Father Flores Lizana, has noted how as the Andean peasantry have become more sophisticated, with many of their children going to university, and as many more city-folk come to the festival to reclaim their Andean past, these *casitas* have become more elaborate, with an even greater level of fantasy.

The same priest has collected copies of petitions left at the nearby Virgin's shrine, where the builders of these houses tuck supplicating notes under the stones around her image. The petitions overwhelmingly ask for better health or for more money, and sometimes forgiveness for having smacked their children. Rarely do they touch on anything political or romantic. The people of the mountains are pragmatic and shrewd, but as these models show, they can still dream. And when they dream, they dream in stone.

I meet Carlos, who has wandered up from the campsite in the early dawn and looks in the fine shape a man can only be who has spent all night comfortably in a tent while his friends have shivered on a glacier. As an architect, he is intrigued by the level of detail in the maquettes before him, and also by the intensity and speed with which the game is played. Within moments Carlos and I are involved in some serious negotiations for his own first house. Despite being an architect, Carlos forgets to ask the right questions, and the vendor has to prompt him: does he need planning permission, how many hectares go with the plot, does he want water rights, or grazing, or *transporte*? To our surprise, a notary almost immediately bustles up to make sure the sale is made official (for which of course, like a real notary, he receives a small fee in the paper money).

And in a way the game serves two purposes: it allows people to dream and to see that dreams can be made manifest, whether they be of land, or marriage, or travel, but it is also heuristic, an education in the processes of how you achieve this: 'These are the questions you should ask/this is what you should expect should happen.'

I buy a house for Sally and me by the river in Urubamba; mark out the garden with eucalyptus and stone walls; then collect the 'deeds' to our property. El Señor de Qoyllurit'i assigns us a plot of 6,600 square metres at a price of $5,000 to build on as we will, as long as it conforms to local planning regulations.

A large, bearded man approaches us with a seaman's intensity, like somebody out of Conrad. He asks whether I am foreign, and from which country; then whether I will act as British Consul and grant him a visa. He produces a beautifully made miniature passport, all of an inch square. I am about to accept it, but Carlos stops me. 'First you must ask him some questions,' he reminds me. So I ask whether he has had an honourable record, whether he has his own business, whether he has ever been in trouble with the law. He replies positively, but then insists that we keep the passport so that we can make 'further enquiries'.

'But how will you ever find us again?' I ask.

'I will,' he says, withdrawing with an intense gaze.

And there is an Alice-in-Wonderland logic to the whole place. All about me I see Peruvians with their heads buried in their tiny dream-sites, as if going down a hole. Some of the buildings are thatched; most have wedding confetti (*pica pica*, as they call it) thrown over them.

Weddings are another cornerstone of the *juego de las casitas*. I leave Carlos for a while and wander through the plots. Everywhere there are couples being blessed and solemnised, easier to do here than in a church, with all the expectations of family and church hierarchy. Many of the ceremonies are unattended by anyone save the 'priest', some local boy playing the role for the day in a mock cassock, who swings incense over these couples and pronounces the vows. There is a long tradition of the *tinquy*, or meeting place, being a bride market as well as a tribal gathering. This is a place for the impetuous Vegas 'let's just do it' wedding, as I am shortly to discover.

Vera Tuleneva taps me on the arm. I have not seen her since she came to the house to talk about Paititi and Bolivia. She wants me to be godfather at her wedding, to someone she now introduces me to for the first time: Mariana. This is a lot of information for me to process, as I was unaware that Vera was gay, much less in a committed relationship. I make a mental note to tell Sally. Mariana is older, an Argentinian woman with a reputation, Carlos tells me later, for wild behaviour and all the impetuosity that goes with the territory for émigré Argentinians.

This is a place where anything is possible, so I say yes immediately. I tell her that Carlos is with me. 'Perfect. He can be the other godfather.'

Before he knows it, Carlos is swept up in the wedding as well. And Vera does not want any old roadside ceremony, at one of the smaller makeshift chapels. She wants to be married at the cathedral of the 'game of little houses', a great rock, like a *huaca*, around which huddle a large congregation of curious spectators. I had already seen the officiating priest at work, standing on the centre of the rock to officiate over the happy couples who came and blessing them with 'holy water' which he dispensed out of a plastic bottle. He was a young fast-witted *cholo*, probably from the city, with a line in patter and smooth asides that had the crowd roaring in appreciation at his broad Rabelaisian humour. At one mock wedding I'd heard him ask the bride 'whether she was still a virgin, with just zero kilometres on the clock', much to her blushing and the crowd's amusement.

There is something transcendent about Vera. Having made her decision to get married – an impulsive one taken only some minutes before, she tells me, when she had wandered up to the 'game of little houses' and realised it was possible – she now has a Russian glow of certainty and substantiation about her.

What I had not expected was the formality of what is to come. Before being led to the 'cathedral', we have to fill in a bewildering series of mock forms, mirroring the real process. With a flourish, a salesman unfurls the arm of his cloak to reveal a set of wedding rings pinned to the black silk lining; Vera and Mariana choose matching ones. Then I lead Mariana into the 'nave' of the cathedral in front of the priest on his great stone above us, with Carlos behind me leading Vera. It is intimidating in that many of the congregation have lined up beside and behind the priest, so are also looking down on us. It dawns on me that of course we don't quite know what they will make of the concept of a gay marriage. This is not San Francisco or Brighton.

At first the crowd assume that either Carlos or I are the bridegroom. It is with some shock that they realise Vera and Mariana are the couple. '*Pero eso no puede ser*, this can't be,' says the priest, 'woman and woman, *mujer y mujer*.' There is much ribaldry from the crowd, with bawdy jokes in both Spanish and Quechua (*¿Quien es el hombre?*, who's the man?'). But the priest, to his credit, quietens them down. 'Well, if they love each other,' he asks aloud, 'why not?

'Do you?' he asks them.

'Yes,' chorus Vera and Mariana, both lightly but with their voices charged with emotion. And Carlos, intoxicated, like me, by the moment, begins a speech in Spanish that would have done credit to Oscar Wilde in his courtroom, with much appealing to how '*el amor es amor dondequiera se encuentra*, love is true love wherever it is found.'

I feel emotionally charged myself, and the crowd, who have already watched several marriages beforehand, move up several notches of excitement at the novelty and strangeness of what is happening. There is even silence when the happy couple kiss (enthusiastically), a silence the priest tactfully breaks with a joke about how careful everyone must be that one of the brides doesn't run off with godfather Carlos, as he seems to be the one handing out most paper notes to everybody.

Carlos and I produce the rings we have purchased beforehand and the bride and bride exchange them. We shower the couple and the congregation with confetti. It is a wild, unbridled instant. Vera and Mariana look ecstatically happy. Even the priest's patter dries up in the face of such joy. And they are led away to have their photo taken together.

Just as at a real wedding, most of the bills (for the rings, the priest's fee, the confetti) seem to come after the event – perhaps another learning exercise for those involved – and Carlos and I, as the *padrinos*, spend a while settling them.

As I finally stumble from the scene, feeling that after my long night on the glacier I am truly flying on different, Andean time, the bearded Conradian man approaches me; in a low voice, he respectfully asks, 'Was all my paperwork in order, in the end? Can you endorse my passport?'

I sign and give it back to him.

'Now I can travel, like you,' he says.

*

It started to snow. Not the genteel snow of a Nativity scene, but hard, hard snow. Within a few minutes the ground was covered. Visibility started going. I made my way back to our tent and huddled inside with some bacon and eggs, washed down by black coffee.

An Australian friend of John's was sitting there, an athletic guy in his twenties called Matt, together with his Peruvian girlfriend Isabella. They had met in Australia, and Isabella's story was an unusual one. Now in her twenties, as a child she had been a 'Cuzco street kid', selling cigarettes to tourists. An Australian woman had taken pity on the miserable conditions the street kids lived in, and had tried to help them, with educational programmes and shelter. With Isabella she had gone further – adopting her, and then taking her back home.

Isabella had become to all intents and purposes an Australian teenager, and now young woman, with Matt as the archetypal Australian boyfriend. He was large, fit, clean-limbed and looked as if he surfed. They had come to Peru because Isabella's natural mother was terminally ill. John had been looking after the couple and told them to find us at Qoyllurit'i if they got into trouble.

Matt was now in a bad way and John was not around. Matt was suffering from the altitude and had been up most of the night vomiting. It was perhaps not tactful to be eating bacon and eggs near him in the circumstances, but he managed a bit of conversation. I gave him some medicine and, together with Isabella, arranged for a horse to carry him down the mountain.

Many others were attempting to do the same thing. The scene

outside, in the fierce snow, was chaotic. While some were leaving the mountain, others were huddling under square blue plastic sheets, which never seemed quite to cover them; a limb would always be poking out somewhere. Children were shivering miserably under thin blankets.

At that moment I saw the unmistakable figure of Peter Frost. I knew that he sometimes came to Qoyllurit'i. He was peering with great interest at the much-prized toilet tent John and I had brought, one of our better pieces of foresight at a festival that seemed to have about ten latrines for 30,000 visitors.

I had not seen Peter since all the arguments had erupted between him and Gary Ziegler over who had or had not been involved in finding the ruins at Corihuayrachina. But I was aware that due to my own association with Gary, and our subsequent discoveries at Cota Coca, relations might be strained. Given that the world of Inca studies was too small for such continuing squabbles, and that Peter was someone whose commitment I admired, it was clearly time for the magnanimous gesture and to advance the hand of friendship.

'Peter, any time you want to use our toilet tent, you can.' A cordial word was spoken on both sides. What our team later dubbed 'the Historic Accord of the Toilet Tent' had been made.

Meanwhile as the storm cleared, the last dancers and musicians streamed back down the mountain, ignoring the snow. Through the white-out, picked out by the last few shafts of sunlight, I could see red flags waving in the air, and the bright feather headdresses of the *chu'unchos*, again accompanying the crosses that were being brought from the glaciers. Carlos and I followed the last of these processions as they turned the last few bends of the hillside to the Sanctuary church. The *ukukus* streamed to either side of each cross as outriders, whipping all those bystanders who did not take off their hats as the crosses passed.

We danced down behind one of the very last *comparsas*, and found ourselves being swept into the shrine itself. Previously there had been such an intimidating line of supplicants waiting around this building that I hadn't tried to get in; being at high altitude is debilitating enough without standing in a queue. But the snow and our accidental timing seemed to allow completely open access.

The Sanctuary dominated the bowl, and I felt that I had seen it from every angle. Yet the interior was not what I expected; it was a long barn of a place, simply constructed and with cheap gilt ornaments hanging down one wall. There were whisperings that the substantial annual donations made by the *naciones* were siphoned off by the Church rather than used to embellish the building.

The place was still filled with the deep and generous spirituality of the Andean people. They had placed large bunches of lilies and other flowers along the aisle, as well as candles everywhere. While the dancers moved down the main aisle, in the candle-lit shadows to either side were little clusters of quiet worshippers, lost in their private worlds.

I waited while Carlos went to be flagellated at the altar. As elsewhere at the festival, the penitent was always embraced first by the *hermano* who was about to whip him. While waiting (and trying not to watch, as it felt like an intrusion), I noticed a man in the deep shadows behind the great door to the Sanctuary, which had been left open during the festival. He had squatted down on his haunches with a candle, and looked as if he had been there for hours, hugging one of the model trucks from the *juego de las casitas*. He seemed completely oblivious of the celebrants streaming out of the church a few feet away, just as they were of him.

Following the others out, I realised why the church had been so easy to get into. The central mass was about to be celebrated by the priests as an outdoor service from the church's terrace; across the bowl, people had risen from their plastic sheets and shaken off the snow to listen. We were directly behind the open-air altar that had been set up; placed beside the crosses that lined it were feathered *chu'uncho* headdresses, an incongruous contrast with the sober vestments of the priests.

I walked back across the bowl during the long service, as if through a field of statues, with the celebrants standing rapt and listening to the priests' voices booming out over the PA system. Then I fell asleep at midday, just where I had left off, with a burning heat in my head, the noise of the festival outside and the sense that I was being buried alive in the middle of it.

*

I could only sleep for a short while. For now came the *coup de grâce* of the festival, the so-called twenty-four-hour walk out through the night and across the hills that Javier had talked about so much. This was the festival within a festival, the moment when the El Señor de Tayankani crucifix was taken from the Sanctuary after the blessing on the glaciers back to its home near Ocongate, with the transference of power of Qoyllurit'i's sacred landscape accomplished.

Only a small minority took this route. Most descended the way I had originally arrived, back to the road-head town of Mahuayani, where buses awaited them. The *hermanos* headed upwards instead, to make their twenty-four-hour pilgrimage over a high pass leading from the Sanctuary around the skirts of the Qoyllurit'i massif.

It seemed perverse, after the days of attrition we had just endured, to be climbing again, when we could see the main stream of pilgrims flowing contentedly away below us back to their beds. As we packed away the tent and gear, I felt that I was already, in the words of the country and western song, 'hurtin' and hurtin' bad'. The last thing I needed was a night of penitential rigour, walking some forty kilometres over the mountains in what looked, from the dark clouds I had seen when I emerged from my tent, to be filthy weather. More snow had fallen while I slept, and a frost had set in.

As before, it was only having companions that kept me motivated. Carlos, ten years older than me and with a heart condition, was determined to do it; Ramiro and John likewise; and meekly to descend the mountain with the other pilgrims would have felt flat.

The path was narrow at first and only allowed a single file. A long thin line of musicians, dancers and *ukukus* led the way to the pass up ahead; Javier and Henri were somewhere in among them. The sensation of 'following the pipers' across the hill helped me forget tiredness and altitude. John, Ramiro and I were walking, while Carlos rode, although we also had mules and another horse in case anyone tired. I rested at a corner and watched Carlos riding up to me, his black poncho swaying with the horse and a battered fedora planted firmly on his head, angelica tucked into the hatband. Beyond in the valley was the Sanctuary, with the remaining blue plastic sheets of those who had not yet left looking like an alluvial deposit from the glaciers.

It was three in the afternoon by the time we had climbed up and over the shoulder of a pass to a wide *pampa*, liberating after the constriction of the Sanctuary bowl. We could see mountain ranges in the distance and it had temporarily stopped snowing; the snow already lying on the ground flattened out perspectives, making a white-on-white landscape. Some of the musicians started to play, and then stopped when they met another group who had already set up their banners and crucifix. The two groups faced each other and began a call-and-response exchange with flutes and drums. I noticed that the brass instruments had been put to one side and were just being carried rather than played, as if the simpler, more traditional, Andean 'fife and drum' combination was enough here, and brass was only needed for the clamour of the Sanctuary. It was also noticeable that the banners had been given to some of the youngest members of the *comparsas* to carry, as if this were a handing on of the baton to a younger generation.

The musicians started off again and we followed. The man in front of me was carrying a big drum on his back and had to bend forward to counterbalance the weight. Further ahead I could see Carlos swaying on his horse, his poncho casting a long shadow on the snow as the sun went down.

The sun was soon obliterated completely, as the snow returned with a vengeance: black clouds blew up from the valley below. It happened suddenly. One moment we were descending past what in Scotland would have been called a tarn, a body of water too small to be a lake, where we had listened to a piper-boy playing to a cross, under a clear sky. The next, a blinding white-out came down with such severity that it was difficult to walk, not least because there was an accompanying bitter wind that drove us all backwards.

I could just see the horses ahead and tried to keep up with them, but there was no sign of John. The man with the drum sank down deep into the snow and just sat there, waiting for the storm to pass.

Struggling on, I had begun to lose my way in the snow and the dark, when a small Andean woman with a lamp appeared at my side, guiding the way. She was short, and held the lamp low so that the light fell on the ground. We carried on together and as the wind was too strong to talk, I just trusted blindly that she knew where she was going. For some reason I remembered *The Wind in the Willows*, and Mole and Rat advancing into the Wild Wood, a story I had been reading to the children. With the wind and the dark, all I could see were the long shadows that the lamp cast on the snow.

I heard voices up ahead, the unmistakable high-pitched camelid squeals of the *ukukus*. A brief clearing of the storm gave me a glimpse of a line of them on the hillside above. We had reached Yanacancha, the first resting-place on the journey, where the *ukukus* traditionally stopped to recuperate before walking through the night. I found Ramiro, Carlos and the horses on the approaches, and we pitched a simple bivouac camp to heat some soup and get a brief rest.

While the soup was cooking, Carlos and I wandered down among the *ukukus*, who had lit guttering fires by the walls of the simple stone corrals that made up the place. The *ukukus* were celebrating, like prefects who have finished term and are now allowed a party of their own. Although there were no bottles to be seen, I got the impression that the strict prohibition on drinking at the Sanctuary was relaxed once they got up here into the hills. The snow was an endless source of amusement to them; some were rolling down the hill in it; another group were making a snowman and trying vainly to fix the head on top.

A *capitán* wanted to address them all, and amidst much laughter climbed the nearby hillside clutching an outsize megaphone, like an old-time movie director. He shouted at the five hundred or so *ukukus* present that they should press on with great care, as some of the passes might be closed by the snow.

We let them leave first and followed on a little way behind. John had by now caught up with us; he had taken a wrong turn in the snow and followed some *ukukus* who, it later transpired, were themselves lost. Restored by analgesics washed down with hot soup, we set off into the black and closed-in night. Not a star was visible. If the Pleiades were indeed due to reappear around this time of year, it was not the night they were going to do so.

The journey begins to take on a dreamlike quality, helpful in that I lose track of time and distance completely. Angelica, the Andean woman who had guided me earlier, falls in beside us again with her lamp. Occasionally the clouds part to reveal the full moon, which lights up the night landscape – ridges shading off into grey, valleys dropping away into black beneath us and sometimes a glimpse of distant Mount Ausangate. At times we stop to drink *mate*, often when we come to a constellation of musicians' torches where they have gathered to play.

Slowly some stars start to appear above us – at one point we turn and seem to be heading straight for the Southern Cross. Below it, on the hills, are small clusters of *ukukus'* torches marking the way ahead, pinpricking the black.

The Quechua place-names roll away: the ascent to Senqa, the pass of Inti-Sulkayoc, the cross at Markaskunka, the high valley of Kachu-wayku, and the punishing slope of the narrow-pathed Leq'epata before the descent to Kak'allaki. At one stopping point, Ramiro discovers a trombone that has been left behind (presumably because the brass instruments are no longer being played). Some miles on down the road we meet the trombone's owner, who has run back for several hours to try to find it, and he falls in with us.

At around two in the morning, we reach a small shrine at 14,000 feet. Big fat candles are burning with extravagance around the small offerings and effigies on the makeshift stone shrine. Just as at the mass, the headdresses of the *chu'uncho* dancers have been placed beside their crosses and banners, as if they wanted to scatter the spirit of the jungle feathers across the mountains.

I'm beginning to feel weak, and lie on the ground for longer than is wise if I want to keep moving later. Ramiro produces a packet of Pringles, that staple food of the Andes, pronounced '*Pring-lees*', to rhyme with 'tease'; I lie prostrate, wolfing them down and forcing myself to drink coca tea. Looking straight up, I see a mackerel sky moving fast above me, as the clouds are driven back over the stars.

We pass little groups of *ukukus* who have stopped for rest, or a brief sleep. The pace, altitude and exposure are beginning to tell, and the *ukukus* have after all spent the previous night on the glacier for their vigil, and many previous nights pushing their bodies with a holy abandon.

A man is lying on the ground. His mouth is open and his skin blue. He looks dead. His musician companions are desperately trying to see whether he still breathes, but from their conversation it is clear they have little hope. Four of them sling his inert body between their arms and stumble off down the mountain with him, while others carry their instruments for them.

We come down to a plain, where a much larger group of *ukukus* have made their camp, surrounded by exhausted musicians who are no longer playing. Out of the darkness, a very young *ukuku* staggers towards us. He seems disorientated, punch-drunk. He is crying. Carlos and I try to talk to him. It seems he has lost his friends, and fallen on a stone; many of the *ukukus* have no torches, often by choice, as it is considered to lessen the challenge of the forced march over the mountains. We try to get a nearby group of *ukukus* to help him, but they are not sympathetic. '*Es un loco*, he's mad,' says one. Just as when I'd seen the young girl *ukuku* fall from the lorry on arriving at Mahuayani, there is a certain toughness about the *ukukus*, and their calling is a hard one; when a comrade falls by the wayside, he is often left there. There is an old *ukuku* saying: '*Ukuku muerto no es llorado. Ukuku muerto es celebrado.* You don't cry for a dead *ukuku*. You celebrate him.'

We start to straggle over the plain and lose each other. In the dark and the confusion, and as we are all tired, things begin to go wrong. First the muleteers panic when they lose their horses. We sit and wait for them, but discover that we have lost John, who always walks slowly, with his head down, and likes to be a loner on these occasions.

None of us, including Ramiro, has made this journey before, and it is not exactly signposted, so we have no idea how far we have still to go. In fact we are in one of the last high valleys before the descent to the village of Tayankani. We can either press on down, or make a camp for what little remains of the night – it is 4.30 a.m. – and hope John finds us, and that the muleteers find their horses. I've also heard that there is a ceremony marking the dawn above Tayankani, so don't want to miss that. Carlos gets into a tent before me, and is asleep, with a hat over his head, before I've had time to follow him.

The only thing that gets me up an hour or so later is hunger, and the nagging reminder that I've been resting in a sleeping bag while a friend is somewhere out on the mountain. It is still before dawn. Carlos has already risen. Outside, I can see him chatting to a few old ladies by the path. I look around blearily. And I realise that over on the skyline behind me there is an extraordinary vision – a host of dancers, musicians and *ukukus* have lined up on the ridge, looking for all the world like the massing soldiers of *Zulu*. Carlos seems blissfully unaware of them. I call him over, and we hurry to see the spectacle.

It is a wild awakening. There must be some thousand dancers lined up on the hill. Having slowly been arriving here through the night, they have now changed into full costumes, luminous in the pre-dawn light; the *chu'uncho*, the jungle dancers, are in one line, while the *colla*, the mountain dancers, are in another. And behind them are the *ukukus*, who likewise have put on their full bear costumes, with the red cross on the black fur.

Every so often one of the *caporales* of each order will run along the line, like a general reviewing his troops on a horse, shouting exhortations at them. They are all facing the range of mountains where the sun will rise. The cacophony of noise is overwhelming. The bands are all playing. And added to the sound of flutes, drums and bells is the massed sound of whistling. It is as if every person there has to add to the dawn chorus. As I drink this in, intoxicated already by lack of sleep and the suddenness of the spectacle, an accordion starts up behind me.

There are a few fires burning near by, the remnants of those lit

267

by people who have been waiting through the small hours. A late group of *ukukus* come running down the mountain, concerned that they may be late for the ceremony, perhaps having overslept wherever they had dropped for the night on the mountain crossing.

Everyone is bracing themselves for the coming of dawn. The sun appears over the mountains, as a wink between the peaks. The noise reaches a climax and then stops completely at a signal from one of the *celadores*, the guardians of the Sanctuary, dressed all in white. And a mass is held as the sun comes up fully.

As the service is intoned, the leaders of each order walk down the lines. The *colla* and the *chu'uncho* kiss the cross that their leader holds, but for the *ukukus* it is a whip that is proffered and that they kiss. I am just behind the *ukukus* and with the first light on them I can see the wild rawness in their faces after their nights of exposure. They have a telluric quality to them, as if etched from stone and *puna*, with the grain of their skin brought out by the blue cold, and also a fierceness that reminds me of pictures of the Hell's Angels at Altamont. The one nearest to me has three gold teeth that glint when he smiles.

I see Javier in the line, his whole face lit up, as if he feels accepted, part of the Andean world. He had already told me that, despite the ostensible mass, this greeting to the sun by the massed corps of dancers and *los hermanos*, 'the brothers', was the most pantheistic moment of all, a moment when the Andean spirit could be seen at its most naked.

The mass ends, and the lines of dancers tense and sway. For the mass is only the necessary preamble to what is to come. The *caporales* go up and down the lines giving final instructions, then take their places at the far end of the line. And the dance begins.

This is a dance at the run. The *caporales* of each order lead hundreds of their men behind them in a dance across the entire valley, peeling away and back towards each other, the *chu'uncho* from the jungle and the *colla* from the highlands weaving in and out of each other; the *ukukus* flanking them to either side, as a protective cordon for what is a *contradanza* between the ancient elements of Peru, the jungle and the highlands.

I run up the hill above, the better to see the enfolding pattern of the dance. Among the other spectators there is much laughter and speculation as to which of the two orders are doing better: '*Mira, ¡Paucartambo avanzan!* Look, Paucartambo [the jungle dancers] are winning.'

The two lines peel away to either side of the valley, making the landscape theirs. It is a living tapestry, weaving the elements of Peru together in a choreography of enormous scale – for the dance continues right out of the first valley and over a series of others that gradually descend towards Tayankani beyond. As they go, the lines crossing each other and re-forming, they make the *inti*-diamond shape representing the sun, the symbol that is universal throughout the Andes.

It is an intuitive choreography impossible to programme, for the *caporales* lead their men across the hills swiftly, at the run, and seem to make their minds up as they go, needing to respond to each other so that the lines can cross. There is much laughter at the crossing points, for the two lines interweave at speed, dancer by dancer, and the possibility of violent collision is ever present. Occasionally one line will outrun the other and have to wait, with much good-natured ribaldry, for their rivals to catch up so that they can interlace again.

In the brilliant dawn sunshine coming in low over the horizon, the colours of the dancers are intense, made more so by the grey winter landscape against which this is all played out, the thin grassland of the *puna* tightened like a stripped hide over the hills.

At one point the line of dancers across the landscape stretches so far that it looks like a Chinese wall rippling across the valleys. It is performance theatre on the biggest stage I have ever seen, an entire landscape danced into life. Perhaps what makes it so moving is that it is happening after the long march through darkness – dawn recognised in its most primal way. There is a sense that night has been dispelled with light and colour and a celebration of the Peruvian soul; it is the end of a long night's journey into day. I feel intoxicated, transported, exhausted. And in need of a good breakfast.

*

Carlos and I followed the dancers down the hill. There was still no sign of John. Ramiro and the muleteer had gone on ahead. As we came down into sight – and sound – of the church at Tayankani, the church bells were completely drowned out by all the harps, violins and instruments now let loose by the musicians, even the brass ones, as if they had been kept in reserve for this moment. From above, we witnessed a final dance in which a shorter line of *colla* danced against the *chu'uncho* in the churchyard.

Just above the hill, Ramiro had set up a stove so we could cook breakfast, and I was relieved to see John with him; after losing us, he had continued on down the mountain and spent a few hours sleeping against a wall. Then his nose for breakfast had led him to Ramiro. We watched together as the *ukukus* below collapsed along the sides of the church after their dancing, apart from those few who were to receive further initiation rites; they were taken off and whipped in the churchyard, although they probably got off lightly as those doing the whipping had hardly any energy left themselves. In another corner were young putative *ukukus* who, having completed the journey, were making their first application to join the *hermanos* the following year. And off to another side was a small area where local couples were getting unofficially 'married', in the same way as I had seen earlier at the *juego de las casitas*, amidst much hilarity and propositioning by unattached bridesmaids of stray passers-by, including me, for an instant marriage.

Beyond Tayankani, the pilgrimage trail wound over a further and last pass to Ocongate, where it met the road. I gratefully flopped onto one of our horses for this last ascent, although I walked down the other side, conscious of the Bhutanese saying: 'Only a rich man can afford to ride up a hill, but only a fool can afford to ride down.'

As we came into the small town of Ocongate, the villagers lined the narrow pathway and applauded all those arriving, as if at the end of a long-distance run. One village boy came up to us: '*¿Vino por encima?* Did you really come over the top?' he asked, unused to seeing any gringos on the pilgrimage.

I was still on a high when we got back to Cuzco. Although it was by now late in the evening again, my body-clock was still riding on the adrenaline of Qoyllurit'i, and I went to Ukukus, the nightclub named after the festival's guardians. The place was heaving with a mixture of dance-floor classics and pumping *techno-cumbia*; in the centre of the club was a large block of ice on a pillar. The owner told me that it had just been brought down from the glacier by some *ukuku* friends of his. Many in the club that night had also been to Qoyllurit'i. As they danced, the clubbers would rub their hands, bodies and faces over the ice, both to cool down and to take on some of the energy of the festival.

And I remembered what Nilda Callañaupa had said about the reason to do this pilgrimage. Nilda was from the same extended family of weavers from Chinchero whom I had spent time with; she had been to Qoyllurit'i many times and told me that her prime reason for going was that 'it makes you more comfortable as a human being to have different parts of the landscape within you'.

RETURN TO LLACTAPATA:
MACHU PICCHU'S OBSERVATORY

IT WAS TIME FOR the family to return to England. While we were sorry to leave Carlos, Claudia and what had become our home in Urubamba, at least we now had a piece of paper from the *juego de las casitas* at Qoyllurit'i showing that one day we might own property there ourselves and return.

Leo had his fourth birthday party at the house just before we left. With his shock of blond hair, he had been a popular mascot figure among the older girls when he paid a visit at the school, and many of Daisy's friends came to his party. My own birthday was around the same time, and Nick Asheshov arrived unexpectedly with champagne and dancing girls – two diminutive and shy Quechua ladies who insisted on dancing with Owen, to his mortification.

Leo in particular had become deeply attached to the household dogs and they would roam after him as he went around the garden, playing in the irrigation pools and ditches. Just a few days before our departure, Claudia came to me in tears; Leo's favourite, Silver, had been run over in the street by one of the trucks that the dogs incessantly chased; we kept the news from him. Leaving was quite sad enough as it was.

Gary Ziegler, Kim Malville and I prepared a lengthy formal report on our findings at Llactapata, which was published in the appropriate academic magazine, the *Revista Andina*, along with peer reviews of our findings by other experts. I was pleased to get the article published in Spanish and in Peru, mindful of Ruth Shady's admonition that so many archaeological reports were never made accessible to the country of investigation.

We also released the news to the press. As Nick Asheshov had always warned, this was not without its difficulties; the story that we had found more of an already known site did not have the simple clarity that news organisations like. In the main the archaeological correspondents of the *Telegraph, Independent, New York Times, LA Times* and other papers published the actual body of the story well. More of a problem were the headlines, where sub-editors would insist on reaching for a 'lost city' banner to put over the article (in the *Sun's* case, the headline 'LOST CITY FOUND' was virtually the whole of the article), although we had carefully avoided this term in our own press release, as misleading and overdramatic.

By the time we got to some of the American regional papers that wanted to pick up on the story, my patience had run thin, and I refused to cooperate with either pictures or interviews unless they guaranteed that 'lost city' would not appear in the headline. The result? 'LOST SUBURB FOUND NEAR MACHU PICCHU' (*Seattle Times*). This was the headline I read when in Seattle visiting Microsoft, who had invited me to help build a virtual-reality Machu Picchu that tourists could wander around over the web rather than have to visit the actual site – one curious by-product for me of the interest that our discoveries had provoked.

Meanwhile the response from fellow Andeanists was gratifying. John Hemming, who had first advised me many years ago on my first visit to Peru, arranged for me to give a lecture in London. Johan Reinhard, the discoverer of the 'Ice Mummies', the sacrificial child-victims on top of mountain peaks, who had himself reported on one of the Llactapata sectors, welcomed our findings and made the important point that Llactapata should now be incorporated inside the Machu Picchu Sanctuary and so conserved. Luis Lumbreras, the head of the Peruvian INC and a distinguished archaeologist, commented that our findings highlighted the importance to the Incas of the whole Machu Picchu area. Most crucially, the considerable publicity meant that the site was brought to the attention of the Peruvian authorities, and its possible value as an archaeological and tourist site established.

I was particularly pleased that Tom Zuidema was so supportive, both in the peer review on our report, which he contributed to the *Revista Andina*, and in his volunteering to return to the site with us the following year for some further work to consolidate our findings. Tom was one of the most senior Andeanists of his generation, with a considerable reputation for his achievements since he had first started coming to Peru in 1952. As a pioneer of archaeo-astronomy, his past students and colleagues had included Gary Urton and Anthony Aveni, whose respective studies of the *quipus* and the Nasca lines I admired. Indeed, it had been Tom's name as a patron that had kept Urton and Aveni out of jail when Maria Reiche had denounced them for trespassing on her *pampa*.

Throughout a long career in the Andes, Tom's area of study had been sacred landscapes and ethno-history. His work on the *ceque* system of the Incas had shown how they divided the area around Cuzco through those complicated but carefully delineated lines connecting the *huacas*, the shrines. Over a lifetime he had also continually been working on the equally complicated Inca calendrical system, about which he was uniquely qualified to write, as he drew on ethno-historical sources as well as the chronicles. Now he wanted to join us on a return visit to Llactapata to help us take even more precise measurements of the astronomical data with a theodolite and other specialised equipment.

Any concern that he would be a Grand Old Man quickly dissipated on meeting him in Cuzco. Tom proved to be mischievous and enthusiastic; his eyes lit up on discovering that we would, despite the skeletal nature of our team, still be taking a 'vodka mule'. On hearing that like just about every other serious investigation in the country we had been faced earlier with a *denuncia*, he declared: 'That's nothing – I've not only had *denuncias* but been thrown into jail.'

He had left Holland shortly after the war and had at first worked as a fledgling anthropologist in Indonesia until his doctoral supervisor had abruptly suggested he switch instead to Peru. When Tom arrived in Peru, he had met the equally penniless Maria Reiche, who was embarking on her long study of the Nasca lines and whom he admired for her persistence if not her intellect, and also John

Rowe, who was to be Tom's occasional rival as the other *éminence grise* of the Andeanist world. After a lifetime of involvement in that world, Tom's knowledge was encyclopaedic and was drawn largely from ethno-history, from acute observation of the contemporary descendants of ancient cultures, a technique that was often neglected by archaeologists who were not always temperamentally suited to opening themselves out in conversation.

Indeed, there had long been a childish rivalry between the twin Andeanist disciplines of anthropology and archaeology, based partly on their methods; archaeologists resented the short cuts by which anthropologists could simply talk to people rather than spend years digging. There were also personality clashes; Tom and John Rowe had not got on when they were in Cuzco in the 1950s and there had been many perceived slights between them – articles unacknowledged, and in particular Rowe's refusal to offer the impoverished Tom lifts to any of the sites he was visiting.

A more profound disagreement had arisen from a difference on the way in which the chronicles should be read, as historical, factual documents or as more literary texts that needed decoding.

From such trivial seeds had grown a long-standing rift between their respective schools, for Rowe had gone on to teach just about every Andeanist archaeologist of note and exerted great influence (one former student told me he dare not publish some radical new theories on a particular site while Rowe was still alive). Tom had likewise taught the most prominent Andeanist anthropologists and archaeo-astronomers.

The trench warfare was conducted at many levels – the most absurd being the refusal of some archaeologists to cite the anthropologists' books even when they closely related to their own work, say in astronomy. The usually mild-mannered Tom could still be roused to fury by the thought of John Rowe, whom he described as 'imperialistic' and 'blinkered', while recognising his considerable achievements as a scholar. Meanwhile one of Rowe's disciples had gone so far as to write that Tom was in denial for not accepting certain chronologies of Inca emperors established by Rowe.

Tom was a formidable talker once he got going – so much so

that I wondered how his ethno-historical sources had ever managed to get a word in edgeways. Despite his many years based in the States, he still spoke with a soft Dutch accent. His favourite word was 'fantastic', as in 'There is a *fantastic* essay by a young French anthropologist on the different Quechua terms for potato.'

Joining Tom were the core of the original team who had gone to Llactapata with me: Gary and Kim, together with the ebullient Nicholas Asheshov, who had just sold his hotel in Urubamba at considerable profit and had married María del Carmen, to the surprise of their friends – surprise in that most of us thought he had been married to her for the past twenty-five years anyway. His nine children had attended the wedding. The top-hatted bridegroom alarmed the family by galloping over the plains of Chinchero to get to the small church at Maras, despite his sight being so impaired – and this was no trick stunt, as his horse-wranglers told me Nick still galloped along the lanes above Urubamba every day.

John Leivers also joined us, looking exceptionally well. After suffering some seventeen bouts of giardia after his years of living rough, he had finally bombarded his stomach with antibiotics of such exceptional severity ('I sourced them on the internet') that even the giardic cysts had given up the fight, and he looked a brand-new man as a result.

We all walked up to Llactapata again from the Aobamba valley. I noticed how the valley floor was being replanted with pisonays and other native trees, and was recovering from the awful landslide of a few years previously. We had come a bit later in the year than before, in order to make observations close to the June solstice, and the red pampas grass had an autumnal glow to it in the evening sun as we climbed the shoulder, past ferns of every description: hart's tongue, lady-fern, ostrich fern, tree ferns higher up and a myriad of other small ones, nameless to me at least. There were begonias everywhere, as well as wild strawberries along the path.

I stopped to talk to the Añanca family, who had long owned a smallholding near the site; Hiram Bingham had recorded meeting Marcello Añanca back in 1912. Silverio, Marcello's great-grandson, was a burly well-built man in his early thirties. He was concerned that the interest in the site resulting from our earlier investigation would jeopardise the family's use of the land for pasture and agriculture; just like the Incas, they exploited the different heights on the slope, growing coffee and bananas on the lower slopes, maize and potatoes up above, with some high grazing as well when they could afford the cattle.

Silverio reported that, as we knew, the Peruvian authorities had come to Llactapata following our report and had officially registered the newly found, different sectors of the site as well as beginning the process of initial preservation. It was gratifying to see that the walls of the main sectors were now propped up with supporting posts, as we walked around with Tom Zuidema, showing him our findings. They had even begun the process of anastilosis, the laborious process of marking up each stone in a building so that it could be taken apart and restored.

However, the INC had done less at Sector III, the area with the ceremonial platform, which Gary and I had measured with such growing excitement when we had first found it. Here the *huaqueros* had come and with ruthless thoroughness virtually demolished the small granite building connected to the *usnu* by a causeway. They had dug such a large hole in its centre that the back and side walls had given way, spilling the finely cut granite ashlars on all sides, a heartbreaking act of pointless destruction, given that all that they were likely to find were a few broken bits of pot. From candles they had left on upturned Gloria milk cans all around to light the scene, we knew the *huaqueros* had worked at night.

It was a reminder that the site desperately needed permanent protection – ideally in some arrangement with the local community at Santa Teresa and with the local smallholders, whereby they could gain tourist revenue in return for maintaining the area. Higher up the slope it seemed unlikely that the INC or, indeed, the *huaqueros* had been able to find the small Overlook Temple. Some days later Gary was able to show the young INC archaeologist supervising the site registration exactly where it was.

Having Tom Zuidema with us meant that we could discuss in more detail the most important aspects of the architecture of

Llactapata that we had revealed on our previous expedition. Most remarkable was that the layout of the main buildings in the Bingham sector of Llactapata seemed to correspond with the layout used at the Coricancha, the main Sun Temple in Cuzco. This insight of Kim Malville's was impressive. Since our original visit, he had been able to demonstrate that the central part of the 'Bingham sector' at Llactapata, with its seven buildings, passageways and courtyards, was astonishingly similar in scale and orientation to the Coricancha.

The Coricancha was the central most important religious building for the Incas, in Cuzco at the heart of their realm; it contained some of their finest stonework, even by Inca standards. When Atahualpa needed gold to ransom himself from the Spanish, he sent to the Coricancha for it to be stripped from the walls.

On the western side of the Coricancha are a group of buildings that, just as at Llactapata, surround a corridor leading to a high-status double-jamb doorway. Kim had shown that the orientation of the corridors at both sites is uncannily similar, both pointing to the same place on the horizon where the Pleiades and the June solstice sun rose. The rooms to either side are also close to identical in size and layout.

We know that the Incas took buildings and town-planning in Cuzco as their model, and then copied this pattern across their realm. A sector of Llactapata seems clearly to have been copied from the Coricancha in just this way, as a miniature 'Sun Temple'.

By that evening, after a full but exhausting tour of the site, including the sector mirroring the Coricancha and also the long sunken corridor pointing towards Mount Machu Picchu and the solstice, Tom was ready to break open the first bottle on the vodka mule. 'What a *fantastic* place – I feel I need a whole second lifetime to see where this is all leading.'

*

I woke during the middle of the night. As I stood looking up at the stars again, and the brilliantly illuminated panorama of Salcantay and the distant peaks, I recalled that similar moment when I was last here, still fresh from England, finding my feet and my vision again. Then I had been anxious whether we would discover anything at all at Llactapata or if it was just a wild-goose chase Hiram Bingham had sent us on. Now I was stargazing with more relaxed and indeed interested eyes, and not just because we had succeeded in our original mission, or because of the many nights I had spent studying the night sky with Carlos and Andrés, the nightwatchman, while living at Urubamba. For astronomy was proving essential to any interpretation of Llactapata.

Of all the stars that fascinated the Incas and their forebears, the Pleiades or 'Seven Sisters' were the ones that mattered most. I knew them well from the winter night skies of Europe, a closely knit group of small twinkling stars just out of arm's reach from Orion the hunter. They were too small to be their own Zodiacal constellation in Western astronomy, but were of consummate importance to the Incas. I had already seen how important they were to the origin of the Qoyllurit'i festivities.

Their very faint twinkling nature meant that the Seven Sisters' visibility could easily be affected by atmospheric changes; indeed, as some stars in the group are fainter than others, the number of 'sisters' that could actually be seen was a good indicator of visibility (one rarely sees all seven, for instance, from light-polluted England). The Spanish chronicler Francisco de Avila noted in 1608 that the Huarochirí Indians near Lima carefully watched the first rising of the Pleiades to note how large and bright they were and believed that this indicated the strength of a future harvest – a custom that continues right up until the present time.

Recent investigations by Benjamin Orlove, a professor at UCLA, have proved a fascinating validation of this. Orlove was intrigued by the way in which contemporary Quechua Indians carefully studied the appearance of the Pleiades. They told him that if the stars looked particularly radiant, that was an indicator that four months later there would be plentiful rainfall and a good harvest. However, if the Pleiades appeared lacklustre and faint, little rain would fall later in the year, making early planting essential.

Orlove realised that the *campesinos* had found a way to predict El

Niño, which, while it precipitates flooding on the coast, can cause a drought in the mountains and ruin the crucial potato harvest (the potato being shallow-rooted and so particularly vulnerable to lack of rain). This led Orlove and his colleagues to wonder whether the transparency of the night sky was somehow affected by El Niño. But it was strange that when the Pleiades were seen clearly, rain was forecast – precisely the opposite of what would happen if cloud cover was building up and that was what was obscuring the stars. Moreover the Pleiades were being used to predict what the weather would be like in four months' time.

It was then suggested that the farmers might be witnessing the effects of very high-altitude clouds – too thin to see, yet dense enough to affect starlight. After trawling through satellite data, Orlove and his UCLA team found that during El Niño years there was indeed an increase in high-altitude clouds in the region during June – and in precisely the part of the sky where the Pleiades first appear.

Quite how the Incas discovered this is unclear, but it would seem likely that they imbibed it from the same ancient Andean spring from which they took so much of their knowledge and which fed back down from millennia before. Bernabé Cobo, the same Spanish priest whose chronicle I had followed when visiting the Island of the Sun, noted that the 'group of small stars commonly known as the Pleiades, which these Indians called Collca [the storehouse]' were the main focus of attention of the Inca astronomers. 'Those Indians who were informed about such matters kept better track of its course all year long than that of any of the other stars.' He added: 'It was called "mother" and it was universally considered to be a major *huaca* [object of worship].'

The date of the heliacal rising of the Pleiades (their first appearance in the night sky) is approximately 9 June at this latitude. They were therefore doubly significant in the Inca world because their reappearance was part of the celebrations leading up to the solstice around 21 June, the start of their year, known as Inti Raymi.

Near the end of April, the Pleiades became invisible again as the sun was too close and the sky too bright. For approximately thirty-seven days the Pleiades could not be seen – and these were considered 'missing days' in the Inca calendar, when sacred time ceased to flow. Then around 9 June the Pleiades appeared in the eastern sky just before dawn, perhaps only for a few seconds before the Sun rose and flooded the sky with light. This was the moment that the 'dawn dance' I had seen at Qoyllurit'i may well have been re-enacting. Because this sighting was so fleeting, the Incas needed markers to indicate exactly where the Pleiades first made their appearance above the horizon – as it so happened, and very conveniently, at almost precisely the same place as the sun rose for the summer solstice twelve days or so later.

And this was why the Pleiades were so important for our interpretation of Llactapata. What Kim Malville had noted on our previous visit, and what had drawn Tom Zuidema here as well, was the orientation of the long 150-foot sunken corridor we had found in the main sector of the site and which was its central dividing feature; it pointed towards the spot on the horizon where the Pleiades were due to rise. Due to their very faintness, this would have been a real aid to the waiting sky-watchers.

Because the corridor was so long and relatively narrow, when viewed from the far rear end the angle of aperture created by the open gateway was precise, and allowed for the rising of the Pleiades and the June solstice sun to be seen with considerable accuracy. Moreover the sunken corridor had no doors leading from it, despite its great length, so it had no other useful architectural function.

This momentous discovery had taken considerable additional research from source materials about the Incas' use of both the Pleiades and the June solstice. It was further confirmation of our major finding about the site: that Llactapata was in effect an observatory for Machu Picchu, fulfilling some of the same functions as the Coricancha did for Cuzco.

I determined that early the next morning I would awake before dawn and head up to see the sun rise down the corridor myself.

*

There was something magical – and in my case rarely experienced – about being the first to rise in the campsite: the green tents glowing in the grey light of pre-dawn, the clouds lying in the valley below us, the moon still visible and the giant peak of Mount Salcantay already gleaming pink from the first sun as it caught the dawn so much earlier than the camp. And of course I was not the first up; Ramiro was already boiling water, the smoke blowing across the grass past the grazing horses.

I took some tea to John Leivers, who had volunteered to come with me. Ramiro cooked eggs and porridge for us before we began the climb. My concern was that the clouds below would lift and obscure our vision of sunrise from the solstice corridor, but John was reassuringly confident: 'They'll either burn off or rise up much later when the morning sun heats them.'

We were walking in the calm of the shade, a few small hummingbirds singing noisily and one of them, a sparkling violeteer, seeming to chase us up the slope. I felt as excited as when I had first come to Llactapata over twenty years before. We climbed the 300 feet to the sector at a good pace; by 6.30 we were jumping down into the long 150-foot sunken corridor and making our way along the dark and overgrown walls, negotiating the supporting posts put up by the INC to hold them in place. Then we were in position at the end of the corridor, awaiting sunrise. We knew from Kim's calculations exactly where on the horizon the sun was supposed to come up at the solstice, and light was already radiating around that point.

But it is one thing to know something theoretically and quite another to experience it in the flesh. When the sun actually rises at great speed and hits us, it is, in the true sense of the word, phenomenal – for the sun casts a direct beam of light directly down the long corridor with incredible precision. The clouds have remained below in the valley, so the sun is at full strength. John stands silhouetted at the entrance to the corridor as the light streams past him. His shadow, with his broad-brimmed hat, goes right down the corridor in the beam of light. The walls of the corridor are lit up from the reflected beam.

I cannot remember a more intense experience in the Andes. It is epiphanic, almost Damascene, in that for so many years I had been sceptical about the astronomical alignments often claimed for Inca sites. But this is incontrovertible, 100 per cent confirmation of the solstice theory. I can feel the sun on my face to prove it; in the manner of the true doubter, my conversion is all the more total for having questioned it for so long. It is the culmination of a change that has been growing in me over the previous year as I absorbed the spirit of ancient Peru on my travels through the country.

I feel for a brief and rare moment that I have touched the hem of an other-worldly and completely different civilisation in all its light and strangeness – a connection to a way of thinking almost washed away by the Western monoculture that has engulfed Peru since the Conquest and seemingly spread into every last crevice of the planet.

Momentarily blinded by the low dawn sun flooding down the corridor, I was brought up short from this vision when I smacked my head into one of the posts the INC had put up to protect the side walls, uttering a cry of pain. John turned from being an epic figure silhouetted by the dawn into his normal blunt, Antipodean self: 'Aw, don't worry, there's not much blood on your face. It's only a graze.'

Sun was likewise streaming into the nearby chamber with the double-jamb doorway; the whole plaza beside it was orientated to face the rising sun and it was easy to imagine just such a scene as I had witnessed at dawn at Qoyllurit'i, but one played out with architectural precision: the priests and Inca astronomers observing the solstice down the corridor; the emperor, just as at the Coricancha, off to one side in his own chamber, also watching the sunrise, while courtiers and others assembled on the plaza facing Machu Picchu, probably including dancers and musicians.

And that was perhaps one of the most intriguing of revelations to come out of Llactapata: that it was symbiotic to Machu Picchu, designed so that one could be admired from the other. I remembered Kim's words when we had first come here together, when he had compared it to the Hindu concept of *darshan*, in which a devotee makes eye contact with a god who then returns the stare.

We had all been up to Machu Picchu just before returning to Llactapata and it was extraordinary how differently we looked at the site with the knowledge that Llactapata would have been in full view to the west. The western side of Machu Picchu had always previously been considered the 'blind side' of Machu Picchu and not of particular interest. Hiram Bingham could not understand why the Sacred Plaza, the most important grouping of buildings anywhere on the site, was open on that side and faced west. He presumed that the Incas had just not got around to erecting another building on that side, whereas in fact they may deliberately have left it open to focus attention towards Llactapata and distant Mount Pumasillo beyond. There is likewise the curved *mirador* facing that way, which has also puzzled previous commentators, and from which I had watched the sun setting on Llactapata. This faces absolutely clearly towards Llactapata, and is made of fine curved ashlars, traditionally used by the Incas only for buildings of the greatest importance, like the Coricancha and the Torreón.

Tom Zuidema, Gary, Kim and I had re-examined the so-called 'Sacristy', one of the finest buildings of all, set off to one side from the Sacred Plaza. Again this is orientated to face away from the rest of Machu Picchu, but directly towards Llactapata. It even has a stone seat-ledge inside from which to view it. And while we had been there, the Peruvian archaeologist based at Machu Picchu, Fernando Astete, had kindly showed me some terraces that had just been cleared and restored on the western side and were far more elaborate than had previously been realised, with niched walls and flying steps, also facing Llactapata.

All this made more sense when one remembers that Llactapata would have been the only Inca site directly visible from Machu Picchu. Kim and Gary theorised that there might have been some ritual progression from Machu Picchu to Llactapata; if so, the Incas had a spectacular road to process along, the so-called 'drawbridge route' across the western cliff-face of Mount Machu Picchu, which leads in the direction of Llactapata and is named after the removable set of logs at the steepest point (a route now closed to tourists since one of their number dropped off it).

One could easily imagine a reciprocal ceremony at the time of the June solstice. While those of the court present at Llactapata would have seen the sun flooding down the long corridor directly towards them, as John and I had, others remaining at Machu Picchu would have seen Llactapata lit up by the first rays. The priests at Llactapata might even have used shields of gold, like the celebrated Punchao, 'the shield of the sun', to reflect the solstice sun back to the watching observers across the valley, as we know they did with reflecting metals at the Coricancha and on the Island of the Sun.

The whole of this last visit to Llactapata was inevitably heightened by my recent travels through the principal sites of ancient Peru, as I had hoped it would be. The relationship of the site to Machu Picchu encapsulated so many of the themes I had seen emerging through a period of four millennia: the natural concern to understand the calendar and climate, given the Andean peoples' acute dependence on it; the architecture of power and ritual; even the division of the site into principal upper and lower, *hanan* and *hurin*, sectors, just as at Caral 5,000 years before.

Above all it exemplified the great achievement of Andean pre-Columbian civilisation: the ability to give meaning to a harsh and difficult environment, to carve order out of the inchoate, perhaps the most primeval of aesthetic impulses, in this case to create a complex sacred landscape where once had been plain rock and water. Any other people would have looked at the terrifyingly precipitate terrain round Machu Picchu, 'a landscape built by titans in a fit of megalomania' as Christopher Isherwood once described it, and turned away.

It exemplified the ancient Peruvian need for other repositories of meaning; without writing, they invested everything they wanted to pass on to their descendants into landscape, rock art, lines across the desert and elaborate weavings. Like the cochineal red of those weavings, much of Peru's past remains visible, stained into the fabric of the country and lived by the descendants of those who built their empires. Indeed, my sense of the country is that it is slowly trying to weave a pattern out of the disparate symbols it has collected over five millennia – in the same way that we all weave our own past to make sense of it, in my case by writing this book.

It was my very last day at Llactapata. I had to leave ahead of the others and then fly out. With just a single mule and *arriero*, I wandered down the ridge, again bathed in late afternoon sun, which was burnishing the pampas grass a soft red. Far below, the Urubamba snaked its way from Machu Picchu and on around the corner towards the distant Amazon. I felt at peace with myself, and I suddenly remembered the words with which John Hemming had first suggested I come here twenty-five years before: 'Anyone can find a ruin in the jungle; but it can take a lifetime to understand what you have found.'

GLOSSARY

NOTE

The spelling of pre-Columbian terms is variable and political. I have largely followed the spelling used in *The White Rock*, trying to keep to those that are most familiar.

As the citizens of Nasca have now elected to be spelt with a 'c', not a 'z', I have respected their lead. Qoyllurit'i is a term that has more spelling differences than most, and important ones in that they can affect meaning. I have followed Jorge Flores Ochoa in using 'Qoyllurit'i'.

adobe Bricks of dried mud bound with straw, widely used in the Andes for construction.

alpaca Domesticated camelid highly valued for its wool; smaller than a llama.

altiplano The high plateau of the Andes, above the treeline.

anadenanthera A low montane shrub, which contains *DMT* (dimethyltryptamine) and is used to produce a hallucinogenic snuff.

anastilosis Technique for reassembling the stones of decayed buildings in their original places, usually by numbering them.

apu Spirit of the mountains.

arriero Muleteer.

arroyo River-channel that is normally dry but fills in the rainy season.

ayahuasca Hallucinogenic drink containing *DMT* (dimethyltryptamine).

Aymara Ethnic group and also language of the peoples living to the south and east of Lake Titicaca.

azimuth The horizontal angle used together with a vertical elevation to give the position of an object in the sky from a given observation point.

biomorph A *geoglyph* of a living organism, be it plant or animal.

cajón Peruvian box-drum.
campesino Worker of the land.
cancha Small group of buildings around a courtyard.
cantina Bar.
Capac-nan The 'royal road' of the Incas from Quito to Cuzco.
caporal Foreman.
Caral Part of a complex of very early civilisations near the Supe valley of central Peru that have recently been dated from *c.*2700 BC to 1800 BC. Caral itself was occupied from around *c.*2600–2100 BC.
celador Guardian, as of the Qoyllurit'i Sanctuary.
ceque Imaginary line radiating out from Cuzco and passing through a set of *huacas*, shrines. Each *ceque* was the responsibility of one of the *panacas*, the royal Inca lineages.
chacra Cultivated field, smallholding.
Chan Chan The capital of the *Chimú*, near the modern city of Trujillo on Peru's north coast.
Chavín de Huantar This ancient site (*c.*1200–200 BC) lies in the mountains on an important trade route between the jungle and the coast. It is an early example of the importance of cross-fertilisation between Peru's different zones, as its builders mixed elements of coastal architecture with jungle images of jaguars and snakes on their stelae and friezes. The influence of Chavín art spread right across the Andes.
chicha Fermented maize drink, traditionally made using saliva.
chicharrones Deep-fried pork, an Andean delicacy.
Chimú Contemporary rivals of the Incas, who expanded their Chimor empire along 800 miles of the northern Peruvian coast and were conquered by the Incas before the arrival of the Spanish.
cholo Indigenous man of the people, a 'lad'.
Choquepukio Huari site near Cuzco, close to the larger site of *Pikillacta*.
Choquequirao Inca site near the Apurímac. The name means 'cradle

of gold' in *Quechua*. Like *Machu Picchu*, it has a dramatic setting on a mountain saddle over a river.

chuño Form of dried potato.

chu'uncho Dancers in 'jungle costume', including a feathered headdress.

coca Plant (erythroxylon) used by Indians for stamina and health and by the drugs trade to extract cocaine. The tea made from it is called *mate de coca*.

cochineal Red dye-stuff obtained from the cochineal insect found on certain cacti.

colla Dancers in 'mountain costume', who often dance contrapuntally to the *chu'uncho*. The original Colla were a tribe contemporary with the Incas.

comparsa A group or company, used here at the Qoyllurit'i festival.

cumbi The finest camelid cloth of the Incas, used only for royal garments.

cumbia Colombian version of salsa, popular across South America. *Techno-cumbia* is a modern hybrid form.

Cusichaca. Complex of archaeological sites at the confluence of the Urubamba and Cusichaca rivers, excavated by Ann Kendall in the late 1970s and early 1980s as part of the Cusichaca Project she initiated.

Cuzco (Cusco / Qosco) Capital of the Inca empire.

delincuente Delinquent, criminal.

denuncia A legal accusation.

DMT (Dimethyltryptamine): the active ingredient in hallucinogenic snuffs such as *anadenanthera* and in the drink prepared as *ayahuasca*.

empanada Stuffed pastry.

Espíritu Pampa Modern-day settlement in the Andean lowlands (around 3,000 feet) near which the Inca city of Old Vilcabamba was found by Gene Savoy in 1964. The name was evocatively translated by Hiram Bingham as 'the Plain of Ghosts'.

estado The rough height of a man, five to six feet, employed by the Spanish for measuring vertical distances.

explorer Term of abuse used by archaeologists.

federales Police agents.

geoglyph Any design made across a landscape, whether abstract or figurative.

guanaco Fast-running camelid related to the llama and the *alpaca*. An exceptionally curious creature, large groups of them will sometimes congregate near hunters to see where the shots are coming from. As a result, their numbers are in decline.

hacienda The house and grounds, usually substantial, of an estate.

hanan Upper moiety or subdivision of an Inca town.

hermano Brother.

huaca Shrine, or sacred place.

huaquero Looter.

Huari (or Wari) Civilisation that flourished in the highlands around Ayacucho from *c.* AD 600–1000 whose influence spread to the coast and the area around Cuzco. The Incas appropriated some Huari legacies such as their use of the *quipu* and of a road system to connect distant colonies.

Huayna Picchu The ruins of *Machu Picchu* lie on a saddle between two mountains, Mount Machu Picchu and the much-photographed Mount Huayna Picchu. *Huayna* in this context means 'lesser', to distinguish it from *Machu*, meaning 'greater', as *Huayna Picchu* is the smaller of the two mountains.

hurin Lower moiety or subdivision of an Inca town.

huayno **music** Mountain guitar music accompanied by high-pitched vocals: an acquired taste.

Inca (Inka) The Incas expanded rapidly from their base in *Cuzco* between *c.* AD 1400 and 1532, establishing their 'realm of the four quarters', *Tahuantinsuyo*, before it was cut short by the arrival of the Spanish.

indigenismo Movement in Peru promoting a return to pre-Columbian values, strong in the 1920s and 1930s. Hence *indigenista*, one espousing *indigenismo*.

Instituto Nacional de Cultura (INC) 'National Institute of Culture' responsible for archaeological monuments in Peru.

inti The sun.

intihuatana 'Hitching post of the sun'. Term used for some Inca sculptures, such as one at the centre of the Sacred Plaza in *Machu Picchu*, and also one lying near the Urubamba river below.

juego de las casitas 'Game of the little houses' acted out at the festival of *Qoyllurit'i*.

kallanka Inca meeting-hall.

Llactapata Site discovered by Bingham in 1912 on a mountain ridge between the Aobamba and Santa Teresa valleys, and then lost again. The name means 'high town' in *Quechua*.

Machu Picchu The best-known of Inca sites, lying on a saddle at almost 8,000 feet between Mount Machu Picchu and Mount Huayna Picchu. It is thought to have belonged to the estate of the Inca emperor Pachacuti.

Majeños Dancers from the Majes valley, where the site of *Toro Muerto* is located.

marinera Peruvian dance in which the couple advance on one another, the woman coquettishly waving her handkerchief.

mate de coca Tea made from *coca* leaves.

mestizo Phrase used after the Spanish Conquest to refer to those of mixed Indian and European blood.

mirador Viewpoint platform; a common feature of some Inca sites and paths.

mita (*mit'a*) Inca system of compulsory community labour.

mitamayo The practice of transplanting populations from one part of the country to perform *mita* in another, with those transplanted known as *mitimaes*.

Moche Small but exuberant civilisation, which flourished on the northern coast of Peru in the first millennium, from around AD 50–700. They left superbly expressive ceramics depicting the human face and finely worked jewellery such as that recently found at Sipán. The ceramics also give a vivid picture of their various sacrificial and sexual activities.

moraya Freeze-dried potato.

moya Literally a garden or orchard, but used more widely to refer to 'a place of leisure' for enjoyment and relaxation, a 'country estate' of the sort the Inca emperors would retire to from *Cuzco*.

Nasca (Nazca) A culture that was at its peak from around AD 1–700, most famed for the great line-markings on the desert plain of Nasca. Some of these *geoglyphs* are geometric, some figurative, like the figure of an enormous hummingbird. The lines have attracted much speculation. The name comes from the nearby town of Nasca.

El Niño Known as 'the Child', because it often occurs around Christmas, this occasional meteorological phenomenon upsets the climatic balance in Peru and can cause severe flooding and drought.

ocarina Clay whistle.

Pachacamac Pre-Columbian pilgrimage site near Lima, and the site of the most venerated oracle in the country when the Spanish conquistadors arrived.

Pachamama Andean deity, loosely translated as 'Mother Earth'.

Paititi 'Lost city in the jungle': probably mythical, frequently searched for and never found.

Palcay Small classical Inca site at head of Aobamba valley.

pampa Literally 'a plain', as in Argentina, but often used in the Andes for any small enclosed flat area.

panaca Group of royal descent and associated estate, perpetuated after the death of an Inca emperor.

Paracas Peninsula on the coast that has given its name to the culture that flourished there from around 800 BC – AD 1. Celebrated for its elaborate funerary textiles, the nearby *Nasca* culture later emerged from it.

petroglyph Drawing or carved design on rock.

Pikillacta The 'Place of the Flea': large *Huari* site near *Cuzco*.

pisco Peruvian brandy; a *pisco sour* is made by combining it with lemon and egg white.

polylepis Ancient pre-Columbian trees planted by the Incas, often forming stands high above the normal treeline; they are a habitat for some of the rarest birds in the world. Unfortunately the trees grow slowly and burn well, so have been much reduced in recent years.

provenance Context in which an archaeological find is made. An artifact 'with provenance' is of far more value than one without.

puna High-altitude Andean grassland, above the treeline.

Punchao The golden image of the sun, at the heart of Inca religious practice.

qeros Drinking vessel.

qolqa Storehouse.

Qoyllurit'i Annual festival held in June near Ocongate and the Ausangate massif to the east of *Cuzco*, in honour of *El Señor de Qoyllurit'i*.

Quechua Dialect adopted by the Incas to be the lingua franca of the empire and still widely spoken. Also used to refer generically to their descendants.

quinoa Colourful plant with a fine grain, grown on the *altiplano*.

quipu The knotted cords used in the Andes to keep records; the mnemonic system has yet to be fully decoded.

quipucamayoc An interpreter of the *quipu*.

ritual Paul Bahn, in *Bluff your Way in Archaeology*, describes this term as an 'all purpose explanation used where nothing else comes to mind'.

Sacred Valley The so-called 'Sacred Valley' or *Valle Sagrado* of the Incas lies along the Urubamba / Vilcanota river to the north of *Cuzco*, where substantial Inca sites were built at Pisac, Yucay and Ollantaytambo. The climate is suitable for growing maize, essential for the ritual drinking of *chicha*, which the Inca practised. It was an important area for them, for agricultural as well as possible religious reasons. However, the actual term 'Sacred Valley' was not used by the Incas themselves, as is often assumed, but was a marketing invention of 1950, designed to promote a driving rally held in the valley that year.

Sechín Archaeological complex, settled between 1800 and 1300 BC. A frieze at Cerro Sechín shows some 350 monumental stone figures, many decapitated.

selva Jungle: the phrase '*ceja de selva*', 'the eyebrow of the jungle', is often used to refer to the high cloud-forest on the descent to the Amazon basin and its more tropical rainforest.

Señor de Qoyllurit'i The Lord of Qoyllurit'i: the figure of Christ as embodied by the shepherd boy of the Qoyllurit'i legend.

stratigraphy Interpretation of archaeological evidence depending on the level in the earth at which it is found.

Tahuantinsuyo The Inca empire, which was divided into four quarters.

tambo Small settlement or lodging-house along Inca highways; also used for storage.

taytacha Banner with a representation of *El Señor de Qoyllurit'i*.

terraform Verb: a term used by archaeologists when they mean 'to landscape'.

Tiahuanaco Ruins near Lake Titicaca, the centre of an eponymous culture, which flourished between *c.* AD 200 and 1000 and extended over highland Bolivia and the far south of Peru. The Incas were much influenced by Tiahuanaco architecture, and appropriated the shrines on the Islands of the Sun and of the Moon as their own.

tinquy A meeting place: used of the highland fairs, which are often marriage markets, and also for the encounters of ritualised combat between communities.

Toro Muerto. Site in the Majes valley near Arequipa, with many *petroglyphs*.

tumi Ceremonial knife.

tupu Pin used by Inca women to hold a shawl in place.

ukukus The guardians of the Qoyllurit'i festival, who wear furred costumes, masks and carry whips to enforce the festival's rules; sometimes called *pablitos*.

ulluchu Fruit used by the *Moche*, related to the papaya, which has anti-coagulant properties and was often associated with ceremonies of human sacrifice; often represented as paisley-shaped in their ceramics.

uña de gato Herb, translated literally as the 'nail of the cat'; used medicinally, for tea and less commonly to flavour *pisco*.

Urubamba Small town on the Urubamba river in the *Sacred Valley* near *Cuzco*.

usnu Ceremonial platform.

Valle Sagrado See *Sacred Valley*.

Vilcabamba An area north-west of *Cuzco*, centreing on the Vilcabamba river, to which the Incas retreated after the Conquest.

viringo Pre-Columbian breed of hairless dog.

Vitcos Inca centre in the *Vilcabamba*, which they used when they escaped from the Spanish after the Conquest.

Wiñay Wayna Attractive site close to Machu Picchu, discovered by the Paul Fejos team at the very end of their expedition in 1941.

zampoña Double-rowed panpipe.

NOTES AND REFERENCES

5 *the pressure of so many clouds.* Elizabeth Bishop, 'Questions of Travel', *Complete Poems* (Chatto & Windus, 1983).

7 *an energetic and capable archaeologist called David Drew.* David Drew went on to make television programmes and to write a book about the Maya, *Lost Chronicles of the Maya Kings* (Weidenfeld & Nicolson 1999). See Drew (1984) for his report on Llactapata.

10 *Pampacahuana – best ruins of all.* This refers to the ruins around the Cusichaca valley, which Bingham was indeed to investigate and excavate later; he also explored the 'Inca Trail', which begins there.

12 *his half-hearted and incomplete description of Llactapata.* The slight nature of Bingham's account of Llactapata must be set in its literary context. The same *National Geographic* report, 'In the Wonderland of Peru', contains the first descriptions of Machu Picchu and of substantial Inca sites at Vitcos and at Espíritu Pampa. Given that any one of these by themselves would have constituted a major discovery, it is perhaps understandable that he did not devote as much attention to Llactapata as he might otherwise have done.

13 *Reinhard mapped the building.* He also reported that looting had taken place at the site: 'Some digging had been done here, including one hole dug recently, i.e. possibly within the past year.' See Reinhard (1990).

17 *'worker colonies' placed discreetly out of royal eyesight up the valley.* As at, for instance, Cusichaca – see Kendall, 'Current Archaeological Projects' (1984) for fuller discussion of this site, as well as a description in *The White Rock*.

18 *Johan Reinhard had shown how carefully aligned.* In his book *Machu Picchu: The Sacred Center* (Lima, 1991: revised edn 2002), p. 19.

18 *Bingham had been so puzzled by this find.* See Bingham, *Lost City of the Incas.* 'Results of Excavations at Machu Picchu' (New York, 1948).

19 *Jay Ague, a geologist at Yale, had gone further.* See Richard L. Burger, 'Scientific Insights into Daily Life at Machu Picchu' in Richard L. Burger and Lucy Salazar-Burger (eds), *Machu Picchu: Unveiling the Mystery of the Incas* (Yale University Press, 2004).

20 *Burger saw Bingham as foreshadowing.* Op. cit.

24 *recent work on what scholars sometimes described as the 'sacred landscape' of the Incas.* See Richard Townsend (ed.), *The Ancient Americas: Art from Sacred Landscapes* (The Art Institute of Chicago, 1992).

26 *The Paul Fejos team simply confused the two sites.* See Paul Fejos, *Archaeological Explorations in the Cordillera Vilcabamba, Southeastern Peru* (1944), p. 17: '[Bingham's expedition of 1915] spent two months clearing and excavating the ruins of Llactapata (also called Patallacta), a short distance *down* the canyon of the Urubamba from Machu Picchu' [my italics]. In fact Bingham excavated the site upriver from Machu Picchu in 1915 ('By Qqente', in Bingham, 'Further Explorations' (1916), p. 445) and left the other Llactapata downriver untouched. Fejos repeats the mistake later in his report, describing Bingham as travelling from Palcay 'along the opposite slope of the Aobamba valley to Llactapata, the scene of the 1915 excavations' (p. 18).

26 *In his book, Fejos states.* Op. cit., p. 19.

27 *some ruins at the head of the valley.* A reference to Palcay (or Llactapampa) – see Thomson, *The White Rock*, for a description of this site.

34 *the intriguing site the Andeanist scholar Johan Reinhard had described finding some years earlier.* This was in 1985. The building was near the route of a likely Inca road that would have run along the ridge, very high in the customary Inca manner, and connected Llactapata with the site of Palcay higher up in the Aobamba valley. Johan Reinhard had been retracing this route from Palcay when he had come across the building. Thinking that Llactapata had been previously investigated (and as he found the ridge building at the end of his expedition when he was running out of water), he had not tried to establish how close it was to the Llactapata site, which he knew to be somewhere in the area. In fact the building lies almost directly above the other sector we knew about, on the fall-line, so the two seem clearly linked. See Reinhard, 'Informe sobra una sección' (1990).

39 *It helped that not all those with us were experts.* Some of the fieldworkers were volunteers who contributed to the field costs. Archaeologists with academic tenure and access to university funds for their expeditions, or who simply stay at home, can be critical of the presence of 'paying clients' on research expeditions, forgetting that this has always been a mainstay of exploration. Some of the members of Scott's ill-fated 1910 expedition to the South Pole, like Apsley Cherry-Gerrard and Lawrence Oates, paid subscriptions for the privilege (£1,000 each, a considerable amount then).

50 *referred to the area of 'Cotacoca'.* In the map drawn by the enterprising prospector Christian Bües in 1921, the nearby river is called the 'Cutacuta'. For more on Bües, see *The White Rock*. Hiram Bingham also passed close to the area in early June 1915, taking photographs of the Lower Yanama valley, and then crossing to the Arma plateau, again without seeing the site (from his unpublished journals, Peabody Museum, Yale). See also Sartiges (1850).

55 *Reinhard noted that the name ... Salcantay.* See Reinhard, *The Sacred Center* (2002), p. 19.

55 *Hiram Bingham on the ruins of Salmite.* 'In the Wonderland of Peru' (*National Geographic*, April 1913), p. 539.

57 *Pedro Pizarro.* See Pizarro (1921), pp. 242–3.

59 *'they were made to mark the presence of man without depicting him'.* John Hemming and Edward Ranney, *Monuments of the Incas* (1990), p. 169.

64 *'shouting at the top of their voices and whipping their dogs so they would bark and howl', according to one chronicler.* Bernabé Cobo, *Inca Religion and Customs* (University of Texas Press, 1990), p. 29.

75 *considerable opposition to the idea that a civilisation could have arisen based just on 'recursos maritimos', maritime resources.* Michael Moseley's

'Maritime Foundations of Andean Civilization' or 'MFAC'
hypothesis proposed that 'thousands of years ago the rich Andean
fishery sustained the growth of early littoral populations, the rise of
large sedentary communities, and the formation of complex
societies and thus established the foundations of coastal civilization.
... MFAC proposed that early fishing societies developed the
organizational foundations for coastal civilization, but civilization
itself arose after 1800 BC with the introduction of pottery, the
intensive cultivation of staples and the construction of large-scale
irrigation systems.' Michael Moseley, 'The Maritime Foundations
of Andean Civilization: An Evolving Hypothesis', in *Perú y El Mar*
(Sociedad Nacional de Pesquería, 2005).

78 *Science magazine were alerted and ran a major article on the subject.* See
Ruth Shady Solis, Jonathan Haas, and Winifred Creamer, 'Dating
Caral, a Preceramic Site in the Supe Valley on the Central Coast
of Peru' (*Science*, 292, April 2001).

79 *Haas and Creamer had started to work in other areas near Caral.* Like
Fortaleza and Patavilca. For more on their 'Norte Chico project',
see Jonathan Haas, Winifred Creamer and Alvaro Ruiz, 'Dating
the Late Archaic Occupation of the Norte Chico Region in Peru'
(*Nature*, 432, 2004).

79 *the memory of Hiram Bingham carrying all his findings at Machu Picchu
back to Yale still rankles.* As of writing, Peru is preparing a lawsuit
against Yale for the return of the artifacts.

86 *more such sites would be uncovered along the Peruvian coast in the years
to follow.* Near by at Chupacigarro, another great circular sunken
plaza has already been uncovered, while at sites thought to be
contemporary with Caral, like Kotosh and La Galgada, new
techniques of archaeological analysis can now be brought to bear.

86 *humans first entered the Americas from Asia around 15000* BC. This
figure is constantly being revised.

88 *Michael Moseley, the Andeanist who influenced a generation.* See Michael
Moseley, *The Incas and their Ancestors* (Thames & Hudson, 1992,
revised edn 2001).

88 *Recent studies on the ice-cores of Andean glaciers.* See Lonnie
Thompson et al., 'A 1500-year Record of Tropical Precipitation

Recorded in Ice Cores from the Quelccaya Ice Cap, Peru' (*Science*, 229, 1985).

94 *nowhere in the Sechín complex do there seem to be any signs of fortifications.* The traditional view, as espoused by Moseley and others, of climate change as being more important than military conflict to the rise and fall of Andean civilisations has been challenged recently. See, for instance, Elizabeth Arkush and Charles Stanish, 'Interpreting Conflict in the Ancient Andes: Implications for the Archaeology of Warfare' (*Current Anthropology*, 46, February 2005).

103 *A local Trujillo scholar has shown how quarter-shares.* Jorge Zevallos Quinoñes, *Huaca y Huaqueros en Trujillo* (Trujillo, 1994).

103 *the Pyramid of the Sun had a more administrative role.* See Steve Bourget, 'Los Sacerdotes en la Sombra del Cerro Blanco y del Arco Bicéfalo' (*Revista del Museo de Arqueología, Antropología e Historia*, Trujillo, 1995).

106 *some were discovered to contain residues of dried human blood.* Steve Bourget, 'Rituals of sacrifice: its practice at Huaca de la Luna and its representation in Moche iconography' in Joanne Pillsbury (ed.), *Moche Art and Archaeology in Ancient Peru* (Yale University Press, 2001).

106 *John Verano wrote a report.* See Pillsbury, ed., op. cit.

106 *in Steve Bourget's description, this was a 'teatro de sacrificio, a theatre of sacrifice'.* Steve Bourget op. cit., 1995.

106–7 *the American E. G. Squier commented.* Squier (1877), p. 130.

108 *Near the Pyramids of the Sun and Moon is the little hamlet of the Campiña de Moche.* The Moche culture takes its name from the village, as near the pyramids, rather than vice versa.

110 *coleccionistas, many of whom were only interested in sending pieces to the States or Europe.* For a general discussion of this worldwide problem, see Roger Atwood, *Stealing History: Tomb Raiders, Smugglers, and the Looting of the Ancient World* (St Martin's Press, 2004).

111 *The German anthropologist Réna Gündüz.* See her *El Mundo Ceremonial de los Huaqueros* (Peru, 2001).

111 *the local, more Indian huaqueros feel that they are just liberating their inheritance from pre-Columbian ancestors.* A similar argument surfaces occasionally at Machu Picchu when the local residents of Aguas Calientes complain that, as their ancestors built the ruins, they and not central government should enjoy the considerable revenue brought by tourism.

113 *Christopher Donnan ... has stated.* Quoted in Alva (1990), p. 23.

118 *At one burial site investigators were surprised to find ... a full foot taller than the average Moche man.* Excavating Dos Cabezas between 1997 and 1999, Christopher Donnan and his team discovered three high-status males buried there, all surprisingly tall, between 5 feet 9 inches and 6 feet tall. The height of a normal Moche adult male was 4 feet 10 inches to 5 feet 6 inches. The team speculated that they may all have suffered from a form of gigantism called Marfan's syndrome, a genetic disorder that causes thin, elongated bones. Marfan's syndrome can also involve potentially deadly cardiovascular problems, which may account for why none of these men was more than twenty-two years old.

120 *some of [the Sipán treasure] resurfaced anyway in museums in Lima.* One such is the privately owned Poli Museum.

120 *[some of the Sipán treasure] was recovered by the FBI from dealers in the States.* A landmark case, as this was the first time stolen pre-Columbian artifacts were returned to Peru.

124 *Moche is now a dead language.* A Moche grammar and some catechisms do survive. See Paul Goulder, 'The Languages of Peru: Their Past, Present and Future Survival' (*Enter Text*, vol. 2, no. 2, Summer 2003, Brunel University).

124 *The El Brujo complex lay even closer to the sea.* This area, by the Chicama river, had long been politicised and was one of the first in Peru to set up worker cooperatives to run the sugar cane plantations.

124 *National Geographic ran an article on [El Brujo].* See *National Geographic*, 109, July 2004.

134 *Chavín's main period of construction and influence has recently been dated from 1200 BC to 200 BC, although it may have started as early as 1400 BC.* John Rick has been quoted as saying that after dating some materials he excavated, he has revised the chronology of structures on the site: 'We've pushed Chavín back in time.' He makes the argument that the culture was 500 to 800 years older than some believed, gaining prominence around 1200 to 1400 BC and fading around 400 BC.

134 *the theocratic nature of later Andean shrines.* Like Pachacamac on the coast.

135 *the Lanzón, the extraordinary statue carved from white granite.* John H. Rowe disliked this name for the statue ('infelicitously called "the Lanzon" in the earlier literature'), preferring 'The Great Image' (Rowe, 'Chavín art', 1962).

137 *Jay has teased out the implications.* Mike Jay, 'Enter the Jaguar: Psychedelic Temple Cults of Ancient Peru' (*Strange Attractor Journal*, 2, 2005).

137 *plants like anadenanthera, which produce DMT, have an intense and immediate effect.* To quote 'DMT guru' Terence McKenna: 'The feeling of doing DMT is as though one has been struck by noetic lightning. The ordinary world is almost instantaneously replaced, not only with a hallucination, but a hallucination whose alien character is its utter alienness. Nothing in this world can prepare one for the impressions that fill your mind when you enter the DMT sensorium.'

137 *DMT is today most often taken as ayahuasca.* See Tahir Shah, *Trail of Feathers* (Weidenfeld & Nicolson, 2001) for an amusing and informative account of this.

146 *toasts would be drunk in matching drinking vessels, known as qeros.* See Jorge Flores Ochoa et al., *Qeros: Arte Inca en Vasos Ceremoniales* (Lima, 1998).

147 *[María Rostworowski] had written the text for a website*: http://incas.perucultural.org.pe/

148 *a group of conservatives, alarmed at the growth of the left-wing indigenista movement.* This attitude was not just held by Latin American conservatives. Evelyn Waugh, writing in the same pre-war period, commented of Mexico: 'The traditions of Spain are still deep in Mexican character and I believe that it is only by developing them that the country can ever grow happy.' *Robbery Under Law: The Mexican Object-Lesson* (1939).

150 *Mario Vargas Llosa, the country's best-known writer, had just pointed out.* Mario Vargas Llosa, 'Los Hispanicidas' (*Caretas*, 1772, 30 April 2003).

161 *Just below the Southern Cross.* See Gary Urton, *At the Crossroads of* *the Earth and the Sky* (University of Texas Press, 1981) for a fuller discussion of Inca sky-watching.

176 *their German colleague Karsten Lambers had put it in his PhD thesis.* 'The geoglyphs of Palpa (Peru): documentation, analysis, and interpretation' (University of Zurich, Switzerland, 2004), available online in PDF format at http://www.dissertationen.unizh.ch/2005/lambers/abstract.html

180 *Bolivian peasants, who still process ceremonially along certain lines at certain times of year.* The 'Sajama Lines' in western Bolivia. See Morrison, *Pathways to the Gods* (1977) and Reinhard (1988). The similarities between the *ceque* system of Inca Cuzco and the Sajama Lines have also been discussed by Morrison, op. cit. (1977) and Bauer, *The Sacred Landscape of the Inca* (1998).

180 *the Nasca people extended and manipulated with an elaborate system of underground aqueducts.* There has been some debate as to who built the irrigation system, but the consensus seems to be that it was the Nasca.

180 *We know from climate research on the ice-cores of glaciers.* See the pioneering work of Lonnie Thompson and colleagues for more detail on this: L. G. Thompson, E. Mosley-Thompson, J. F. Bolzan and B. R. Koci, 'A 1500-Year Record of Tropical Precipitation Recorded in Ice Cores from the Qualccaya Ice Cap, Peru' (*Science*, 229, 1985).

181 *the Hotel Nasca Lines.* Known in Maria Reiche's time as the Hotel Turistas. She lived in Room 130.

182 *She even took Aveni and Zuidema out into the desert to show them how she measured the lines.* One of Maria Reiche's main interests, in addition to the astronomy of the geoglyphs, was the unit of measurement with which they were constructed.

184 *the suggestion that the Nasca not only processed on the lines but danced along them.* A suggestion first made by the Peruvian historian Hans Horkheimer in the mid-1940s. See Aveni, *Nasca: Eighth Wonder of the World?* (2000), pp. 89–90, for a discussion of Horkheimer's contribution.

187 *other [Nasca] themes emerge, usually associated with human sacrifice.*

There is some indication that the Moche may have extended their influence to the Nasca in the later period of both cultures.

187 *a feline, winged deity.* María Rostworowski calls this deity 'Con' in 'Origen religioso de los dibujos y rayas de Nasca' (*Journal de la Société des Américanistes*, 79, 1993).

188 *To all intents and purposes the Nasca culture disappeared.* Or at least their geoglyphs. The ceramics were investigated by Max Uhle in the early twentieth century.

189 *according to the archaeologist Francis Pryor.* In *Seahenge: New Discoveries in Pre-historic Britain* (HarperCollins, 2001).

192 *Before we got to Toro Muerto, we stopped at one of the many ancient cemeteries.* Called Cochate.

193 *One entire volume of Petroglifos del Perú was dedicated almost exclusively to Toro Muerto.* Volume 4.

198 *A few quipus have known 'provenance'.* See also Charles C. Mann, 'Unraveling Khipu's Secrets' (*Science*, vol. 309, 12 August 2005).

199 *A team led by the same Gary Urton.* See his *Signs of the Inka Khipu* (University of Texas Press, 2003). Urton is currently Dumbarton Oaks Professor of Pre-Columbian Studies in the Archaeology Department at Harvard.

201 *William J. Conklin.* Quoted Mann, op. cit.

202 *cardinals were able to obtain a much richer scarlet cloak after the conquests of Peru and Mexico.* Renaissance artists such as Michelangelo were able to achieve a carmine red as well. For a fuller discussion of the New World influence of cochineal on Europe, focussing on Mexican production, see Amy Butler Greenfield, *A Perfect Red* (Doubleday, 2005).

207 *Choquepukio lay on top of a small tableland just off the main highway.* Near the little village of Huacarpay.

207 *one of their principal sites, at a nearby town called Huaro, had been discovered only in 1995.* By Julinho Zapata.

209 *As Hiram Bingham had pointed out on his first visit in 1911.* See Bingham, *Inca Land* (1922).

212 *recent subtle studies of Inca historiography.* See Bauer, *The Development of the Inca State* (1982), Rostworowski, *Historia del Tahuantinsuyu* (1988), Julien, *Reading Inca History* (2000).

212 *Arminda Gibaja, Gordon's Peruvian colleague, had made an important discovery some years previously.* In 1997.

214 *But while I was still talking to Gordon, at just after 11 in the morning.* The figurine was found on Friday, 18 July 2003.

215 *Juan de Betanzos, who married an Inca princess, recounted how a set of miniature gold figures.* See Juan de Betanzos, *Narrative of the Incas*, trans. Hamilton and Buchanan (University of Texas Press, 1996), p. 48: 'All around the font they buried some small gold statues, each one about the length and thickness of one finger. Before these little statues were buried in this way around the font, they made as many small squadrons as lineages of the city of Cuzco. Each statuette represented the most important lord of each of these lineages.'

218 *the step and diamond motifs of an older Andean style, that of Tiahuanaco.* The stepped Tiahuanaco motif can also be seen at the Inca sites of Qenko and Pisac, and at the Fountain of the Ñusta in Ollantaytambo. See John Hemming and Edward Ranney, *Monuments of the Incas* (1990).

218 *Father Bernabé Cobo, a Jesuit priest who visited the island in the early seventeenth century.* 1610–15.

219 *There is a point where the peninsula narrows and forms a natural point of control.* Yungayo.

219 *much to Cobo's disgust.* See Cobo, *Inca Religion and Customs* (University of Texas Press, 1990). In the chapter on sin (pp. 123f.), Cobo also notes that the Colla local to Titicaca were particularly strong observers of the pre-Columbian tradition of confession, to the extent that he wondered whether they were the originators of the custom.

222 *Bernabé Cobo records with some amazement.* Op. cit., p. 94.

222 *Hiram Bingham tried humanely to counterbalance when he visited in 1915.* See Bingham, *Inca Land* (1922).

224 *in some places they [the Tiahuanaco and Huari] seem to have coexisted without conflict.* Like Cerro Baúl in the Moquegua valley. See Patrick Ryan Williams and Donna Nash, 'Imperial interaction in the Andes: Wari and Tiwanaku at Cerro Baúl' in W. Isbell and H. Silverman (eds), *Andean Archaeology* (New York, 2002).

225 *Bauer and Stanish argue that Chucaripupata was already 'a pilgrimage centre of regional significance' for the Tiahuanaco.* To the extent, according to Matthew Seddon who worked with Bauer and Stanish, that they modelled this site in miniature on the temple of their capital to the south of the lake.

227 *At the very last gate, Pillcopunku, in the words of one Spanish chronicler.* Ramos Gavilan (1621), quoted in Brian S. Bauer and Charles Stanish, *Ritual and Pilgrimage in the Ancient Andes: The Islands of the Sun and the Moon* (2001), p. 225.

230 *a local gang of workers from the little village near by.* Of Challapampa.

232 *unedited papers of Juan Ramirez.* Quoted Flores (1997), p. 48.

251 *This temporary disappearance of the Pleiades was used as a seasonal indicator.* Randall gives their heliacial set in Cuzco as 24 April and their rise as 9 June; Randall, 'Qoyllur Riti, An Inca Festival' (1982).

252 *Qoyllurit'i ... a necessary propitiation of the spirits to look after the people's livestock.* This might also explain the high camelid voices with which the *ukukus* spoke, about which there were many rival theories: why did the 'bear men' speak like alpacas? One leading Peruvian anthropologist, Jorge Flores Ochoa, believed that the *ukukus* had nothing to do with bears, the more popular interpretation of their role, but simply represented alpacas themselves. See Jorge Flores Ochoa, *El Cuzco* (1990).

252 *The Q'eros people ... congregated around the Q'eros rock and waited until other pilgrims departed.* Jorge Flores Ochoa, op. cit.

253 *There was even a [Qoyllurit'i] ceremony held in its honour in distant New York.* See Javier Ávila Molero, 'El Taytacha Qoyllur Rit'i en Nueva York' (*Revista Andina*, 37).

268 *a contradanza between the ancient elements of Peru, the jungle and the highlands.* The *contradanza* as practised in colonial Peru has an interesting ancestry. The 'country dance' of late medieval England was danced at court functions during the reign of Queen Elizabeth I. It also became popular on the Continent and as it was accepted into European court society it became more formal. From there it became popular in South America and Peru. *Contradanza* is not originally a Spanish word, being the Spanish form of the French *contredanse*. This would seem to make sense in French ('against-dance') as two rows of dancers face each other, but may actually be a corruption of the English 'country dance' (see OED).

278 *The Coricancha was the central most important religious building for the Incas.* Because 'Coricancha' means 'Temple of Gold', an assumption is often made that its purpose was solely related to the sun, hence 'El Templo del Sol', 'Sun Temple', but this was the name given to it subsequently by the Spanish, in whose minds 'gold' meant 'sun', and it seems that it was used for other stars, such as the Pleiades, with temples also dedicated to the moon and Venus. See Bernabé Cobo, op. cit.

278 *On the western side of the Coricancha are a group of buildings that, just as at Llactapata, surround a corridor leading to a high-status double-jamb doorway.* It had been this same double-jamb doorway that had allowed us first to identify the sector as the one that Hiram Bingham had found.

278 *the orientation of the corridors at both sites is uncannily similar.* For a full description of this orientation, with diagrams, and for other more technical aspects of the research at Llactapata, see the article by Malville, Thomson and Ziegler, 'El Observatorio de Machu Picchu: Redescubrimiento de Llactapata y su Templo Solar', *Revista Andina*, 39 (Cuzco, 2004), translated at www.thomson.clara.net/Llactapata.html. See also Malville, Thomson and Ziegler (2006).

279 *They [the Pleiades] were too small to be their own Zodiacal constellation in Western astronomy.* The Pleiades lie on the far edge of the Taurus constellation. The Hyades, the central star cluster in Taurus, were used likewise by the Greeks, as their heliacal rising in the Northern Hemisphere marks the start of the autumn rainy season: hence Tennyson's reference to the 'rainy Hyades' in 'Ulysses'.

279 *Recent investigations by Benjamin Orlove.* See Benjamin S. Orlove et al., 'Ethnoclimatology in the Andes' (*American Scientist*, vol. 90, no. 5, 1 September 2002).

280–81 *For approximately thirty-seven days the Pleiades could not be seen.* Tom Zuidema suggests that each of the 328 *huacas* of the *ceque* system of Cuzco corresponded to a day when the Pleiades was visible. See Zuidema, *Inca Civilization in Cuzco* (1991).

281 *the angle of aperture created by the open gateway was precise.* About 4°
when viewed from the far end of the corridor. See Malville,
Thomson and Ziegler, op. cit.

282 *the sun casts a direct beam of light directly down the long corridor with
incredible precision.* Purists will point out that the earth's axis has
tilted slightly since the time of the Incas; however, the difference
between the June solstice point of today and that of 500 years ago
is minimal.

283 *the emperor, just as at the Corincancha, off to one side in his own chamber.*
In the Coricancha it is thought that the emperor sat in the chamber
on the left (when viewed from the courtyard) of the double-jamb
doorway.

284 *the curved mirador facing that way [west], which has also puzzled
previous commentators.* With the exception of Johan Reinhard, who has
suggested that it was orientated towards Mount Pumasillo. See
Reinhard, *Machu Picchu: The Sacred Center* (1991).

284 *some terraces that had just been cleared and restored on the western side
... facing Llactapata.* Interestingly the approach from the west, past
these terraces and up an extremely steep slope, was the one first
taken by Herman Tucker and Paul Lanius, Bingham's colleagues,
when they returned to Machu Picchu at his request later in 1911,
some months after he had spent a brief afternoon there. Lanius
described this western approach as 'one of the steepest slopes I
have ever climbed'. The pair were in some ways the forgotten
'discoverers' of Machu Picchu, needing several weeks to clear and
photograph the site. It was Tucker who took the pictures that really
entranced National Geographic when they saw them and persuaded
Gilbert Grosvenor to send a full expedition back to Macchu Picchu
the next year, 1912, for further investigation and photography.

For more detail on the role that the photographic chronicling of
Machu Picchu played in its initial exploration, see Thomson,
Machu Picchu and the Camera (Penchant Press, 2002).

285 *One could easily imagine a reciprocal ceremony at the time of the June
solstice.* This may have been repeated at sunset on the December
solstice when the sun would have set behind Llactapata. See also
David Dearborn, Katharina Schreiber and Raymond White,

'Intimachay: A December Solstice Observatory at Machu Picchu, Peru' (*American Antiquity*, 52, 1987).

285 '*a landscape built by titans in a fit of megalomania*' as Christopher Isherwood once described it. In *The Condor and the Cows* (Random House, 1949), when he visits Peru. This also contains a memorably honest account of Cuzco: 'No sense in my trying to describe Cuzco; I should only be quoting from the guide-book. In fact, after two days sightseeing, I am so bewildered by impressions that I scarcely know what we have actually seen and what we have read.'

SELECT BIBLIOGRAPHY

For some civilisations (like Caral, Chavín and the Moche at El Brujo), ongoing research is best accessed at the official websites run by the archaeologists concerned, which are also listed below.

CARAL

Haas, Jonathan, Creamer, Winifred and Ruiz, Alvaro, 'Dating the Late Archaic Occupation of the Norte Chico region in Peru', *Nature*, 432 (2004).

Moseley, Michael, *Maritime Foundations of Andean Civilization* (Cummings, 1975).

Shady Solis, Ruth, *Caral, Supe: La Civilización más Antigua de América* (Lima, 2003).

Shady Solis, Ruth, website on Caral: http://www.caralperu.gob.pe/

Shady Solis, Ruth, Haas, Jonathan, and Creamer, Winifred, 'Dating Caral, a Preceramic Site in the Supe Valley on the Central Coast of Peru', *Science*, 292 (April 2001).

SECHÍN

Bischof, Henning, 'Los relieves de barro de Cerro Sechín, evidencias de un culto marino en el antiguo Perú', *Boletín de Lima*, 55 (1988).

Cordy-Collins, Alana, 'The Cerro Sechín Massacre: Did it Happen?' (San Diego Museum of Man, 1983).

Maldonado, Elena, *Arqueología de Cerro Sechín: Tomo I. Arquitectura* (Pontificia Universidad Católica del Perú, 1992).

Pozorski, Sheila and Pozorski, Thomas, *Early Settlement and Subsistence in the Casma Valley, Peru* (University of Iowa Press, 1987).

Samaniego, Lorenzo et al., *Arqueología de Cerro Sechín: Tomo II. Escultura* (Pontificia Universidad Católica del Perú, 1992).

Tello, Julio, 'Wira Kocha', *Inca*, vol. I, no. 1 (1923).

MOCHE

Alva, Walter, 'Into the Tomb of a Moche Lord', *National Geographic*, vol. 174, no. 4 (1988).

Alva, Walter, 'The Moche of Ancient Peru: New Tomb of Royal Splendor', *National Geographic*, vol. 177, no. 6 (1990).

Alva, Walter and Donnan, Christopher, *Royal Tombs of Sipán* (University of California, 1993).

Bawden, Garth, *The Moche* (Blackwell, 1996).

Berrin, Kathleen (ed.), *In the Spirit of Ancient Peru: Treasures from the Museo Arqueológico Rafael Larco Herrera* (Thames & Hudson, 1997).

Bourget, Steve, 'Children and ancestors: ritual practices at the Moche site of Huaca de la Luna, north coast of Peru', in Elizabeth P. Benson and Anita G. Cook (eds.), *Ritual Sacrifice in Ancient Peru* (University of Texas Press, 2001).

Donnan, Christopher, *Moche Art of Peru* (University of California, 1978).

Donnan, Christopher, *Moche Portraits from Ancient Peru* (University of Texas Press, 2004).

Gündüz, Réna, *El Mundo Ceremonial de los Huaqueros* (Peru, 2001).

Pillsbury, Joanne (ed.), *Moche Art and Archaeology in Ancient Peru* (Yale University Press, 2001).

El Brujo Archaeological Site and Huaca Cao Viejo, website: http://researchweb.watson.ibm.com/peru/brujo.htm

Rafael Larco Herrera Museum, website: http://museolarco.perucultural.org.pe/

Sipán website: http://www.unired.net.pe/sipan/

CHAVÍN

Burger, Richard L., *Chavín and the Origins of the Andean Civilization* (New York, 1992).

Jay, Mike, 'Enter the Jaguar: Psychedelic Temple Cults of Ancient Peru', *Strange Attractor Journal*, 2 (2005).

Reinhard, Johan, 'Chavín y Tiahuanaco', *Boletín de Lima*, 50 (1987).

Rowe, John Howland, 'Chavín art: an inquiry into its form and meaning' (New York Museum of Primitive Art, 1962).

Tello, Julio, 'Discovery of the Chavín culture in Peru', *American Antiquity*, vol. IX, no. 1 (July 1943).

John Rick, website on Chavín: http://www.stanford.edu/~johnrick/

Luis Lumbreras, website on Chavín: http://chavin.perucultural.org.pe/

NASCA

Aveni, Anthony F. (ed.), *The Lines of Nasca* (American Philosophical Society, Philadelphia, 1990).

Aveni, Anthony F., *Nasca: Eighth Wonder of the World?* (British Museum Press, 2000).

Chatwin, Bruce, 'Maria Reiche – the Riddle of the Pampa' (*Sunday Times*, 1975), reprinted in *What Am I Doing Here?* (Jonathan Cape, 1989).

Hawkins, Gerald, 'Prehistoric Desert Markings in Peru' (National Geographic Society Research Reports, 1967).

Isla, Johnny and Reindel, Markus, 'New Studies on the Settlements and Geoglyphs in Palpa, Peru', *Andean Past*, 7 (2005).

Kosok, Paul, *Life, Land and Water in Ancient Peru* (Long Island University Press, 1965).

Lancho Rojas, Josué, *María Reiche: La Dama de las Pampas* (Lima, 1984; revised edn 2005).

Morrison, Tony, *Pathways to the Gods* (Lima, 1977).

Reiche, Maria, *Mystery on the Desert* (Heinrich Fink, 1968).

Reinhard, Johan, *The Nazca Lines: A New Perspective on their Origin and Meaning* (Lima, 1988).

Reinhard, Johan, 'Interpreting the Nazca lines', in Richard Townsend (ed.), *The Ancient Americas: Art from Sacred Landscapes* (Art Institute of Chicago, 1992).

Silverman, Helaine, *Cahuachi in the Ancient Nasca World* (University of Iowa Press, 1996).

Silverman, Helaine and Browne, David, 'New Evidence for the Date of the Nazca Lines', *Antiquity*, 65 (1991).

Silverman, Helaine and Proulx, Donald, *The Nasca* (Blackwell, 2002).

HUARI

McEwan, Gordon F. (ed.), *Pikillacta: The Wari Empire in Cuzco* (University of Iowa Press, 2005).

Isbell, William, *Mummies and Mortuary Monuments: A Postprocessual Prehistory of Central Andean Social Organisation* (University of Texas Press, 1997).

Isbell, William and McEwan, Gordon F. (eds.), *Huari Administrative Structure: Prehistoric Monumental Architecture and State Government* (Dumbarton Oaks Research Library, 1991).

ISLAND OF THE SUN

Bandelier, Adolph F. A., *The Islands of Titicaca and Koati* (New York, 1910).

Bauer, Brian S. and Stanish, Charles, *Ritual and Pilgrimage in the Ancient Andes: The Islands of the Sun and the Moon* (University of Texas Press, 2001).

Pentland, Joseph Barclay, 'Report on the Bolivian Republic' (Public Record Office, Foreign Office file 61/12, microfilm 2045, 1827); trans. as *Informe Sobre Bolivia* (Editorial Potosí, Bolivia, 1975).

Ramos Gavilan, Alonso, *Historia del Santuario de Nuestra Señora de Copacabana* (1621), ed. Ignacio Prado Pastor (Lima, 1998).

Reinhard, Johan, 'Underwater archaeological research in Lake Titicaca, Bolivia', in Nicholas J. Saunders (ed.), *Ancient America: Contributions to New World Archaeology* (Oxbow Books, 1992).

Stanish, Charles, The Islands of the Sun and Moon website: http://www.sscnet.ucla.edu/ioa/stanish/islands/index.html

INCAS

Ascher, Marcia and Ascher, Robert, *Code of the Quipu: A Study in Media, Mathematics and Culture* (Michigan, 1981).

Bauer, Brian S., *The Development of the Inca State* (University of Texas Press, 1982).

Bauer, Brian S., *The Sacred Landscape of the Inca: The Cuzco Ceque System.* (University of Texas Press, 1998).

Bauer, Brian S. and Dearborn, David, *Astronomy and Empire in the Ancient Andes: The Cultural Origins of Inca Skywatching* (University of Texas Press, 1995).

Bingham, Alfred, *Portrait of an Explorer: Hiram Bingham, Discover of Machu Picchu* (Iowa State University Press, 1989).

Bingham, Hiram, 'In the Wonderland of Peru', *National Geographic* (April 1913).

Bingham, Hiram, 'Further Explorations in the Land of the Incas', *National Geographic* (May 1916).

Bingham, Hiram, *Inca Land* (Boston, 1922).

Bingham, Hiram, *Machu Picchu: A Citadel of the Incas* (New Haven, 1930).

Bingham, Hiram, *Lost City of the Incas* (New York, 1948, reissued Weidenfeld & Nicolson, 2002, with an introduction by Hugh Thomson).

Burger, Richard L. and Salazar-Burger, Lucy, 'Machu Picchu Rediscovered: The Royal Estate in the Cloud Forest', *Discovery*, 24 (1993).

Burger, Richard L. and Salazar-Burger, Lucy (eds.), *The 1912 Yale Peruvian Scientific Expedition Collections from Machu Picchu: Human and Animal Remains* (Yale University Publications in Anthropology, no. 85, 2003).

Burger, Richard L. and Salazar-Burger, Lucy (eds.), *Machu Picchu: Unveiling the Mystery of the Incas* (Yale University Press, 2004).

Dearborn, David and Schreiber, Katharina, 'Here Comes the Sun: The Cuzco–Machu Picchu Connection', *Archaeoastronomy*, 9 (1986).

Dearborn, David, Schreiber, Katharina and White, Raymond, 'Intimachay: A December Solstice Observatory at Machu Picchu, Peru', *American Antiquity*, 52 (1987).

Drew, David, 'The Cusichaca Project: the Lucumayo and Santa Teresa Valleys' (*British Archaeological Reports*, international series 210, Oxford, 1984).

Fejos, Paul, *Archaeological Explorations in the Cordillera Vilcabamba, Southeastern Peru* (Viking Fund Publications in Anthropology, no. 3, New York, 1944).

Gasparini, Graziano and Margolies, Luisa, *Arquitectura Inka* (Venezuela, 1977); trans. Patricia J. Lyon as *Inca Architecture* (Indiana University Press, 1980).

Hemming, John, *The Conquest of the Incas* (Harcourt Brace, 1970; revised edn British Papermac, 1995).

Hemming, John and Ranney, Edward, *Monuments of the Incas* (Boston, 1982; revised edn University of New Mexico Press, 1990).

Hyslop, John, *The Inca Road System* (Academic Press, New York, 1984).

Hyslop, John, *Inka Settlement Planning* (University of Texas Press, 1990).

Julien, Catherine, *Reading Inca History* (University of Iowa, 2000).

Kendall, Ann, 'Current Archaeological Projects in Central Andes: Some Approaches and Results' (*British Archaeological Reports*, 210, Oxford, 1984).

Lee, Vincent R., *Forgotten Vilcabamba* (Sixpac Manco Publications, 2000).

Malville, Kim, Thomson, Hugh, and Ziegler, Gary, 'El redescubrimiento de Llactapata, antiguo observatorio de Machu Picchu', *Revista Andina*, 39 (Cuzco, 2004); trans. as 'Machu Picchu's Observatory: the Re-Discovery of Llactapata and its Sun-Temple' (http://www.thomson.clara.net/llactapa.html).

Malville, Kim, Thomson, Hugh, and Ziegler, Gary, 'The Sun Temple of Llactapata and the Ceremonial Neighborhood of Machu Picchu', in Bostwick, Todd W. and Bates, Bryan (eds.), *Proceedings of the Oxford VII International Conference on Archaeo-astronomy* (Pueblo Grande Museum Anthropological Papers no. 15, Phoenix, 2006).

Morris, Craig and Thompson, Donald E., *Huánuco Pampa: An Inca City and its Hinterland* (Thames & Hudson, 1985).

Murra, John V., 'Cloth and its Functions in the Inca State', *American Anthropologist*, vol. 64, no. 4 (1962).

Murra, John V., *The Economic Organisation of the Inca State* (JAI Press, 1980).

Niles, Susan, *The Shape of Inca History: Narrative and Architecture in an Andean Empire* (University of Iowa Press, 1999).

Ochoa, Jorge Flores, *El Cuzco: Resistencia y Continuidad* (Cuzco, 1990).

Randall, Robert, 'Qoyllur Riti, An Inca Fiesta of the Pleiades: Reflections on Time and Space in the Andean World', *Bulletin de L'Institut Français d'Études Andines*, XI (Lima, 1982).

Reinhard, Johan, 'Informe sobre una sección del camino Inca y las ruinas en la cresta que baja del nevado de Tucarhuay entre los ríos Aobamba y Santa Teresa', *Revista Sacsahuaman*, 3 (Cuzco, 1990).

Reinhard, Johan, *Machu Picchu: The Sacred Center* (Lima, 1991; revised edn 2002).

Rostworowski de Diez Canseco, María, *Pachacutec Inca Yupanqui* (Lima, 1953; revised edn 2001).

Rostworowski de Diez Canseco, María, *Historia de Tahuantinsuyu* (Lima, 1988); trans. as *History of the Inca Realm* (Cambridge University Press, 1999).

Rowe, John Howland, 'An Introduction to the Archaeology of Cuzco', *Papers of Peabody Museum of American Archaeology*, vol. xxvii, no. 2 (Cambridge, Mass., 1944).

Rowe, John Howland, 'Inca culture at the time of the Spanish Conquest', in *Handbook of South American Indians* (Bureau of American Ethnology, Bulletin 143, vol. 2, Washington, 1946).

Rowe, John Howland, 'Machu Pijchu a la Luz de Documentos del Siglo XVI', *Kultur*, 4 (Lima, March–April 1987).

Salomon, Frank, 'Testimonies: the makings and reading of Native South American historical sources', in *Cambridge History of Native South Americans* (Cambridge University Press, 1999).

Sartiges, Comte de (writing under pseudonym of M. E. de Lavandais), 'Voyage dans les Républiques de l'Amérique du Sud', *Revue de Deux Mondes* (Paris, 1850).

Savoy, Gene, *Antisuyo* (New York, 1970).

Thomson, Hugh, *The White Rock: An Exploration of the Inca Heartland* (Weidenfeld & Nicolson, 2001).

Thomson, Hugh, *Machu Picchu and the Camera* (Penchant Press, 2002).

Thomson, Hugh, Cota Coca Report 2004, with Gary Ziegler: http://www.thomson.clara.net/cotacoca.html.

Thomson, Hugh, Llactapata report with Kim Malville and Gary Ziegler: http://www.thomson.clara.net/llactapa.html, cf. Kim Malville et al.

Urton, Gary, *At the Crossroads of the Earth and the Sky* (University of Texas Press, 1981).

Urton, Gary, *The History of a Myth: Pacariqtambo and the Origin of the Inkas* (University of Texas Press, 1990).

Urton, Gary, *Signs of the Inka Khipu* (University of Texas Press, 2003).

Valencia, Alfredo and Gibaja, Arminda, *Machu Picchu: La Investigación y Conservación del Monumento Arqueológico después de Hiram Bingham* (Lima, 1992).

Wright, Kenneth R. and Valencia, Alfredo Z., *Machu Picchu: A Civil Engineering Marvel* (ASCE Press, 2000).

Ziegler, Gary, *Beyond Machu Picchu* (Crestone Press, Westcliffe, 2000).

Zuidema, R. Tom, 'Catachillay: the role of the Pleiades and Southern Cross and Alpha and Beta Centauri in the calendar of the Incas', in Anthony Aveni and Gary Urton (eds.), *Ethnoastronomy and Archaeoastronomy in the American Tropics* (Annals of the New York Academy of Sciences, 1982).

Zuidema, R. Tom, *Inca Civilization in Cuzco* (University of Texas Press, 1991).

Zuidema, R. Tom, *The Ceque System of Cuzco: The Social Organization of the Capital of the Inca* (E. J. Brill, 1964).

CHRONICLES

Betanzos, Juan de, *Suma y Narración de los Incas* (1551); trans. Roland Hamilton and Dana Buchanan as *Narrative of the Incas* (University of Texas Press, 1996).

Cieza de León, Pedro de, *Crónica del Perú* (1550–3).

The Incas of Pedro de Cieza de León, introduction by Victor von Hagen (University of Oklahoma, 1959).

Cobo, Bernabé, *Historia del Nuevo Mundo* (1653); trans. and ed. Roland Hamilton as *History of the Inca Empire* (University of Texas Press, 1979) and *Inca Religion and Customs* (University of Texas Press, 1990).

Cusi, Titu, *Relación de la Conquista* (1570), in *En el encuentro de dos Mundos: los Incas de Vilcabamba*, ed. María del Carmen Martín Rubio (Madrid, 1988); trans. Ralph Bauer as *An Inca Account of the Conquest of Peru* (University Press of Colorado, 2005).

Guaman Poma de Ayala, Felipe, *Nueva Corónica y Buen Gobierno* (c.1580–1620), ed. John V. Murra and Rolena Adorno (Mexico, 1980).

The Huarochirí Manuscript, eds. Frank Salomon and Jorge Urioste (University of Texas Press, 1991).

Pizarro, Pedro, *Relación del Descubrimiento y Conquista de los Reinos del Perú* (1571); trans. as *Relation of the Discovery and Conquest of the Kingdoms of Peru* (New York Cortes Society, 1921).

Vega, Garcilaso de la, *Los Comentarios Reales de los Incas* (1609–17); trans. as *The Royal Commentaries of the Incas* (University of Texas Press, 1966).

GENERAL

Adorno, Rolena, *Guaman Poma: Writing and Resistance in Colonial Peru* (University of Texas Press, 2000).

Allen, Catherine, *The Hold Life Has: Coca and Cultural Identity in an Andean Community* (Smithsonian University Press, 1988).

Arkush, Elizabeth and Stanish, Charles, 'Interpreting Conflict in the

Ancient Andes: Implications for the Archaeology of Warfare', *Current Anthropology*, 46 (February 2005).

Benson, Elizabeth P. and Cook, Anita G. (eds.), *Ritual Sacrifice in Ancient Peru* (University of Texas Press, 2001).

Bowen, Sally, *The Fujimori File: Peru and Its President 1990–2000* (Lima, 2000).

Chambi, Martín, *Photographs, 1920–1950* (Smithsonian Institution Press, 1993).

Drinot, Paulo, 'Historiography, Historiographic Identity and Historical Consciousness in Peru', *Estudios Interdisciplinarios de América Latina*, vol. 15, no. 1 (2004).

Flores Lizana, Carlos, *El Taytacha Qoyllur Rit'i* (IPA, Cuzco, 1992).

Frost, Peter, *Exploring Cusco* (Lima, 1979; revised edn 1999).

Higgins, James, *Lima: A Cultural and Literary History* (Signal, 2004).

Keatinge, Richard W. (ed.), *Peruvian Prehistory: An Overview of Pre-Inca and Inca Society* (Cambridge University Press, 1988).

Menzel, Dorothy, *The Archaeology of Ancient Peru and the Work of Max Uhle* (University of California Press, 1977).

Meisch, Lynn (ed.), *Traditional Textiles of the Andes* (Thames & Hudson, 1997).

Morris, Craig and von Hagen, Adriana, *The Inka Empire and its Andean Origins* (Abbeville Press, 1993).

Moseley, Michael, *The Incas and their Ancestors* (Thames & Hudson, 1992; revised edn 2001).

Núñez Jiménez, Antonio, *Petroglifos del Perú* (Havana, 1986).

Orlove, Benjamin S., Chiang, John C. H., and Cane, Mark A., 'Ethnoclimatology in the Andes', *American Scientist*, vol. 90, no. 5 (September 2002).

Paternosto, César, *The Stone and the Thread: Andean Roots of Abstract Art*, trans. Esther Allen (University of Texas Press, 1996).

Peñaloza, Cucho and Galarza, Sergio, *Los Rolling Stones en Perú* (Lima, 2004).

Poole, Deborah, *Vision, Race and Modernity: A Visual Economy of the Andean Image World* (Princeton University Press, 1997).

Ramirez, Juan Andrés, 'La Novena al Señor de Qoyllur Rit'i, *Allpanchis* 1 (Cuzco, 1969).

Rostworowski de Diez Canseco, María, *Curacas y Sucesiones: Costa Norte* (Lima, 1961).

Rostworowski de Diez Canseco, María, *Etnía y Sociedad: Costa Peruana Prehispánica* (Instituto de Estudios Peruanos, Lima, 1977).

Sallnow, Michael J., *Pilgrims of the Andes: Regional Cults in Cuzco* (Smithsonian Institution Press, 1987).

Squier, George, *Peru: Incidents of Travel and Exploration in the Land of the Incas* (New York, 1877).

Stanish, Charles, *Ancient Andean Political Economy* (University of Texas Press, 1992).

Thompson, Lonnie et al., 'A 1500-Year Record of Tropical Precipitation Recorded in Ice Cores from the Quelccaya Ice Cap, Peru', *Science*, 229 (1985).

Townsend, Richard (ed.), *The Ancient Americas: Art from Sacred Landscapes* (Art Institute of Chicago, 1992).

INDEX